BOOKS BY BOB THOMAS

JOAN CRAWFORD

A Biography by
BOB THOMAS

SIMON AND SCHUSTER · NEW YORK

(1) The author and the publisher are grateful for the following permissions:

Photoplay Magazine, for material on pages 118–119

Doubleday & Company, Inc., for an excerpt from *Portrait of Joan*, by Joan Crawford, © 1962 by J. C. Steele. Reprinted by permission of Doubleday & Company, Inc.

Published by Simon and Schuster
A Division of Gulf & Western Corporation
Simon & Schuster Building
Rockefeller Center
1230 Avenue of the Americas
New York, New York 10020

Designed by Elizabeth Woll
Photo Editor: Vincent Virga
Manufactured in the United States of America

1   2   3   4   5   6   7   8   9   10

Library of Congress Cataloging in Publication Data

Thomas, Bob
  Joan Crawford, a biography.
  Includes index.
  1. Crawford, Joan, 1908–1977.
2. Moving-picture actors and actresses—United States—Biography.   I. Title.
PN2287.C67T5   791.43'028'0924 [B]   78-14250

ISBN 978-1-5011-9435-1

Contents

Joan Crawford is doubtless the best example of the flapper,
the girl you see in smart night clubs,
gowned to the apex of sophistication,
toying iced glasses with a remote, faintly bitter expression,
dancing deliciously, laughing a great deal,
with wide, hurt eyes.
Young things with a talent for living.

—F. Scott Fitzgerald

Prologue

The Oscar: 1946

SHE DESERVED THE PRIZE, she realized, but would they give it to her? They had always looked down their noses at her, ever since she arrived in Culver City as Lucille LeSueur. She knew that they whispered about the blue movie. She remembered the haughty disdain of Mrs. Cudahy, the long months after the marriage to young Doug before she was permitted to enter Pickfair. She had heard the scorn for her thin arched eyebrows, her heavy lipstick, her padded shoulders. They almost celebrated as her career dwindled with each reworking of the Crawford formula.

But by God, she had showed them! While her rivals at MGM— Norma Shearer, Greta Garbo, Jeanette MacDonald—had vanished from the screen, Joan had returned in triumph. She had dangerously absented herself from the world's theaters for two years, an eternity in the life of a star. It was an arduous time, during which the lack of income and a calamitous third marriage had depleted her savings. She waited and waited, and found *Mildred Pierce.*

She was nominated for best performance by an actress in 1945, along with four newer stars, Ingrid Bergman, Greer Garson, Jennifer Jones and Gene Tierney. As the ceremonies approached, Joan was afflicted by the worst of her demons, her fear of rejection. She telephoned her publicist, Henry Rogers.

"Henry, I can't do it," she said desperately.

"Do what, Joan?" he asked.

"Go to the Academy awards."

"But you must! It will be the biggest night of your life."

"Henry, I'm so frightened! I know I'm going to lose."

"What makes you think so?"

"They won't vote for me."

"Nonsense. They love a comeback story, and yours is the greatest ever. You're going to win, Joan. I can feel it."

"And supposing I do. Then I'll have to get up in front of all those people and make a speech. You know how that terrifies me. I'll be tongue-tied, and I'll make an ass of myself."

Rogers could not convince her. He called Jerry Wald, the producer of *Mildred Pierce*, and told him of Joan's reluctance.

"Joan, you've *got* to go to the awards," Wald argued. "It will mean a great deal to the picture to have you there."

"And to you, too, Jerry?" she asked.

"Yes, it will mean a great deal to me, too."

"You know I'd do anything for you. I'll try, Jerry. I'll honestly try."

But she couldn't. Now she was confronted with another grave problem: how could she stay away from the awards without displeasing Jerry Wald, to whom she owed the revival of her career? It was astonishingly simple. Christian Science had taught her that purity of thought cures disease. Could she not give way to disease by neglecting the principles of Mary Baker Eddy?

Joan's temperature had risen to 104. She was examined by her physician, Dr. William Branch, who declared that she could not leave her house on the night of the Academy awards.

They started to arrive at seven. With the firm belief that his client would win, Henry Rogers had invited photographers to the Crawford house, and they came in numbers. Especially the fan-magazine photographers, who adored Joan for her many kindnesses. Warner Brothers press agents came to record the event for the studio's publicity releases. Joan's makeup man and hairdresser were present, out of allegiance to her and to make certain that she looked her best for the photographs. Also Joan's lawyer, her business manager, her masseuse—all of those who possessed a fierce loyalty to Joan and hence were the persons she felt most comfortable with.

Dr. Branch was among the growing crowd in the Crawford bedroom. "Now, I don't want Miss Crawford to become excited," he said dubiously.

"If you don't win, we're all going to picket the Academy," said a photographer. Joan managed a wan smile.

Over the radio came the suave tones of Charles Boyer: "Nominees for best performance by an actress in 1945 are: Ingrid Bergman in *The Bells of St. Mary's*, Joan Crawford in *Mildred Pierce*, Greer Garson in *The Valley of Decision*, Jennifer Jones in *Love Letters*, and Gene Tierney in *Leave Her to Heaven*. The winner is . . . Joan Crawford in *Mildred Pierce!*"

The cheers and shouting over the radio from Grauman's Chinese Theater were obliterated by the celebration on Bristol Avenue. Even Dr. Branch overcame his caution and shouted the victory of his longtime friend and patient. "It is the greatest moment of my life," said Joan Crawford with utter conviction.

Ann Blyth, Joan's daughter in *Mildred Pierce*, was the first to arrive from the theater; she was in a body cast after breaking her spine. The two actresses embraced amid tears. Van Johnson joined the gathering; he was a self-proclaimed charter member of the Joan Crawford Fan Club. Michael Curtiz came into the room with the Oscar he had accepted for Joan, and the room went white with flashbulbs. He and Joan greeted each other like old lovers, not the fierce antagonists they had been when he directed her in *Mildred Pierce*.

"Usually I'm ready with the wisecracks," remarked the red-eyed Crawford. "But I can't say anything. My tears speak for me."

Dr. Branch allowed Joan to go downstairs—miraculously, her fever had broken. But after she had spoken to each member of the press and friends who had come to Brentwood to offer congratulations, the doctor insisted that she had to retire. She submitted to one last photo request, from Jack Albin, who asked her to pose asleep with her Oscar.

She arose early, her health fully recovered. The house was filling up with floral displays of every kind. Telegrams arrived in bundles, and Joan insisted on reading each one. They came from the messenger girls at Warner Brothers studio, propmen and electricians at MGM, her butcher, from Douglas Fairbanks Jr. and Franchot Tone, from telegraph operators themselves. They came from Ray Sterling, her Kansas City sweetheart—who had been the first to see promise in Billie Cassin—and from James Wood of Stephens College, dear Daddy Wood, who had been the second. And from her old boss, Louis B. Mayer, and Clark Gable and Spencer Tracy, who had been her lovers. And from the same MGM producers who had proclaimed Joan Crawford washed up three years before.

Newspapers all over the world printed front-page stories telling how Hollywood's Cinderella won the prize without going to the ball. Joan was euphoric, but not so overwhelmed that she lost her sense of discipline. She made certain that Christina and Christopher performed their chores and went off to school with polished shoes and clean fingernails. She began dictating replies to those who sent flowers and messages; each would receive a personal, signed letter.

She had made it back to the top, and she, of all people, realized what work and self-denial were required to stay there. She also knew how lonely it could be. She had toughened herself to loneliness. She had tried marriage three times, and she would not face that hurt again. She had her career and the children. She had a myriad of acquaintances and a few who were loyal enough to be called friends. No matter that she was alone. Hadn't she been that way for most of her forty years?

I

*From Billie Cassin to
Lucille LeSueur:
1906–1925*

1

JOAN CRAWFORD the movie star rarely became tired, such was her boundless energy. But during moments of extreme fatigue she would suddenly and uncontrollably revert to an accent as heavy as a Panhandle cowboy's. "Ah jes' cain't seem to understand the dialogue," she would tell an astonished director.

No amount of correcting could restore the diction of her role as a society belle. Such occurrences baffled Joan. She could not understand why she would regress to her Southern beginnings. Lawton, Oklahoma, is farther south than Little Rock or Memphis, and the Confederate influence was still strong in Lawton in the early part of the century. And she may have lived longer in Texas than she admitted.

In her autobiography, *A Portrait of Joan*, she tells of leaving San Antonio at the age of six weeks. In interviews early in her career, she gave the figure as three months, six months, and a year. But in a remarkable series of biographical articles written by John C. Moffitt for the Kansas City *Star* in 1932, he cited her "childishly vague memories" of San Antonio: "of being cold at night, of a woman in a checkered apron who gave her round cookies with fat currants in the centers, and of her mother crying."

The best evidence points to the birthdate of March 23, 1906, for Lucille Fay LeSueur, despite her claim for almost fifty years that she was born on March 23, 1908. The exact date may never be known, since Texas law did not require birth certificates until 1908. Little is known about her father, Thomas LeSueur. He was French-Canadian, and in family portraits appears as an erect, humorless man with strong features and large, deep-set eyes. He married Anna Bell Johnson, part-Irish, part-Scandinavian; a lovely young woman with an oval face and long auburn hair. They had three children: Daisy, who died as an infant; then Hal Hayes LeSueur, born in 1904; and finally Lucille. The family lived, according to Joan, on South Cherry Street in "a drab little rented house on the wrong side of the tracks." Tom LeSueur was a "contractor," which meant that he picked up laboring jobs wherever he could. Eventually the task of supporting a wife and two small children proved too much for him, and he abandoned them. Anna LeSueur sought a new life for her little family in Lawton, and there she met and married Henry Cassin.

Joan saw her real father again in 1934. After she had become a movie star a man wrote from Waco, Texas, that he believed she was his daughter. She was dubious, since other correspondents had made that claim, but when he sent a photograph of himself, Joan's mother confirmed that he was indeed Tom LeSueur. He and Joan exchanged letters for five years, and then she suggested he come to Hollywood. He arrived when she was filming *Chained* with Clark Gable. Hal called her on the set and announced he was bringing their father that afternoon. "You'll know him," Hal said. "He's very tall and he has your eyes."

Joan's emotions were in a turmoil. For all of her twenty-eight years, her father had been a real figure in her mind. His image in faded family photographs had been impressed on her memory, and as a child she had conjured fantasies of what her life would have been like if he hadn't left. She was certain that he and her mother would have remained a loving couple, that his stern but affectionate hand would have given his daughter and son the right kind of upbringing. That father out of the old photographs came to life in her girlhood dreams, a darkly handsome figure who picked up his crying daughter and stroked her until the pain vanished.

Joan had no writers to tell her how to play the scene of a woman meeting her father for the first time. She approached the tall, serious-looking man tentatively. Hal took her hand and brought her closer. Tom LeSueur's big hand enveloped Joan's and he kissed her palm. "Hello, baby," he said shyly.

Joan said later: "I saw my father several times during his brief stay in Hollywood, but it was always the same—both of us trying to make a relationship that existed in name only a living thing. We never quite succeeded. On his last day in town, he visited me again on the set. I had only a few minutes with him when I was called for a scene. Just as I went into it, I looked across the stage and saw that his eyes were filled with tears. He waved goodbye, blew me a kiss and left. I never saw him again."

2

SHE STOOD in the wings, a tiny figure in a bright-red, accordion-pleated dress. Her big eyes grew larger as she watched the black-faced comic shuffle around the stage to "Camptown Races," played by the five-piece orchestra in the pit. The little girl's feet started to slide over the rough wooden backstage floor, trying to duplicate the comic's loose-jointed dance. "You're gittin' it, honey," said the comic as he came offstage. He patted her on the head and went on to his dressing room.

"Billie Cassin, you'd better get on home." She turned around and smiled at the familiar broad face. "Oh, Daddy, can't I stay and watch the acrobats?" she asked.

"No, dear, your mama will be sore enough about you stayin' this long. Now, scoot!" Billie kissed him on the cheek and scampered out the stage door. She saw the sun disappearing beyond Cache Creek and suddenly was worried. Time had stopped for her in the theater; now she was late for supper. She raced down the dirt street to the four-room Cassin house and hurried up the walk.

As Billie had feared, her mother was furious because the girl was late for supper.

Billie stood dejectedly in the middle of the kitchen floor while her mother reached behind the stove for the whip of sapling boughs. She deliberately tried not to make any noise as they lashed bloody welts across her legs. She looked at her brother, Hal, who was smiling over his bowl of white bread in warm milk, topped with melted butter and brown sugar. Billie stuck out her tongue at him and stomped into her bedroom. She picked up her baby doll and curled on the bed with it, the agony of her legs diminishing as she remembered the painted face and the leaping feet before the footlights of her father's theater.

Billie was always getting in trouble—she was an unabashed tomboy, and that's how she got her name. Hal thought "Billie" suited her better than the "Lucille" she had been born with, and while she was always tagging after Hal and his friends, he was always trying to escape her. "Billie, I want you to play with the girls," her mother ordered, and she applied the switch when Billie disobeyed. Billie never mentioned how the neighborhood girls teased her: their mothers didn't want them playing with the daughter of Henry Cassin, whose reputation in Lawton was highly questionable.

Lawton, Oklahoma, was the center of her world. Billie Cassin was one of the 7,788 citizens of the town, located near the Wichita mountains in the southern part of the state. It had been a territory only a few years before, and statehood had made citizens feel that Lawton was going to prosper with its cotton fields and oil derricks. Certainly Henry Cassin thought so, and he bought the Lawton Opera House; he also operated an open-air theater on C Street.

Henry Cassin could never be accepted by the citizenry of Lawton. The townspeople were hard-striving and serious-minded, with little regard for someone who trafficked in show business. Henry's manner and appearance offended them. He was a small man who dressed with flamboyance and wore glittering rings on his stubby fingers. People wondered how he could afford such jewelry on his earnings from the opera house, and there were whispers that he was engaged in something illegal. When schoolmates made such accusations, Billie fought with them, and her misbehavior brought more beatings from her mother.

Anna Cassin could not understand why Billie would not behave. Why couldn't the girl be like her brother, Hal, who never talked back to his mother and was always willing to run errands and help around the house? Anna saw in Billie a familiar willfulness that disturbed her. Anna herself had obstinately ignored the advice of her parents, with resulting grief. She had been warned that the marriage to Tom LeSueur would bring her grief, and it did. Anna had known the lonely fear of being left with two small children and no way to support them. She had hurried into the marriage with Henry Cassin as the only means of survival. He was an amiable man, but Anna felt none of the excitement she had known with young Tom LeSueur. She blamed herself for the sorrow that had befallen her, and she recognized her own youthful tendencies in Billie.

Billie adored the theater. She gave special attention to her school lessons because she was allowed to stand backstage only if she brought home good marks. The theater made life bearable for Billie. The performers accepted her as the boss's kid, and they smeared her face with rouge and greasepaint, taught her how to dance the cakewalk and the buck-and-wing. She listened wide-eyed to their tales of playing the circuit as far as the Yukon and dodging sheriffs after minstrel shows in the South, and she didn't realize that her heroes and heroines were the dregs of vaudeville, rejected misfits with scant talent who were reduced to touring Oklahoma for little more than subsistence.

The high-pitched barn behind the Cassin home was the scene of Billie's own shows. That was where Henry Cassin stored the threadbare scenery from his theaters, and Billie enlisted her playmates to imitate the world she had seen onstage. The neighborhood girls thought she was putting on airs, and they declined to play, but the boys found it exciting to dash about like musketeers and pilgrims under Billie's direction.

One day when Billie was six she cut her foot. She had grown bored with her piano lesson and decided to play on the front lawn. She leaped off the porch and landed on the jagged piece of a bottle. The glass ripped through her tendon and artery, and the pain was so acute that she lost consciousness. Don Blanding, the boy across the street, was returning to his house for a package he had forgotten and discovered the small figure on the lawn. He carried her into the house and called the doctor.

"She'll never be able to walk without a limp," the doctor pronounced after he had sewn Billie's foot together. Two operations later he made the same prediction. Billie refused to believe it. The intense pain kept her awake at night and in the darkness she determined that she would dance again.

Billie spent long months in bed. Each day she looked forward to the time when Henry Cassin came home, for he brought her candy and new dolls, and he filled her with backstage stories—a fight between two acrobats over their girl partner, a wild performance by a drunken fire-eater. Then her daddy read to her from Grimm's fairy tales.

Before she fell asleep, Henry Cassin assured her, "Don't you worry, little Billie, you're gonna dance again." He was convinced. Cassin possessed the sunshiny confidence of a man who believed he could bring entertainment to the citizens of a southern Oklahoma hamlet. He had persisted, despite the rebuffs of the staid elements of the community. He applied the same positivism to Billie and her injured foot. The doctor's opinion didn't matter; Billie could *will* her own recovery.

When her mother was away at the store, Billie began the first faltering steps. After a few weeks she began to dance. She borrowed the kitchen clock and timed how long she could dance until the pain overcame her. Five minutes. Then eight. By the end of summer Billie could dance for half an hour without collapsing. She realized she had beaten the doctor's prediction.

Billie was exploring one day in the cellar where her mother kept the jellies and preserves. She discovered a burlap bag too heavy to lift. It fell over, and out tumbled a profusion of bright, glittering coins. She hurried upstairs to show them to her mother. Instead of being overjoyed, Mrs. Cassin was disturbed. "Don't you ever mention this to anyone—*ever!*" she told Billie.

That night Billie noticed urgent whispered conversations between her mother and father, and the next day Billie was told that she and Hal were going on a train to visit their grandparents in Phoenix. It was a confused and troubled parting for the little girl, who had never been away from her parents before. She noticed her father's worried face as he waved goodbye to her and Hal from the Lawton station.

"I hope nothing's wrong," she said to her brother. "He's such a nice daddy." She noticed that Hal snickered, and she asked him why.

"Aw, he's not our daddy," the boy said.

"What do you mean?" she demanded.

"Our daddy's in Texas. His name is LeSueur, and that's our name, too. Here, look." He took a photograph out of his bag. It was a family portrait, and Hal pointed to a dark man with a mustache. "That's your real daddy."

Billie lay awake in her berth most of the night, trying to make sense out of what her brother had told her. It was hard for her to grasp. She had known only one father, the warm, incurably optimistic Henry Cassin, who had led her by the hand into the enormously attractive world of the theater, whose quiet understanding had proved her refuge from the discipline of her mother. Now her unfeeling brother had told her that Henry Cassin wasn't her father after all; Billie was the daughter of some stern-featured man in a faded photograph. She was perplexed and silent during the visit to her grandparents.

Henry Cassin went on trial as the alleged accomplice of the gold embezzler. He was acquitted, but the stigma pursued him relentlessly in the small town. Anna persuaded her husband that the family needed a new start, and Henry moved his wife and two stepchildren to Kansas City.

Never again would Billie know the same closeness with the man she had thought was her father. No more the hand-in-hand walks to the Saturday matinee at the theater, no more climbing into his lap as he smoked his cigar over the evening newspaper.

The Lawton years exerted a profound influence over Joan Crawford. She never escaped the guilt that she alone may have caused the family's downfall by her discovery in the cellar. Fearful remembrances returned to her in later years: An unexpected surge of wind recalled the terror of waiting underground for an Oklahoma cyclone to pass over. During a dance for *Our Blushing Brides,* she fell to the studio floor in excruciating pain, the same she had experienced after she leaped off the porch in Lawton. After she had become a movie star, she collected two thousand dolls and kept them in a special bedroom of her home. She admitted that when her life seemed troubled, she closed the door behind her and curled up with her dolls.

Don Blanding, the Lawton boy who summoned a doctor when Billie Cassin slashed her foot, became a popular versifier, and he wrote of his onetime neighbor:

> She was just a little girl
> Who lived across the street,
> All legs and curls and great big eyes

And restless, dancing feet,
As vivid as a hummingbird,
As bright and swift and gay,
A child who played at make-believe.

3

FORTUNE STILL ELUDED Henry Cassin after he moved his small family to Kansas City. His trial seemed to have placed a curse on the family, destroying his relationship with Anna and tarnishing his hope to make a new start in life. He is first listed in the city directory of Kansas City in 1917, with his residence at 403 East Ninth Street, in the heart of the downtown district, where he and Anna leased a third-rate hotel and managed it for transients.

Billie Cassin was overwhelmed by Kansas City—the clangor of streetcars that passed the family's small apartment, the rumble of brewery drays over cobblestone streets, the noise of brass bands at Liberty Bond rallies to finance the war. After the small country school in Lawton, Scarritt Elementary School seemed huge and unfriendly. The city children made fun of her home-sewn dresses and refused to include her in their games. The school principal, Harvey S. Walter, took notice of her.

"Hello, there, Billie," he said, kneeling so his eyes were on the level with hers.

"Hello, Mr. Walter," she said shyly.

"Your teacher tells me you're trying very hard to learn your lessons. Good for you! I want you to keep up the good work, and if you have any problems, you bring them right to me. Understand?"

"Yes, Mr. Walter." Every time she saw the principal on the

playground and in the hallways, he gave her a warm smile. Billie began bringing her schoolwork home every night, so her grades would justify Mr. Walter's faith in her.

Henry Cassin's hotel venture proved a failure. The place was too rundown to attract anything but drifters, and too many of them fled without paying their bills. Anna Cassin berated her husband for the folly of the investment, and Billie heard them quarreling far into the night.

Since Anna Cassin was working long days in the hotel, she had no time to look after Billie. Henry Cassin, who had been reared a Roman Catholic, suggested that the girl enter a convent school. Anna agreed, and she enrolled Billie in St. Agnes School at Scarritt and Hardesty streets, creating another unsettling change for Billie Cassin. Encouraged by Principal Walter, she had just begun making friends at Scarritt Elementary and was getting better marks in her classes. Now she found herself behind the stone walls of St. Agnes, dressed with fifty other girls in blue-and-white gingham uniforms. After the kindness of Mr. Walter, the nuns seemed cold and exacting. At night Billie went to bed in a dormitory and longed for the chance of climbing onto Daddy Cassin's lap and falling asleep in his arms. Yet as the weeks continued, Billie became more comfortable at St. Agnes. She learned that many of the girls came from poor homes and were just as scared as she was, and she sensed that behind the sternness of the nuns was a loving spirit and genuine concern for the well-being of the girls.

One weekend when Billie returned to the hotel, she noticed a change. No longer did she smell the aroma of Cremo cigars, the sweetly pungent odor of toilet water and worn tweed. "Where's Daddy?" Billie asked.

"He's gone," her mother replied.

"When is he coming back?"

"Never. He's gone for good."

"No, no!" Billie started to shriek.

"Now, listen to me!" her mother said. "There's going to be some changes. I've got a job, managing a laundry. But that won't bring enough. Hal will have to quit school and go to work. And I can't afford to keep you at St. Agnes."

Billie was beginning to rue the impact of constant change. She had been forced to leave Scarritt Elementary just as she was starting to form new friendships. Now that she was beginning to enjoy the order and discipline of St. Agnes, she would be yanked out to become a stranger in yet another school, and instead of sleeping in the cool, gray-walled dormitories of the convent, she would be sharing dingy rooms with her mother and Hal.

"I can't leave St. Agnes; I can't!" Billie cried.

"We have no money, Billie!" her mother shouted.

"Then I'll work at school," the girl insisted. "I know the sisters will let me stay if I work, I know they will."

Her mother preferred not to have a young daughter to contend with, and she knew that if Billie could stay at the convent, she would be assured hot meals and a free education. Mrs. Cassin conferred with the mother superior, and the agreement was reached that Billie would be able to remain at St. Agnes during the week, waiting on tables for her room and board; on weekends she would return to her mother.

At the age of eleven Billie Cassin started supporting herself, beginning a lifetime of almost unremitting work. She had to leave her morning classes early to set up the tables for lunch, and she was late to her first afternoon class because of dishwashing. Classes held no great interest for Billie, so she was happy to spend the time in the kitchen and dining hall. Nor was she concerned about waking up before the other girls to help with breakfast, or working after supper. That meant less time for reading books, which bored her. On Saturdays she began inventing chores to occupy her until late afternoon, because then she had an excuse to go home late. More and more she dreaded the weekends and the return to the drab three rooms that her mother and Hal occupied behind the laundry. She hated the smell of lye and solvent that pervaded her home, and she hated what the drudgery of washing and ironing was doing to her mother.

Billie would never feel close to her mother, for she believed that her mother still grieved over the loss of Daisy and compared Daisy's sweet manner to Billie's tomboyish rebelliousness. Hal had always been the favored child, and whenever Billie and Hal were fighting, it was always Hal who won his mother's support. Billie remembered close moments with her mother, particularly when she had injured her foot. But with the failure of her mother's second marriage and her grueling life at the laundry, Anna Cassin became remote and embittered.

Once in a rare while Billie was able to enjoy tranquillity with her mother. When Anna Cassin had saved enough money, she invited Billie to Sunday dinner at a tearoom on Eleventh Street. Over beef-and-kidney pie they chattered about events of their individual lives—Billie laughed gaily as she told of tricks the St. Agnes children played on the unsuspecting nuns, Anna told of misplaced orders and lost shirts at the laundry. Afterward they strolled down to Main Street and studied the window displays at the Emery, Bird, Thayer Company, Billie admiring and her mother deploring the daring new short skirts. One Sunday Anna had saved enough to treat Billie to a movie. They saw Mary Pickford in *Little Lord Fauntleroy* and cried happy tears. Anna always walked with Billie back to St. Agnes and they parted with hugs and kisses. Billie went to bed with warm thoughts. She reviewed the pleasant time she had spent with her mother and wondered why such occasions had been so rare.

Daddy Cassin always remained in Billie's thoughts. She told the other girls at the convent about how they would walk together to the theater in Lawton and how he would let her watch the show from the wings. Billie even reenacted the performance, deftly imitating the toe dancers and the soft-shoe performers. On her way home every Saturday, Billie strolled through downtown Kansas City, hoping she would see Daddy Cassin once more. Bewildered by the blur of passing faces, she stared at the sidewalk, searching for his small feet in bulldog shoes.

One day she found them. She looked up and saw the broad smile on Daddy Cassin's face. She jumped into his arms and hugged him. "Oh, Daddy, I've missed you so much!" she cried.

"And I've missed you, Billie," he said, kissing her cheek. "C'mon, I'll buy you an ice-cream soda." He led her by the hand to a corner drugstore and lifted her onto a stool before the white-marble counter. Billie ordered a chocolate soda with two scoops of vanilla ice cream, and she continued sipping noisily through the straw after the glass had been emptied. She couldn't take her eyes from Daddy Cassin's round face.

He asked about her school, and she painted a glowing picture of her life at St. Agnes. "What are you doing, Daddy?" she inquired, and he replied, "Right now I'm waiting for a big deal to come through. Matter of fact, I'm on my way to an appointment right now." Both were tearful when they parted, and he said assuringly, "Don't worry, honey, I'll come see you." But he never did.

Billie had lied about St. Agnes. She had become increasingly unhappy at the school, not because of the nuns, whom she found stern but loving, but because of the attitudes of the other students. She wore the same uniform that they wore, but they treated her differently. They considered her a servant, not an equal. She brought their meals, cleaned up after them, ran their errands. She wasn't included in their games or even their conversations. Billie was deeply hurt to be considered an inferior.

She was relieved when she finished the grammar-school curriculum of St. Agnes, but for her mother it was merely another crisis. She had no money to keep her daughter in school, so she hunted for another place where the girl could work for her lessons. An advertisement in the Kansas City *Star* offered employment for a girl at the Rockingham Academy in Kansas City.

Mrs. Cassin took Billie to a district of elegant homes and wide lawns, and found a large house with a sign in the window: GIRL WANTED. Mrs. Emma Hessel, principal of Rockingham, explained that Rockingham was a boarding and day school for children of the better families of Kansas City. She would be willing to enroll Billie in the school in exchange for a few light duties around the house. It seemed the ideal solution to Mrs. Cassin's problem, and an agreement was reached.

Billie discovered that she was in charge of the cleaning and maintenance of the fourteen-room mansion that served as a school for children of the rich, and realized that her work in the convent had been a vacation compared to what Mrs. Hessel expected of her. Billie had to get up at dawn, wake the small children, bathe and dress them, cook all the meals for thirty children, and keep the mansion immaculately clean. If she failed in her duties, she was beaten with a broom handle. She fell into bed at midnight, facing the same drudgery at dawn. Her only solace came from the other students. She enjoyed playing mother to the small children, tucking them into bed and reading them fairy tales until they fell off to sleep. When one of the older girls observed Billie's long days with pity and offered to help in the chores, Mrs. Hessel overheard and dragged Billie down two flights of stairs, then beat her with the broom handle and kicked her.

Billie never told her mother about her abuse at Rockingham Academy; she feared Mrs. Hessel would make more trouble for her if she did. Anna Cassin was now living with a Mr. Hough—Billie never knew his first name. Whenever Billie came home on weekends, Mr. Hough alternated between finding fault with the girl and lapsing into long periods of hostile silence. Communication with her mother had been difficult since the family moved to Kansas City, but now it was virtually impossible. As for Hal, he was too concerned with his own pursuits to bother with his little sister. So Billie returned to the small rooms behind the laundry less and less, even though her life at Rockingham was equally intolerable. One night she left the mansion, hoping to find some way that she wouldn't have to return. She couldn't go home and face the stern questioning of Mr. Hough. She wandered through the park past midnight, and a policeman stopped her, escorting her back to the school. She took off her shoes and tried to return to her room without detection, but Mrs. Hessel was waiting for her and delivered a merciless beating. Billie tried to run away again, but returned with the saddening realization that she had no place to go. The misery continued for three years. Then, suddenly, in her final year at Rockingham, life became more bearable.

Adolescence had provided Billie with a fetching kind of beauty, and the older boys at Rockingham were beginning to notice. One of them asked her to attend a neighborhood dance.

"I'd love to," Billie replied excitedly. Then she added with caution, "But maybe you'd better ask Mrs. Hessel first." To Billie's surprise, the principal approved. Mrs. Hessel reasoned that if the rich boys at the school admired Billie enough to invite her to dances, the girl's presence at Rockingham could prove to be an advantage. From then on, the beatings ceased.

Billie was thrilled at the prospect of her first date, and the girls in Billie's class who had seen her during her years at Rockingham rejoiced with her. One of them volunteered a blue chiffon dress slightly torn under one arm, which Billie easily mended. She gazed at herself in the full-length mirror and discovered what the Rockingham boys had recognized: she was pretty. Perhaps even beautiful. Her eyes, she had always been told, were her best feature, but she also had a perfectly proportioned oval face, with a slim, straight nose and full lips. She had freckles, of course, but a few dabs of a powderpuff could eliminate them. Her hair was a rich brown and it combed easily. Her figure retained some of the aspects of her tomboyish childhood; her shoulders were athletic, her hips narrow. But her chest eliminated any question of whether she was a girl.

She concluded her self-assessment with approval, then prepared for her entrance. The boy was waiting at the bottom of the long oak staircase, corsage in hand. Billie stood at the top of the stairs for a moment, waiting for him to notice. He looked up and stared at the young beauty in blue chiffon. Under his admiring gaze she walked deliberately down the stairs, a half-smile on her lips. It was a scene she would draw from in later years.

The entire evening was a glorious dream. A college band played the latest jazz tunes, and Billie danced unceasingly, hair flying. She still felt infused with energy when she went to bed at the school that night, and she lay awake reliving every dance. She hadn't felt such happiness since the times backstage with Daddy Cassin in Lawton.

The invitations to dances came often, and many nights Billie sneaked out of the school to accompany boys to parties. Mrs. Hessel raised no objection and even contributed a couple of frocks from a bargain store. Billie's mother was pleased to see the girl finally getting some enjoyment out of life, and she took Billie to the basement of a department store. They selected a taffeta dress with shirrings, rosebuds and silver lace, marked down to $4.95. Billie wore it the night she won her first dance contest—at the Jack-o'-Lantern Club on the northwest corner of Westport and Main streets.

After Billie had spent three years at Rockingham, Mrs. Hessel informed her that she had finished the equivalent of her high-school education—there were no more courses for her to take. Billie felt she had learned nothing because of the cruel labor she had been required to perform, but she was given her credits and released from the school. She found a job selling notions at a small department store for twelve dollars a week, and Mr. Hough exacted half of her salary for room and board behind the laundry. Billie used much of the remainder to buy new clothes on the employees' discount.

The dances continued, and at a prom in Kansas City College gymnasium she met the first in a long series of males who would exercise a profound influence on her life and career. He was Ray Sterling, an intense, ambitious youth with handsome blond looks, and he became attracted to Billie not only because of her striking appearance and enormous energy but also because he saw more depth and perceived more potential in her than anyone else had realized, including Billie herself.

"Billie, you're trying too hard to have a good time," he told her. "That's understandable, because you've got a lot of catching up to do. But you can't take it all at once, or it won't have any value for you. You'll just burn yourself out." He told her she didn't have to dance every dance. She didn't have to wear so much makeup, to talk so loud, laugh so much. Billie listened curiously. No one had spoken to her like this before, and his advice made sense. She couldn't always follow it, but she tried, because she wanted to please Ray. Most of all, she wanted to grow. She listened as he shared books and music with her, and she decided not to settle for a department-store job but to broaden her knowledge by going on to college.

Someone else also had faith in Billie Cassin: Mr. Walter, the principal of Scarritt Elementary, who was now secretary of Stephens College, a small girls' school at Columbia, Missouri. Like Ray Sterling, Mr. Walter believed that Billie should go on to college, and reviewing her credits from Rockingham he said they would be sufficient for her to enter Stephens, which was experiencing hard times and needed all the students it could find.

Billie pleaded with her mother, and Anna Cassin agreed to let her daughter enroll at Stephens—provided she could support herself. That had been arranged by Mr. Walter, who found Billie work as a waitress in the school dining room. Anna took money from her savings to buy dresses for Billie, and in the fall of 1922 the girl went off to Stephens College, registering with her birthdate of 1906.

The first weeks went well. She was experienced at serving meals, and her job didn't occupy too much of her time. She enjoyed exchanging experiences with the other Stephens girls, who were far more sophisticated than those she had known in Kansas City. The boys at the university soon besieged the pretty brunette with the dancing feet, and many nights she sneaked back into the dormitory after a fraternity dance at the nearby University of Missouri, unreported by a sympathetic watchman.

Mr. Walter had suggested Billie should become a teacher. So did the president of Stephens, Dr. James Wood, a remarkable educator and empathetic man who maintained a personal interest in his students.

"You would make a fine teacher, Billie," Dr. Wood told her. "You have energy and enthusiasm and the eagerness to help other people. All you need to do is apply yourself to your studies. You can do it if you try." She began to decline invitations from fraternity boys and spent an entire week at the dormitory trying to make sense out of her assignments. It didn't work. She had slept through too many classes at Rockingham and had known too many indifferent teachers. She was totally unprepared for college.

Her depressed spirits were raised one afternoon when she was asked by one of the most popular girls in school to pledge her sorority. "Of course! I'd love to!" Billie replied. "Wonderful!" said the girl. "Wait here until I talk to the rest of my sorority sisters. I'll be right back."

Billie was so thrilled with the news that she had to tell someone, so she started writing a letter to Ray Sterling. But she was interrupted by a knock at her door. Her friend from the sorority stood in the doorway. "I don't know how to tell you this, Billie," she stammered. "When I suggested that you pledge the sorority, I didn't realize you were working your way through school. You see, we don't take in girls who work. I'm sorry." Billie sat alone in her room as the sky darkened outside. She roused herself only when the maid arrived to tell Billie it was time for her to set the tables for supper. Joan Crawford never forgot the hurt. When she became a Hollywood star, she answered every fan letter she received. Except those that began, "Remember me? We were in school together at Stephens. . . ."

Billie decided to escape. With midterm examinations approaching she realized she would disgrace herself in the eyes of Daddy Wood, as the students called him, so she packed all of her belongings and sent a collect wire to Ray Sterling, asking him to meet her at the Kansas City railroad station.

She was waiting for the train on the Columbia, Missouri, platform when she heard a voice behind her: "Where are you going, Billie?" It was Daddy Wood. The dormitory watchman had alerted him that one of the girls had packed her things and was leaving the school.

"Why are you running away?" Daddy Wood asked.

"Because I don't belong here," Billie answered. "I'm too dumb. I don't understand what the teachers are talking about."

"You aren't 'dumb,' Billie. You're a smart girl. You simply didn't get enough preparation for college in your earlier schooling."

"It's too late to catch up. I'm leaving."

"Not like this, Billie. Don't sneak away in the night as if you had done something wrong. I want you to come with me."

"Where?"

"To my office. I want you to call your mother and tell her it just isn't working out and you're coming home. We'll give you a proper discharge from Stephens. Later, when you're better prepared, you can come back."

"No, I don't want to come back. I don't want to serve meals to the rich girls. I want to have pretty clothes like they have, and I'm not going to get them by being a schoolteacher. I want to be a *dancer*."

"All right, Billie, then *be* a dancer. I know you can be a *good* dancer. You're a special kind of girl, Billie; I recognized that from the start. You have it within you to accomplish whatever you set out to do. Never quit. Don't run away because something seems to be too great a challenge."

A decade later Joan Crawford would express her gratitude: "I'll always love Dr. Wood of Stephens College. He was the first person to tell me that my aspirations are all right. He was the first person to speak as though I might *realize* them. In that little talk at the train station at Columbia, he gave me more to benefit me through life, more human education than all the hours in the classroom put together. He'd be surprised to learn the places where I have heard him repeating his words—while I was a member of a cheap road show, while I was kicking in the chorus on Broadway, in cabarets and Hollywood dance halls. I could always hear him say, 'Don't run away; let your record do you justice.' And I've always tried to obey him."

On her return to Kansas City, Billie Cassin entered the training program at the Bell Telephone Company but found the work of a telephone operator unbearable. She took a job wrapping packages at the Wolff Clothing Store for twelve dollars a week, then moved to another store, Rothschild's, which paid her a dollar more, and finally worked for fifteen dollars a week at Emery, Bird, Thayer, selling women's wear.

The situation at home was no better. Mr. Hough continued to resent her presence and complained there was no room for her in the apartment. Fortunately Billie found solace from the tension at home and the dreariness of selling clothes in the stimulating company of Ray Sterling. They went on moonlight rides to Cliff Drive and Penn Valley Park, and they talked about their futures.

"He believed in me," Joan Crawford remembered. "He knew all about the laundry, the schools, the beatings. He knew the gossip which always encircles a girl who is working her way through life and snatching her fun in the dance halls. Yet he believed I was going to amount to something. He believed I had a beautiful *soul* as well as a dancing *body*."

Ray didn't scorn Billie's ambitions of becoming a dancer, as did her mother and Hal. When Billie told Ray of hearing about an audition for a traveling show, he told her, "Go after it." During her lunch hour she hurried to the Baltimore Hotel and stood in line with other girls who were trying out for the chorus of a show starring Katherine Emerine, a popular entertainer in the Midwest. When Billie's turn came, she performed a few steps to the off-key piano in the empty ballroom.

The man with a cigar in his face said, "You'll do, honey. Twenty bucks a week. We start in Springfield, Missouri, next week. What's your name?"

Billie had been thinking about it. "Lucille LeSueur," she replied.

The man with the cigar smiled. "Well, honey, you sure picked a fancy one!"

4

LUCILLE LESUEUR WAS one of sixteen chorus girls who kicked their legs and sang behind Katherine Emerine as she interpreted the latest tunes from New York operettas for an audience in Springfield, Missouri. After two weeks the show folded, and Lucille LeSueur had barely earned enough money for her train fare back to Kansas City. The star of the show expressed interest in the raw, eager girl in the back row of the chorus. "You don't have much talent, Lucille, but I like your enthusiasm," said Miss Emerine. "If you ever come to Chicago, look me up. Here's my address."

Selling corsets and frocks on the third floor at Emery, Bird, Thayer Company again, Lucille was miserable. Even though the Emerine troupe had played only to half-empty houses, the experience convinced her that she had to fulfill her dream of becoming a dancer. But how? A final, acrimonious quarrel with her mother settled Lucille's mind; she would go to Chicago and accept Katherine Emerine's invitation to look her up.

"But how could I leave Ray Sterling?" Joan Crawford wrote in an early magazine autobiography. "He was my pal, my friend and my sweetheart. He, who had given me the very ambition which was now urging me to go thousands of miles away from him. How often does ambition force a woman to face such a separation? Yet, if she subjugates her career for a man, she may spend the rest of her life wondering to what heights she might have climbed had she followed her inclinations. And if she goes, there comes a time when she wonders if, after all, home and innocence-of-the-world might not have meant a more pacific, happy existence."

Lucille boarded the train to Chicago without a telephone call, without a note to Ray Sterling. As she stared out the parlor-car window at the green Missouri farms, she felt heartsick. Not about leaving Kansas City. She was glad to escape the unpleasant memories—the loss of Daddy Cassin, the beatings at Rockingham, her rejection because she was a servant, the bitter wrangles with her mother. Her only regret was leaving Ray. He had offered brightness and hope to her life. She realized that if she had called him, he might easily have persuaded her to stay in Kansas City. Probably they would have married and settled down, and she would never have known a destiny beyond being Mrs. Raymond Sterling.

Later Joan Crawford related differing versions of Lucille Le-Sueur's arrival in Chicago. She either had two dollars left at the end of her train ride from Kansas City, or she had five dollars. She either shared a taxi with a kindly old gentleman she met on the train, or she enlisted the services of a gruff but understanding cabbie. No matter. Instead of arriving at the elegant home of Katherine Emerine, Lucille found herself in front of a seedy rooming house in a dreary district of Chicago.

"She's not here," said the landlady. "She's on the road."

Lucille's heart sank. Katherine Emerine was her only connection in Chicago. But then she remembered a name Miss Emerine had mentioned—Ernie Young. He was a casting agent and producer, and she had worked for him in Chicago. Lucille walked to a corner drugstore and consulted the telephone book. Ernie Young was listed with an office in the Loop. The druggist supplied directions, and Lucille made her way by streetcar and bus to Ernie Young's office in downtown Chicago.

She arrived to find a dozen girls waiting for an audition. Blondes, brunettes and redheads of all sizes, painting fingernails, combing bobbed hair, studying themselves in mirrors. Lucille waited for an hour, and then the urgency of her situation roused her to action. She burst into Young's office over his secretary's protest.

"I may not be as beautiful as those girls out there," she began in a state of frenzy, "but I've only got two dollars and I've some experience in a Katherine Emerine show, and I can't go back to Kansas City. Please don't kick me out."

Ernie Young smiled. "Nobody's going to kick you out. Now, just calm down and tell me what this is all about." He realized immediately that she wasn't as beautiful as the girls in the outer office; she was short for a chorus girl and a bit overweight, but she had an engaging manner, and she could turn on a winning smile when she relaxed and exerted some charm. Ernie Young and his wife auditioned her in a rehearsal hall and the agent told her, "You're going on tonight in the chorus at the Friars' Inn. Twenty-five bucks a week." Another chorus girl demonstrated the simple routines, and Lucille fell right into step. After a week she was sent to Oklahoma City as part of a revue designed to entertain convention salesmen, then to an engagement at the Oriole Terrace in Detroit.

Lucille had been a fast student in Chicago and Oklahoma City, quickly imitating the movements and routines of the other chorines, but the thirty girls in the Oriole Terrace line were veterans who demolished their competition, and they made Lucille dress behind a curtain so she couldn't copy them. A single member of the chorus felt compassion for the green kid from Kansas City. She demonstrated how to apply alluring makeup, how to save the highest kick for the final number, how to use her unforgettable lips and glance suggestively over her shoulder at the male customers. After eight weeks at the Oriole Terrace, Lucille LeSueur was one of the stalwarts of the chorus. She had no trouble learning the eight new routines that were scheduled each week, and the stage manager promoted her to the position at the end of the line, where she would be the last girl to leave the stage. With each change of costume Lucille assumed a new identity, and the exhilaration compelled her to smile, even laugh as she was dancing—her exuberance was enormously appealing.

J. J. Shubert recognized her appeal one evening. She was not the most beautiful girl in the line nor a very good dancer, but she had an engaging way of fixing her eyes on the patrons and seeming to enjoy herself immensely while entertaining them. The theatrical tycoon was trying out a new revue in Detroit, and he took some companions to the Oriole Terrace for a nightcap. He studied the young dancer as she clomped on the stage in wooden shoes for the

Dutch number, then returned for the gypsy ensemble in a swirling multicolored skirt and jangling bracelets. It didn't bother J.J. that the dancer spun too near his table and sent glasses crashing to the floor.

"Are you the girl who knocked the glasses off my table?" he asked backstage.

"Yes, sir," Lucille replied.

"I'd like you to see the matinee of a show I'm presenting, *Innocent Eyes*. Tomorrow afternoon. If you're interested, I might give you a job. I'll have a pass in your name at the box office."

The matinee of *Innocent Eyes* opened an entirely new and dazzling world for Lucille LeSueur. After the makeshift costumes and haphazard choreography of the Oriole Terrace, she was overwhelmed by the opulence and the precision of the Shubert show. Scene after scene presented visual delights, with showgirls descending staircases in sequined gowns and feather boas. The star of *Innocent Eyes* was the French entertainer Mistinguette, and although Lucille couldn't understand the words she sang, the magnetism of her personality was unmistakable. And her legs! The audience applauded whenever she revealed their perfect form.

Lucille was in heaven when she reported backstage to J. J. Shubert. He asked if she could learn the dance routines. Absolutely, she replied, and he invited her to join the show. It would open in ten days, on March 20, 1924. The company would be leaving at two A.M. after the Saturday-night performance.

"Don't be late, Lucille," Shubert called.

"Not on your life, Mr. Shubert."

Lucille had two more nights to dance at the Oriole Terrace. She longed to tell *someone* about her great fortune, especially the one chorus girl who had helped her, but she didn't dare. She was afraid the management would hold her to the two-week notice that she had learned was customary when quitting a show. If that happened, she would miss *Innocent Eyes*. She had her suitcase packed, and when she finished the final number at one A.M., she hurried to the train station and joined the Shubert troupe.

Lucille scarcely slept on the train to New York. To her surprise, the other chorines of *Innocent Eyes* demonstrated the show's dance steps in the train vestibule, taught Lucille how to make quick changes so she could return for the next cue. A few years later Joan

Crawford recalled, "I was a girl, at last, being understood by other girls who wanted to be understood also. I imagine people think chorus girls are just a gaudy crew bent upon being Wall Street's collective mistress. I thought so myself until I became one of them. Hard? Yes, they're hard. They can't be sensitive and be successful. It just isn't in the Broadway racket."

Lucille, five feet four inches tall, was a "pony"—the term for a smaller dancer. Her favorite number was "Organdy Days," a sentimental ballad by Sigmund Romberg and Jean Schwartz. Lucille and the other dancers wore billowy organdy gowns and the chorus boys were immaculate in white tie and tails. Mistinguette sang in her accented English, "When hearts are young . . . in organdy days." *Innocent Eyes* was well-received, and Lucille felt proud to be a part of a successful production. She felt prouder when she was promoted two weeks after opening, moving from the back row of the chorus, third from the left, to a position in the front row. Now she could write to Ray Sterling and to her mother, relating her New York triumph.

Lucille seemed to make friends with ease. Frances Williams, a featured member of the cast, recognized that Lucille was new to New York, and she helped her get established at a respectable boardinghouse that catered to the theatrical trade. Lucille moved in with another chorus girl, Mitzi DuBois, and they took turns cooking meals over the gas fixture. Another member of the *Innocent Eyes* chorus, Lewis Offield, became one of her best friends, for they had much in common. Both came from Missouri—Lew was born in Sedalia. Both had the driving ambition to succeed in show business. Perhaps because they were so similar, no romance developed. Lucille enjoyed the brotherly closeness of Lew, something she had never known with Hal.

The Shuberts enforced a strict rule that a chorus boy and girl could not leave the Winter Garden together, so Lew and Lucille left the stage door separately, then met at the trolley barns behind the Winter Garden Theater. They often practiced a few dance steps on the pavement, then set out to explore Manhattan, riding the bus up Riverside Drive and sitting on park benches overlooking the Hudson. They strolled down Fifth Avenue, and Lucille stood for minutes before the displays of fine dresses in the store windows.

"I'm going to have things like that," she declared.

"Damn right you are!" Lew replied.

They frequented a diner off Times Square and stared dreamily at the marquees of the theaters. Everywhere they looked, lights were flashing with stellar attractions: George M. Cohan in *Song and Dance Man*, Walter Hampden in *Cyrano de Bergerac*, Eleanora Duse making her farewell appearance. Lee Tracy was starring in *The Show-Off* and Otis Skinner in *Sancho Panza*; Bert Wheeler, Fanny Brice and Paul Whiteman were headlining the *Ziegfeld Follies*, and Ziegfeld was presenting Eddie Cantor in *Kid Boots*. André Charlot produced a revue with new English performers Gertrude Lawrence, Jack Buchanan and Beatrice Lillie. Also playing were Fred and Adele Astaire in *Lady Be Good*.

"What do you want more than anything in the world?" Lew Offield asked.

"Me?" said Lucille LeSueur. "I want to be the most famous ballroom *dancer* in the world. Someday I'm going to dance with Maurice, the big dancing star. I dream about it all the time. How about you?"

"I dream of being a big musical-comedy star. I want to have a style that everybody will imitate, like Harry Richman. Now, there's a guy with real style."

Their friendship continued until *Innocent Eyes* went on the road. Lew was promised a raise and a specialty number, while Lucille decided to stay in New York and dance in the next Shubert show at the Winter Garden, *The Passing Show of 1924*. But four years later they met again in Hollywood. At a movie premiere at Grauman's Chinese Theater, Joan Crawford recognized the figure in white tie and tails as he walked up the aisle in front of her. "You looked just like that in *Innocent Eyes*," she said, and Jack Oakie swung around and crooned, "When hearts are young in organdy days . . ."

Not all of Lucille's New York friendships were platonic. At first she went out with college boys that Frances Williams had introduced her to, and the dates were as pleasurable to Lucille as the fraternity dances at college. Her roommate, Mitzi, scoffed, "You're a sucker to go out with those babies when you could be dining with sugar daddies at Delmonico's." But Lucille was unimpressed by the "johnnies" who sent orchids backstage to the chorus girls. One suitor Lucille could not resist was a Broadway actor, star of his own production. He sent flowers to Lucille LeSueur, and she was duly impressed. He took her dancing, and he exercised his considerable magnetism on her. Not only was Lucille overwhelmed by him but she observed how her reputation among the other chorus girls soared just because she was seen with him. Lucille thought she was in love. But then one day after a matinee, the doorman handed Lucille a note: "Please may I see you?" It was signed, "Another chorus girl." Lucille went to the stage door and found a pretty girl who introduced herself as Mary Orr. She asked if Lucille would have dinner with her before the evening show. Over dinner Mary Orr explained that she had been having a romance with the same actor for more than a year and considered herself engaged to him. She had been shattered when he suddenly started devoting his evenings to Lucille. "I'm not asking you to give him up," said Mary Orr. "I just wouldn't like to see you have your heart broken, the way mine was."

It was a revelation for Lucille, and she ended her romance with the fickle actor. Nevertheless the incident disillusioned her, and she poured out her feelings in a letter to Ray Sterling. Friendship and loyalty meant nothing in New York, she wrote; deceitful, selfish persons sought cruel advantage of young girls alone in the city. Ray replied to her on November 9, 1924: "New York, as I gather, is like a melting pot of all classes and a cesspool of all licentiousness. It is only natural that those with more money than morals should be drawn to that gathering of beauty that is the theatrical world. . . . The cads who infest the world you work in are not fit examples of New York, dear. They are but the flies who gather around the sugar bowl. There must be many good people in the city who are as good as the others who are no good."

Ray's letter contributed to Lucille's homesickness. She decided to go back to Kansas City for Christmas. She needed train fare, and her $35-a-week salary wasn't enough. She confided her problem to Nils T. Granlund, the stage manager of *The Passing Show*, who had a reputation for being sympathetic to chorus girls' problems. "I'll tell you how you can make some extra dough, Lucille," said Granlund. "You work up a number or two, and I'll get you an audition at Harry Richman's joint."

Lucille asked her escorts to take her to nightclubs in Harlem, where blacks danced the Charleston. She found it enormously appealing, a mixture of flailing elbows and twisting knees that blended perfectly with the frenetic jazz. She realized she had the energy for it, having concluded that energy rather than technique was her prime asset as a dancer.

She practiced the dance before the mirror of her apartment, devising a routine to a gramophone record of "When My Sweetie Walks Down the Street." When she auditioned for Harry Richman, he recognized the appealing novelty of the dance. He was also impressed by Lucille's vivacity, and he hired her on the spot.

Each night after the curtain of *The Passing Show*, she hurried to 157 West 56th Street, where the singer maintained his speakeasy, the Club Richman. Two weeks before her planned return to Kansas City, Lucille received a telephone call from Granlund. "Harry Rapf is in town," he said.

"Yeah? Who's he?" Lucille asked.

"Who's he? A big shot from Metro-Goldwyn-Mayer. He's looking for girls to sign for the studio."

"That's nice."

"He saw the show last night at the Winter Garden. He wants you to make a test."

"A test? For what?"

"For a picture contract, dummy."

"Not interested."

"Are you *crazy*?"

"Look, Granny, I want to be a dancer. The best there is. That's *my* ambition."

"*You* look, Lucille. You *can't* pass up a chance like this! Dammit, a million women would give their eyeteeth to make a screen test for MGM. I won't let you say no!"

Lucille's roommate, Mitzi, agreed with Granlund: it was the opportunity of a lifetime. Finally Lucille said, "All right, I'll do it. But I'm not the least bit interested in becoming an actress."

She took the subway uptown to an address Granlund had given her. Inside a barnlike structure twenty chorus members and bit players were waiting. Lucille joined them and waited two hours, chatting with other chorus girls and leafing through copies of *Variety*. Finally her name was called.

"This better not take long," Lucille said. "I gotta be at the Winter Garden in an hour."

"Don't worry, honey, we'll have you out of here in no time," the assistant director promised. He positioned her in front of a movie camera and began instructing, "Turn to the right. . . . Now to the left. . . . Let's see your legs. . . . Now smile. . . . *Big* smile. . . ." After three minutes he said, "Okay, honey, that's all."

"That's all?" Lucille asked.

"Yeah. We'll call you."

Surprisingly, he did. She was asked to return a few days later for another test. Afterward she was told to step into an office and meet Mr. Rapf and Mr. Rubin. Harry Rapf had been a vaudeville performer and later an agent who drifted into the movie business and became an aide to Louis B. Mayer (before the merger with Metro and Goldwyn). He was a nervous, compulsive man with an instinct for public taste. J. Robert Rubin was an urbane, accomplished attorney who served as assistant district attorney and deputy police commissioner before joining the burgeoning film industry as counsel and negotiator. Both had detected in Lucille's test a refreshing naturalness that contrasted with the studied charm of the other chorus girls.

Rubin was astounded that Lucille's big eyes did not light up at the mention of Hollywood. "Wouldn't you like to go out there and become an actress?" the lawyer asked.

"No, I want to be a dancer," Lucille replied.

"Your first test was very good, honey," said Rapf. "If your second test confirms our thinking, we may make you an offer that will change your mind. We'll call you next week."

"I won't be here. I'm going home to Kansas City for Christmas."

"Can we have your address in Kansas City?" Rapf asked.

"Yeah, sure." Lucille gave little thought to the movie test as she began her two-week vacation from *The Passing Show*. On the train going west she envisioned her reunion with Ray Sterling and how she would tell him about all of her adventures in Manhattan. She prayed that her success in New York would ease the perennial tension between herself and her mother.

She was bitterly disappointed. Her hopes for a joyful Christmas reunion with Ray failed; he had left the city to spend the holidays with his parents. She had expected a happy time at home, but her mother had been abandoned for a third time. Anna castigated her daughter for going off to New York when she should have stayed home to help support her mother. She accused Lucille of leading an immoral life in the theater world. Lucille answered bitterly that her life was her own, since she had supported herself from the age of eleven without her mother's help.

Desperately she telephoned a fraternity boy who had enjoyed her company on several dates. "I learned some great new dances in New York," she said enthusiastically. "How about taking me to the Jack-o'-Lantern, and I'll teach them to you?"

"Gee, I'd like to, Billie," he replied, "but I've got all these Christmas parties to go to. Maybe some other time. . . ." The next day was Christmas, and Lucille LeSueur received a telegram: "YOU ARE PUT UNDER A FIVE-YEAR CONTRACT STARTING AT SEVENTY-FIVE DOLLARS A WEEK. LEAVE IMMEDIATELY FOR CULVER CITY, CALIFORNIA. CONTACT MGM KANSAS CITY OFFICE FOR TRAVEL EXPENSES." On New year's Day, 1925, Lucille LeSueur carried her suitcase through Union Station and boarded the Sunset Limited for California.

5

LUCILLE LESUEUR STEPPED down from the train platform and into the blinding sunshine. The other travelers left the train and were greeted by friends and relatives, then made their way to the terminal. Lucille was left alone, close to tears. She knew little about Hollywood and had seen only eight movies in her life. But Nils Granlund had told her she would be received like royalty if she went to Hollywood with an MGM contract. She gazed forlornly down the empty platform. Finally a figure appeared. He was compact and breezy, about her age, a fresh-faced young man in a checkered suit. "Are you Lucille LeSueur?" he asked. She nodded. "Hi. I'm Larry Barbier of the publicity department. Got any more luggage? No? Okay, let's go."

A studio limousine was waiting outside the terminal. Barbier talked eagerly as they traveled through the Los Angeles streets, but Lucille was scarcely listening. Nothing in her travels through the Midwest and the East had prepared her for Los Angeles. Row after row of bungalows in gay pastel colors, palm trees seven stories high with trunks as slender as flagpoles, boys on bicycles, shirtless in January. They drove leisurely westward on Washington Boulevard and stopped before the Washington Hotel. It was no better than the fleabags she had known in Chicago and Detroit, and Barbier recognized her disappointment. "I know it ain't the Waldorf," he said, "but it's easy on the pocketbook and you can walk to the studio. It's only six blocks away. We'll get you settled in your room, then I'll drop you at Harry Rapf's office and you can sign your contract."

From the outside, Metro-Goldwyn-Mayer studio was impressive—colonial columns facing on Washington Boulevard. The inside was a jumble of makeshift buildings and stages, many of them hastily constructed since the merger of the three film companies eight months before.

Barbier escorted Lucille on a tour of the studio, stopping at stages where William Haines and Norma Shearer were appearing in *A Slave of Fashion*, Lillian Gish and John Gilbert in *La Boheme*, Lon Chaney and Mae Busch in *The Unholy Three*. Lucille hadn't heard of most of the stars but she was intrigued by the electrifying atmosphere of the movie sets and by the vitality and sense of purpose that surrounded her.

However, she quickly learned that her five-year contract did not offer the security she had imagined. The studio retained the option to drop her after the first six months and at any six-month period thereafter. Her tenure would depend on how well she photographed, and on her second day at the studio she faced a test far more extensive than the ones she had undergone in New York. She couldn't afford to fail because she felt she had nowhere left to go.

The businesslike director instructed Lucille to convey a variety of emotions. Then he asked her to cry. She conjured scenes from her childhood, the departure of Daddy Cassin, the beatings at Rockingham, and her tears descended. "Very good, Lucille," said the director. "Now I want you to look angry." But the tears wouldn't stop. She continued to sob amid the growing realization she could fail the test unless she proved she could really act.

"Hey, you're a dancer, aren't you?" She looked up at the Irish face of Tommy Shagrue, an electrician. He had been a vaudeville ·dancer, and he challenged her to repeat his steps. Within a few minutes the tears were forgotten, and Lucille continued with her test. The incident taught Lucille just how important crew members could be, and it proved to be a moment she never forgot. Until his death, red-haired Tommy Shagrue found employment on every Joan Crawford movie.

The Lucille LeSueur test was neither a success nor a failure. She displayed enough emotion, especially in the crying scene, to warrant keeping her under contract for six months. But the girl from the Shubert show seemed no different from the dozens of pretty girls who were pouring into Culver City since the studio merger. Her large eyes were striking, but her face appeared too full and nondescript. Lucille, however, was determined to prove herself at Metro-Goldwyn-Mayer. She stopped at the newsstand outside the Washington Hotel to buy movie magazines, reading each issue from beginning to end. Clara Bow and other stars, Lucille learned, had to rise at dawn so they could get into their costumes and put on their makeup in time for shooting, so Lucille set her alarm clock to ring at six-thirty every morning. She showered, dressed, ate a quick breakfast and ran all the way to the studio. When she got there, she found nothing to do. No one seemed to care that Lucille LeSueur was being paid seventy-five dollars a week for absolutely nothing.

She visited Larry Barbier in the publicity department. He introduced her to his boss, Pete Smith, the gifted publicity chief Mayer had stolen from Paramount. Smith peered through his glasses at the healthy, broad-shouldered dancer. "I think we can do something with you, Lucille," he said.

He had an idea. Unlike publicity photographs of movie stars, which were always shot in static poses, Smith had noticed that the Los Angeles *Times* was publishing sports photographs full of action: quarterbacks could be seen scoring touchdowns, baseball players hitting home runs. Smith found out the names of the *Times* photographer and his camera—Don Gillum and Graflex—and he hired both. Lucille LeSueur and another contract player, Dorothy Sebastian, were sent to Ocean Park beach, to the University of Southern California track, to Griffith Park. "Now, I want the girls in *action*," Smith instructed Gillum. "Get them swimming, running, tossing footballs, any goddamn thing, as long as it's *action*." When the photographs reached newspaper editors' desks across the country, they were welcomed and printed. Lucille LeSueur's face and figure became known to newspaper readers—but not to moviegoers. She had made only one appearance in a motion picture, and it was anonymous. Norma Shearer was playing a double role in *Lady of the Night* as a juvenile delinquent and a judge's daughter. In one scene the two girls confronted each other, and the back of Lucille's head portrayed the other girl while Norma was in close-up. Lucille studied the lovely young actress from Canada and admired her total assurance in front of the camera. Lucille also noticed a stranger on the set, a small, darkly handsome young man who stood alone far behind the camera, studying the scene intently as he flipped a gold coin. "That's Irving Thalberg," the propman whispered to Lucille.

At first Lucille had been reluctant to visit the movie sets for fear she would be thrown out. "Don't worry about it, dear," counseled the woman in charge of the extras' dressing room. "They're so busy they won't notice." And indeed Lucille found she could stride onto a set as if she were assigned to the production, and no one would object if she stood behind the lights and watched. She studied the scenes as they were repeated over and over again, and at night she played the female role before the mirror in her hotel room, interpreting emotions in her own style.

The MGM performers began to notice the constant visitor. Eleanor Boardman struck up an acquaintance with Lucille and listened to her complaint about inactivity. "Go see Harry Rapf," Miss Boardman told Lucille. "He's responsible for bringing you out here. Tell him you want to work—or else."

Lucille asked for an appointment with Harry Rapf. Ten days later she was granted one. The executive stared at the young contract player and then remembered the big-eyed chorine of *The Passing Show of 1924*. His interest grew. He used his influence to get Lucille her first screen role.

Pretty Ladies was a pastiche concocted by Adela Rogers St. John and adapted by a onetime assistant of D. W. Griffith, Alice D. G. Miller. The flimsy backstage story provided the excuse for the spectacle of the *Ziegfeld Follies*, reproduced silently with impersonations of Will Rogers, Eddie Cantor, Gallagher and Shean, plus Ann Pennington portraying herself. Zasu Pitts, Tom Moore, and Lilyan Tashman played the major roles, with Conrad Nagel, Norma Shearer and George K. Arthur as lesser figures. Lucille LeSueur had a brief dressing-room scene with Zasu Pitts and performed in the chorus.

Lucille made friends with other dancers, especially Myrna Williams, a Montana girl who had grown up in Los Angeles and danced in prologues at Grauman's Chinese. Myrna admired Lucille for her vivacity and enthusiasm; Lucille perceived that Myrna was equally determined, but pursued her ambition in a cool, almost detached manner. Myrna was attractive to men, but she kept them at bay with her quiet dignity. Lucille couldn't do that. She enjoyed the attention of men, though not from Harry Rapf, who was newly aware of his big-eyed protégée. He pressed his claim as Lucille's seigneur and might have succeeded except for the attentiveness of Mrs. Rapf.

Lucille was quickly cast in two more films. *The Only Thing* was written by Elinor Glyn from her new novel and "made under Miss Glyn's personal supervision." The plot cast Eleanor Boardman as princess of a mythical kingdom and Conrad Nagel as an English duke who saves her from marriage to a repulsive king. Lucille had a tiny role as a lady-in-waiting.

Old Clothes was a step forward. It starred Jackie Coogan, Metro's most important contribution to the merger with Mayer and Goldwyn. Lucille played a homeless girl taken in by Jackie and his older partner in the rag business. Eddie Cline directed Jackie and Lucille in touching scenes when they exchanged confidences.

Obviously Lucille LeSueur was a comer. But Pete Smith was convinced she couldn't make it with that name. The publicity chief laid his case before Louis Mayer. " 'Lucille LeSueur' sounds too stagy, even if it is the girl's name," argued Smith. "And it sounds too much like 'LeSewer.' I think we ought to change it." Mayer granted permission, and Smith went to work. Why not conduct a nationwide publicity contest to find a name for the promising new actress? A McFadden fan publication, *Movie Weekly*, agreed to sponsor the contest, and each week it carried photographs of Lucille LeSueur with entry blanks for submission of new names. The winner was "Joan Arden," and Lucille LeSueur became Joan Arden for a few days until a bit player protested that the name belonged to her. The second choice was submitted by Mrs. Marie M. Tisdale, a crippled woman who lived in Albany, New York. She won five hundred dollars, which she applied to medical treatment.

Lucille watched helplessly as the studio tinkered with her identity. The transformation from Billie Cassin to Lucille LeSueur had been confusing enough. She felt as if two persons had resided inside her body—the Billie of her youth and the Lucille of her brief career as a performer. Just as she was starting to adjust to a life as Joan Arden, she was suddenly given a name she detested.

"Joan *Crawford*!" the former Lucille complained to her new friend William Haines. "It sounds like 'Crawfish.'"

" 'Crawford's' not so bad," the actor replied. "They might have called you 'Cranberry' and served you every Thanksgiving with the turkey." Thereafter his name for her was Cranberry.

II

Joan Crawford—
The MGM Years:
1925–1943

6

"LET ME GIVE you some advice," said William Haines to his new friend at MGM. "You've got to draw attention to yourself. There are fifty other girls trying to get roles in pictures, and the producers don't know one pretty face from another. You've got to make yourself known."

"But how?" Joan asked.

"Get yourself some publicity. Go to dances and premieres. Let people know that Joan Crawford is *somebody*."

The proposal appealed to Joan. She had spent enough evenings within the four walls of her dingy hotel room and yearned to see what Hollywood was really like. She found plenty of young men who were ready to show her. There were lunch dances on Wednesday and Saturday at the Montmartre on Hollywood Boulevard, and tea dances at the Cocoanut Grove. Afterward, the Pom Pom Club and the Garden Court Hotel had orchestras, so Joan and her escort could dance through both afternoon and evening. She did so with great vigor, for she had professional skill and had learned the Charleston and black bottom when she appeared at the Club Richman in New York. Her restless feet flew, and other dancers backed away and stared in envious wonder at her athletic energy. Many nights she carried home silver-plated loving cups for her prowess with the Charleston, often returning them to the management and collecting a much-needed fifteen dollars.

Billy Haines's idea succeeded. The studio executives were beginning to notice Joan Crawford, and she was cast with Constance Bennett and Sally O'Neil in *Sally, Irene and Mary*, based on the Broadway musical by Eddie Dowling and Cyrus Woods. It was a backstage story about three ambitious chorus girls and thus ideal casting for Joan. She approached the role overly confident, and her director, Edmund Goulding, told her, "You're giving too much, Joan." He was a suave, cultured Englishman who had drawn smooth performances from such actresses as Gloria Swanson and Greta Garbo. "You can't play every scene at fever pitch," Goulding said. "You'll wear out the audience. Hold back. Control the emotion and it will seem even stronger. A stifled scream is more effective." It was the first time a director tried to teach her, and she listened. She also learned about the camera and how to move within its range. She became good friends with Sally O'Neil, who had also emerged from the chorus, but Joan always addressed her other costar as "Miss Bennett." She came from a famous theatrical family and seemed unapproachable.

When the renewal of her first option raised her salary from seventy-five to one hundred dollars a week, Joan moved out of the Washington Hotel into a rented bungalow. It was the first real home she had known since her Lawton childhood, and she furnished it, on the installment plan, with enthusiasm. Later she remembered it as "a nightmare of fringe, lace, tassels, pink taffeta draperies and ridiculous long-legged dolls."

While Constance Bennett and Sally O'Neil moved on to more important roles, Joan Crawford was relegated to innocuous ones. She was cast as a Prohibition agent in a frivolous comedy, *The Boob*, directed by William Wellman and starring George K. Arthur and Gertrude Olmstead. Next she was loaned to First National to provide the romantic interest in Harry Langdon's first feature comedy, *Tramp, Tramp, Tramp*. Joan realized that if she was going to succeed at MGM, she would have to do it on her own. Norma Shearer's career was guided by her production boss, Irving Thalberg, whom she married in 1927, and Marion Davies became the mistress of William Randolph Hearst, who poured his publishing millions into her movies. Joan Crawford had no patron, but she did have friends. A special friend was Johnny Arnold, the cameraman on *Sally, Irene and Mary*. "Your face is built," Arnold told Joan.

"What do you mean?" she asked.

"It isn't like any other actress's. The bones are made just right for the camera. There's only one trouble."

"What's that?"

"The camera can't see them. You have to lose weight."

Immediately Joan gave up starches and sweets and existed on steak and grapefruit for breakfast, steak and tomatoes for lunch, steak and tomatoes for dinner. Within weeks she dropped twenty pounds, and the change was dramatic. Her eyes seemed immense, leading to rumors that she had undergone an operation in which the skin was slit to make them bigger. No longer was she apple-cheeked; her flesh became elegantly molded to the bones. One important MGM executive began to take an interest in her career. Paul Bern, the small German-born actor and film director, had earned the respect of Irving Thalberg with his acumen about stories and personalities. An unattractive, spidery man, he was nevertheless adored by some of the most legendary beauties in Hollywood. He understood their need to be appreciated for more than their faces and figures, and he penetrated their souls—but because of a physical inadequacy, not their bodies. Jean Harlow later married him.

Joan Crawford both adored and feared Paul Bern and complained to him about her inactivity.

"But what have you done to improve yourself?" he asked.

Bern strove to transfer his own good taste to the girl who had been Billie Cassin only a couple of years before. He gave her designer dresses, unwittingly two sizes too small, but she wore them anyway, and tore them in strenuous dances. Bern even sent her an ermine wrap, but she returned it. With Bern's help Joan Crawford began drawing more attention from the MGM executives. She worked again with Edmund Goulding in *Paris*, playing an apache dancer caught between her lover, Douglas Gilmore, and a traveling American millionaire, Charles Ray, then in the twilight of his career as the ingenuous hero.

In 1927 Joan raced through six movies. They were no more than program pictures to fulfill MGM's commitments to supply product to theaters. But Crawford's name was paired with important male stars, and she was learning acting techniques from them and from journeyman directors such as Jack Conway, W. S. Van Dyke, Tod Browning and Edward Sedgwick. She later declared that her best teacher was Lon Chaney. Offstage he was a mild, shy man but on the set his concentration on his menacing role was so all-absorbing that his fellow actors were terrified. As an armless circus performer in *The Unknown,* he was required to light cigarettes and use knives and forks with his feet, even throw daggers at his beautiful assistant, played by Joan. She marveled at how Chaney spent hours alone in his dressing room perfecting the role, and how he never allowed his own persona to enter his screen character.

Joan's progress as an actress drew the attention of Louis B. Mayer, and he ordered a new contract drawn up at $250 a week. She was thrilled. For the first time in her life she had enough money to do anything she wanted. She bought a Ford roadster and drove it proudly through the studio gate every day. One day Joan returned home from MGM to find her brother stretched out on the living-room sofa.

"Hi, Billie," Hal said breezily. "I figured I might as well come out here and become a movie star. If you can do it with that funny face and all those freckles, why can't I?"

He had been working in a dreary job as a department-store clerk in Kansas City while his sister enjoyed the glamorous life in Hollywood. He couldn't imagine how Billie had become a movie star. He had never considered her beautiful, and he had always derided her pretensions of being a dancer. Certainly if MGM was willing to pay her a large salary to appear in movies, an acting career would be easy for him. He was handsome enough to become a star. He had the LeSueur eyes, wavy brown hair and an ingratiating smile. Joan was able to get him bit parts and extra work at MGM, but he lacked his sister's driving ambition. Instead of cultivating directors and learning how to act, Hal devoted his time on movie sets to lining up dates. Time after time he borrowed Joan's car and wrecked it after a binge, so that she had to hire a taxi in the morning to reach the studio in time. She found herself spending all her time at home cooking Hal's meals and cleaning up after him.

Nevertheless she decided to rent a three-bedroom bungalow on Genesee Street and send for her mother. Even with her pay raise the expense would strain her finances, but she was sending checks to her mother in Kansas City anyway, so her mother might as well take over the job of keeping house for Hal.

At last, Joan thought, the hard times behind the laundry were over. But except for sunshine and better meals, California life did little to change relations among the LeSueurs. Hal continued to belittle his sister and remain independent, and her mother always sided with Hal in any argument, even though Joan was now the breadwinner for the entire family.

Mrs. LeSueur, as she now called herself, discovered something new and wonderful—department-store charge accounts. Joan noticed that her mother and Hal were becoming fashionably dressed, but she never saw any store bills—Mrs. LeSueur was hiding them. Joan discovered the fact when she was threatened by the Broadway Department Store with a lawsuit for nonpayment of her account. Both her mother and Hal had developed new circles of friends in Los Angeles, and Joan often found the house filled with dinner guests when she arrived from the studio. She always went to bed early so she could be rested for work in the morning, but partying kept her awake. Joan realized she needed a house of her own. She found a comfortable bungalow on Roxbury Drive in Beverly Hills, but the $18,000 price frightened her. She went to Louis Mayer for advice. He told her she had a promising future at the studio. "Buy that house, Joan," he said. "The studio will lend you the money for the down payment."

"Oh, thank you, Mr. Mayer!" Joan said. It was the first of her well-calculated consultations with her boss, who adored playing the paternal role, especially with beautiful young actresses.

In 1926 Joan Crawford was named a Wampas Baby Star. The Western Association of Motion Picture Advertisers, a fraternal organization of press agents, annually selected the dozen most promising young movie actresses and presented them amid hoopla at a luncheon or dinner. The class of 1926 was Wampas' finest crop: Crawford, Mary Brian, Dolores Costello, Mary Astor, Vera Reynolds, Janet Gaynor, Sally O'Neil, Dolores Del Rio, Fay Wray, Joyce Compton, Marcelline Day, Edna Marion, Sally Long. For the girl who was spurned by a Stephens sorority because she waited tables, the selection as a Wampas Baby Star was a delectable pleasure. Joan tried to make the group like a sorority, and she organized regular lunches at the Montmartre, where the Wampas girls chattered about their careers and romances.

Joan enjoyed forming friendships with women and gathered her own little circle, which included the Young sisters, Polly Ann and Betty Jane, Dorothy Manners and Audrey Ferris. "Joan was the queen and we were her ladies-in-waiting," Dorothy Manners recalled. "She put on a show wherever she went. At a wedding, she was the bride. At a funeral, she was the corpse." The ladies-in-waiting shared the queen's love of dancing, and they gathered at Joan's regular table for the tea dances at the Cocoanut Grove. She insisted that Jimmy Manos, the headwaiter, reserve the table under the palm tree closest to the entrance so she and her friends could observe everyone as they came and went. One afternoon Joan found the table occupied by Jane Peters (Carole Lombard). Joan raised such a ruckus that Jimmy Manos never tried to seat anyone else under the first palm.

One day when Joan called to pick up Polly Ann and Betty for a tea dance at the Cocoanut Grove, the girls' mother said, "You've got to take Gretchen."

"Oh, Mother, she's too young," Polly Ann complained. "She'll just be in the way."

"Either Gretchen goes or you and Betty don't go," her mother replied. Joan agreed to add the thirteen-year-old Gretchen to the carload of girls. Gretchen, who was to be known on the screen as Loretta Young, was uncommonly mature for her age. Her fresh beauty made an immediate impression with the males at the Grove, and she became the focus at the Crawford table. "This is the last time we bring Gretchen," Joan grumbled. She could not tolerate sharing the spotlight with a thirteen-year-old, or anyone else.

Joan rarely lacked attention. Given a partner who was even a passable dancer, she could monopolize any dance floor. The Grove and the Montmartre were filled with handsome, suntanned young men, both rich and poor, but Joan made no class distinctions. She enjoyed dating Danny Dowling, who worked as a dress extra and was a splendid dancer, as much as she did Tommy Lee, son of the auto and radio millionaire Don Lee. Michael Cudahy of the meat-packing family was another favorite. Howard Hughes, Marion Morrison (John Wayne), and J. Paul Getty attended the tea dances but were too shy to ask Joan Crawford to dance.

Jerry Chrysler was a special Crawford partner. He was slender, athletic, and wild, and he and Joan won a loving cup at the Grove one night. Still damp with sweat, he took her for a fast drive in his roadster. "Put on your coat, Jerry, you'll catch cold," she urged him. "Nah, the cold air feels great," he said. He was hospitalized when he contracted pneumonia, and was almost delirious when Joan visited him. She used all her acting skill to hide her fears for his survival—a scene she was to reenact with Gene Raymond in *Sadie McKee*. Jerry Chrysler died.

Joan rallied her circle of girls, instructing them to meet at their regular table for lunch at the Montmartre. She arrived in black dress and a wide black veiled hat on loan from the MGM wardrobe department. After lunch she loaded the girls into the powder-blue Pierce Arrow Phaeton she had borrowed from Michael Cudahy, and stopped at a florist shop to pick up her order. "Jerry" was spelled out in gardenias against a background of yellow chrysanthemums. At the funeral parlor Joan walked up to the coffin, placed the floral display on top, knelt and sobbed, "Goodbye, Jerry, dear." Jerry's mother was so upset by the scene that she had to be carried out.

Mike Cudahy was the first great love of Joan's Hollywood life. With her beautiful face and athletic figure, and Mike's handsome face and coal-black hair, they were a striking couple. He had everything—wealth, position, looks, an easy manner—the answer to Billie Cassin's dreams. He could even dance well, and many times Mike and Joan were awarded the cup for the Charleston contest. With his allowance of $1,600 a month he could lavish presents on her and take her anywhere. "They were a couple on the dance floor to knock your eye out," Adela Rogers St. John wrote. "Joan wore black a lot in those days, with big picture hats, and much too much makeup. Scarlet lips, mascaraed lashes, flaming hair—hard, haughty, pitifully defiant. Substituting excitement for happiness, drama for contentment, and laughing just a little too loudly in the face of Hollywood's disapproval." Mike Cudahy was nineteen, carried a hip flask, and on many nights took too many swigs from it. After he passed out, Joan drove to the Cudahy mansion, signaled for the butler to assist Mike inside, then took a taxi home. She would always lecture him the next day, urging him not to throw his life away. Later Joan would recall: "Mike was the answer to that mother-love yearning within me. I was determined to do for Mike what Ray Sterling had done for me. I wouldn't let him drink when he was with me. I wanted Mike to be perfect, to be the one man I had always envisioned in all my dreams. When we were out dancing we were like two happy children. But when we took long drives, sat in the moonlight just talking and talking, I was always trying to instill Mike with the same faith in life and in work that Ray had instilled in me. I used to think of the moonlight drives in

Kansas City and how I had sat and listened. Now I made Mike sit and listen." She had more than Mike's drinking to contend with. There was also his mother.

Mrs. Cudahy lived with her son and two daughters in a huge Italian château above Hollywood Boulevard. No one had ever seen her go out of the house. For twenty years she had lived behind drawn velvet draperies, and there were rumors that Mr. Cudahy had died mysteriously. She was a towering woman who dressed only in long gowns. Joan recalled that her skin, after all those reclusive years, "was white and languid as linen."

Joan had been dating Mike for a year when Mrs. Cudahy summoned her to tea. Joan wore her most conservative dress and sat demurely on the huge sofa as Mrs. Cudahy poured tea. The older woman asked polite but uninterested questions about Joan's work before admitting that she herself had never seen a motion picture. Finally she arrived at her reason for the meeting.

Mrs. Cudahy said bluntly that she didn't believe Joan was a good influence on her son. He spent too much time with Joan in nightclubs, stayed out too late, drank too much. It would be better if Michael and Joan didn't see each other.

Joan responded angrily. It was not *her* fault that Michael lacked ambition and drank too much. She had told him again and again that he should make something of his life, but she got no support from Michael's mother, who gave him money to satisfy his whims and never urged him to go to college or find a job. Joan wouldn't stop seeing Michael. She believed she *was* good enough for him, and she would continue her efforts to make a man out of him.

The romance lasted for another year, but her lectures had no effect on Mike. He drank more heavily, and he couldn't understand why she had to go home before midnight just because she was working the next day. Her patience grew thin, and finally she told Michael she didn't want to go out with him anymore. She philosophized about the breakup in an interview: "When a love affair begins, it is like a new dress. It may be your favorite. There's an accident. You tear it. You love it so that you patch it—cleverly, daintily, so no one can see it. Yet *you* know you have patched it. The next time, perhaps, you burn it. Again you patch and conceal it. But again you know it is no longer perfect. Finally after much patching and mending you can no longer feel, even to yourself, that the dress is 'as good as new.' You may still think it is the prettiest dress of your wardrobe, but it is *patched beyond wearing.* The only thing to do, then, is to be brave and discard it! Bury the shreds in the prison of your heart as you bury the shreds of your dress in your mending basket. Remember only its first beauty when it was new and glittering and attractive!"

Joan was upset over the breakup with Mike Cudahy. She hated failure and was distressed that she had been unable to inspire Mike as Ray Sterling had inspired her. She also feared that her career was foundering. The other actresses at MGM—Norma Shearer, Greta Garbo, Marion Davies, Eleanor Boardman, Lillian Gish—were getting the important roles while Joan played in the studio's program pictures. Each morning before she reported to the studio, Joan stopped at the tiny St. Augustine's Catholic church across Washington Boulevard. She prayed that her hard work at the studio would be rewarded with stardom, and that she would someday find the love that had eluded her from her earliest years.

7

JOAN CRAWFORD'S CAREER CONTINUED from one potboiler to another—*West Point, Rose-Marie, Across to Singapore*. She looked around her on the MGM lot and realized that a dozen other actresses were fulfilling the same function: supplying romantic interest for the studio's male stars. All would be discarded as soon as their youthful beauty began to fade, she knew. To escape such a happening, she would need to assert herself, and that meant confronting the studio's young production chief, Irving Thalberg. She understood the risk. Despite his fragile appearance, Thalberg had been known to crush those who questioned his decisions. "Why do you save all the good roles for your darling Norma?" Joan demanded. "Don't you think I deserve some consideration?"

"Joan, your career is coming along nicely," Thalberg replied with icy reserve. "You still have much to learn. If you tried something too ambitious, it might be disastrous. You wouldn't want to be laughed at, would you?" She had breached the studio code of etiquette, and for penance was cast in a Tim McCoy western, *The Law of the Range*. Joan refused to acknowledge that she was being punished. She told Tim McCoy, "I'm going to enjoy working with you and your cowboys if it kills me." She rose early, forced herself to be comfortable in the company of horses, and became one of the gang. Having served her sentence, Joan was cast with John Gilbert in a gangster drama, *Four Walls*.

Then it happened. Hunt Stromberg had prepared *Our Dancing Daughters*, although like other Thalberg employees he received no film credit as producer. The screenplay was written by Josephine Lovett from her original story, an innocuous tale of high living in the jazz age, and though it was no better or worse than other scripts ground out by MGM in 1928, Harry Beaumont directed with vitality, and made good use of the Cedric Gibbons sets, which captured the art deco of the period. For the first time Joan Crawford was cast in a role in which she felt perfectly comfortable, and that was an extension of her own character. Like Diana of the film, she adored the life of fast cars and endless dancing, but although she was "doubtless the best example of the flapper," she considered herself a young woman of high principle and inner yearnings.

Our Dancing Daughters was a huge success, and the critics recorded the emergence of Joan Crawford. The New York *World* wrote: "Of Miss Crawford it may be predicted that in case her managers continue to find such breezy little comedies for her, she will realize what apparently has been her ambition for at least two years, and get going as a star in her own right. She has good looks, sprightliness, intelligence and a good sense of humor. She dances with great grace and versatility and she knows when—and how— to call a halt." For the first time, Joan Crawford was not merely the sweetheart of John Gilbert or William Haines or another MGM star; she herself was the star of *Our Dancing Daughters*. She was so excited about the event that she drove around Los Angeles to theaters playing the film and photographed her name on the marquee with a small box camera. Letters began to pour in from young women who wrote that they wanted to be "just like Joan Crawford," and she answered every letter in her own handwriting. Louis B. Mayer recognized Joan's achievement in *Our Dancing Daughters* by doubling her salary to $500 a week. It all had happened just as she had prayed every morning at St. Augustine's. Now she yearned for the other part of her prayer to come true.

He bore one of the ten most-famous names in the world. More people could identify his father than name the photographs of George V of England, Pope Pius XI, Thomas Alva Edison or George Bernard Shaw. To Douglas Fairbanks Jr. it was both a privilege and a burden—mostly a burden, after twenty years of being referred to as Young Doug.

The elder Fairbanks was a vigorous, vain, self-worshipping man. He had just achieved fame as a stage actor when his wife, Beth Sully, heiress to a cotton fortune, gave birth to a son on December 9, 1907. (Like Joan Crawford, he later subtracted two years from his official age.) Soon Doug Fairbanks Sr. became a favorite motion-picture star, with little time for either his wife or son. "I was never cut out to be a father," Fairbanks complained. "It isn't that I don't like Junior, but I can't feel about him the way that I should."

The reason is not hard to discern: Junior presented a threat to Doug's seemingly inexhaustible youth and intimated Doug's mortality. What's more, Junior was not the boy who should have been Doug Fairbanks' son. Junior was fat and slow, and instead of playing baseball with the other kids, he stayed in his room and made sketches. Only once did he evoke his father's admiration. Junior had fallen and torn his knee, but he did not so much as whimper or cry when iodine was poured into the wound. Junior recalled, "It was one of the proudest moments of my youth, as this behavior was remarked on by my father for some weeks afterward."

Doug and Beth divorced in 1918 when Junior was ten, and Junior saw little of his father until he was grown. Doug married Mary Pickford in 1920 and established Hollywood's royalty, whereas Beth's $400,000 settlement from Doug vanished in a disastrous marriage. Beth took her son to Paris, where she figured they could live on less money. In 1923 Jesse L. Lasky saw a chance to cash in on the Fairbanks name and offered to hire fifteen-year-old Junior for a movie at a thousand dollars a week. To Beth it was a godsend for her finances. To Doug Sr. it was a betrayal.

The confrontation took place in Doug and Mary's suite at the Hotel Crillon. Doug was furious. He was also shocked to find that at fifteen Junior was already taller than his father. Doug accused the boy of profiting from the family name; his inexperience would shame him and his father. Young Fairbanks accused his father of neglect; he had no right to interfere.

Neither Fairbanks yielded. Junior went to Hollywood to star in *Stephen Steps Out* with Theodore Roberts and Noah Beery, and Doug told his attorney to remove Junior from his will. Doug also castigated Lasky and threatened anyone who might try to help Junior's career, defending himself in interviews: "The boy's too young and he really doesn't know what he's doing. I wanted him to have the best education possible, but I don't think that's possible now."

Stephen Steps Out proved one of the failures of 1923, while *The Thief of Bagdad* was an enormous hit. Junior returned to Paris in defeat, but his mother brought him back to Hollywood a year later. This time young Doug Jr. started at the bottom, playing small roles with such stars as Warner Baxter, Will Rogers and Ronald Colman. The elder Fairbanks remained opposed to his son's career and proclaimed, "There's only *one* Fairbanks." But Mary Pickford was fond of young Doug and tried to soften his father's attitude; so did Doug's brother Robert. Doug relented somewhat, but he was now in his mid-forties and terrified by the prospect of losing his vigorous screen image. "Being called Dad makes me feel so terribly middle-aged," he complained.

Doug Jr. had lost his fat and had exercised his body into athletic trimness. Instinctively he rejected his father's image and strove to be an aesthete, reading poetry, making sketches and cultivating the refined speech he admired in Ronald Colman and other British actors. During lulls in his movie career young Doug acted in local productions of *Romeo and Juliet*, *The Jest* and other plays. On October 17, 1927, he opened in *Young Woodley* at the Majestic Theater in downtown Los Angeles. The role was one he enjoyed, a sensitive young Englishman who has an idealistic love for the wife of his school's headmaster. Mary Pickford persuaded her husband to attend the opening night and to bring along a group of his famous friends, and for the first time in his life Doug was truly impressed with his son. He whispered to Mary during the performance, "He's good; he really *can* act."

Another first-nighter was equally impressed. Joan Crawford had been squired around town by Paul Bern after the end of her romance with Michael Cudahy. Ever striving to improve Joan's taste, Bern took her to the opening of *Young Woodley*. She was overwhelmed. "I had met Douglas at a party a few months before and thought him pompous," she later recalled. "Those who are unsure of themselves always think people with poise are putting on an act. However, that night his sensitive, tender performance touched me deeply."

Douglas, too, had been unimpressed at their first meeting. He had seen her "kicking her feet and smiling and joking and I wondered why I felt so sorry for her when she gave every outward appearance of being so happy." When Bern took Joan backstage after the performance, she praised the young actor's work, and he was impressed by her sincerity. Later that night she dispatched a telegram that confirmed her enthusiasm: "I sobbed. I stamped my feet. Your performance was the greatest since Lionel Barrymore in *The Jest*." Douglas telephoned his gratitude and asked if they could dine before his evening's performance. She declined. She claimed she was busy for the rest of the week, too. "That aroused my curiosity, and I laid siege to her," Fairbanks said. "After a while she consented to go out with me and we soon were laughing over the way we had detested each other."

After he returned from playing *Young Woodley* in San Francisco, Douglas pursued Joan in earnest. He called her every day at MGM and sent her poems illustrated with his own drawings. Joan was enthralled with Douglas. He was gentle, considerate, chivalrous—everything she had wanted in a man. She tried to change herself to suit him. During her tea-dance days she would laugh thunderously, but now she became extremely subdued. Once she had chewed gum constantly, believing the exercise was good for her chin; now she gave up gum. She dressed more conservatively and asked friends to pronounce her name as Jo-Ann, not Joan. She began reading books that Douglas recommended—Proust, Ibsen, Shaw, Nietzsche—and they talked for hours about their aspirations. When Douglas expressed doubt about pursuing his father's profession, Joan lectured him sternly. "You can do anything you set your mind to," she insisted. "Be strong! Tell yourself, 'I can do it! I know I can!' "

She was terrified about meeting his parents. Douglas invited his mother to accompany them to a movie. Beth was astonished when Joan read a book during the drive to the theater; Joan was too scared to speak. It's doubtful if Beth would have considered any girl good enough for her son—but certainly not Joan Crawford. The senior Fairbanks reacted violently to reports that his son might marry Joan Crawford. "You must stop them!" he instructed Beth.

Predictably, parental opposition only deepened the love between Douglas and Joan. There was more between them than merely the sexual attraction of two beautiful young people. For Douglas it was his first real love. He had always been under Beth's watchful eye, with never an opportunity for romance. At last he could assert his manliness. To Joan Douglas represented a chance for the love that had always eluded her. With youthful bravado she had declared to an interviewer: "The wedding ring! That's one thing I hope I'll always be able to dodge. I know too much about it after studying other professional women who are married. Never! Not so long as I can support myself."

Now she could support herself handsomely, but she longed to marry. She wanted a husband who could protect her and fight her battles. She tired of the lonely struggle, and she feared that dealing on an equal level in the man's world of motion pictures was making her less feminine. She was thrilled when on New Year's Eve, 1927, Douglas proposed that they become engaged. Joan accepted.

Young Woodley had impressed film producers, and the film career of Douglas Fairbanks Jr. improved. He made his own potboilers—*Dead Man's Curve*, *Modern Mother*, *The Toilers*—but he also was directed by young Frank Capra in *The Power of the Press*. Now it appeared that Douglas Fairbanks Jr. would not be overshadowed by the ascending career of Joan Crawford, and they formally announced their engagement on October 8, 1928.

Pleased with the connection to Hollywood's first family and heartened by good returns from Joan's latest film with William Haines, *The Duke Steps Out*, Louis B. Mayer anointed Joan with the status of *star* and announced that her next film would be *Our Modern Maidens*, costarring her fiancé, Douglas Fairbanks Jr.

Joan and Douglas were thrilled to be working together. They had dressing rooms adjacent to each other, and they announced their presence to each other with a special whistle. They confounded their fellow workers by speaking a form of pig latin that only Joan and Douglas could understand. After completing *Our Modern Maidens*, they placed their footprints in the forecourt of Sid Grauman's Chinese Theater, then went off to get married in New York. It seemed judicious to perform the ceremony as far removed from Pickfair as possible, and they were wed June 3, 1929, in St. Malachy's church. Father Edward Leonard, Douglas' spiritual adviser, performed the ceremony. Among the few guests were Beth Sully Fairbanks and Jack Whiting, the Broadway song-and-dance man she was to marry in two months. Douglas Fairbanks Sr. sent a belated message of congratulation.

The newlyweds had time for only a brief honeymoon at the Algonquin Hotel in Manhattan before they had to return to Hollywood and movie assignments. Before their marriage, Joan had been encouraged by another salary hike at MGM to pay $40,000 for a white-stucco Moorish house at 426 North Bristol Avenue in Brentwood, halfway between Beverly Hills and the Pacific Ocean. Since Douglas was in debt and could not afford to buy a house, he and Joan agreed to make the Bristol house their home. During the first months of their marriage both worked hard at their studios, and they cherished the evenings and Sundays they could spend alone together. Their happiness was complete, except for one vexation that remained unspoken yet clouded their marriage: they were not invited to Pickfair.

To Joan it didn't matter; in fact, she hoped never to face the fearful challenge of meeting Hollywood's royalty in their legendary palace. Yet she knew how important it was to Douglas to be acknowledged after his father's long neglect, and she sensed how hurt her husband had felt because no word came from Pickfair.

Eight months after the wedding of Joan and Douglas, the engraved invitation arrived: "Mr. and Mrs. Douglas Fairbanks request the honor of your presence at a dinner honoring Lord and Lady Mountbatten at Pickfair. . . ." The invitation had been prompted by Mountbatten's own request to the older Fairbanks: "Doug, old boy, I simply must meet that ravishing new daughter-in-law of yours."

Joan was frantic. "I can't go!" she insisted.

"Darling, you can't refuse," Douglas said gently. "It wouldn't be polite."

"But I'm frightened. I'll make a fool of myself. I'll disgrace you."

"You won't do any such thing. You'll be the most beautiful woman at the dinner."

She fretted all week over what to wear, finally choosing a virginal white gown. In the limousine ascending Summit Road she became nauseated and leaned over, expecting to throw up. Douglas, spectacularly handsome in white tie and tails, helped her out of the car. She stood facing the door and whispered, "Dodo, take me home; I can't go in." Douglas smilingly took her arm and escorted her across the tall porte cochere.

"Good evening, Mr. Douglas," said the butler. "Good evening, Mrs. Fairbanks."

Joan gazed fearfully up the staircase that led to the main hall, and leaned against her husband as they climbed the stairs. Greeting them at the top was Douglas Sr. Joan tripped as they reached the final step. "Oh, dear, I think I've lost my shoe," she said.

"Allow me," said the elder Fairbanks, and he knelt down and slipped the shoe onto Joan's foot.

"Mr. and Mrs. Douglas Fairbanks Junior," the chief butler announced. Joan descended the three steps to the drawing room on her father-in-law's arm, her husband following proudly behind. They advanced toward the tiny figure in regal white, a diamond tiara on her head. Mary held out her white-gloved hand and said in her small, warm voice, "Joan, dear, welcome to Pickfair."

The visits to Pickfair became frequent—and punishing for Joan. Douglas was delighted that his father was finally taking an interest in him, and the elder Fairbanks no longer considered his son a threat. They could be buddies, not father and son, because Doug could not bear to be called "Dad"; nor did Douglas appreciate the term "Junior." So his father called him Jayar, and Jayar called his father Pete. On Sundays they played golf together, swam together, then went to the United Artists studio for a steam bath together. Joan was left in a chair in the Pickfair living room working endlessly on embroidery or knitting. Miss Pickford retired for a nap in the afternoon, but Joan remained seated in her chair lest she be considered rude. In the evening she sat quietly at the formal dinner, afraid to say anything. The tension between her and Mary was noticeable. Every Sunday Mary gazed intently at Joan's abdomen, terrified that Joan would become pregnant and make her a step-grandmother. Mary didn't know that Joan was trying to have a baby but was suffering a series of miscarriages.

Relations between Joan and the elder Doug were more pleasant. He called her Billie and kidded her in a genial way, and his practical jokes relieved the stuffiness of the Pickfair gatherings and made Joan temporarily forget her fright. But she never felt completely comfortable.

"I was doing fine until I hit Pickfair," she remarked later. "I was out to tear up the world—in the fastest, brashest, quickest way possible. Then I saw myself through the Pickfair eyes—and every last bit of my self-confidence dropped away from me. Shyness overwhelmed me, and I got a terrific inferiority complex. Immediately I set out to change myself in every way."

It was the kind of fairy-tale marriage that Billie Cassin had fantasized about. Two of the world's most attractive individuals, they reveled in each other's bodies and explored each other's minds. In private and in public, each was always touching the other. He called her Billie and she called him Dodo, and they seemed oblivious of others at dinners and parties as they spoke their private pig latin, exploding in riotous laughter at a risqué reference or a mutual joke. She bought him a huge electric train for Christmas, and he added to her collection of dolls that jammed an entire bedroom. He recited Byron and Keats while she knitted furiously, making him one sweater after another. He acted out swashbuckling roles, clambering over the roof and sliding down drainspouts. She encouraged him to greater deeds and sought to correct the weakness that she detected from his years of living alone with Beth. Once she tested his Spartanism by forcing him to enter a frigid swimming pool one inch at a time. After their marriage she found his finances in total disarray; although she herself was just learning about the management of income, she helped him out of debt.

Joan was learning to change her own style. No more was she seen in the slinky dresses that exposed her superb legs. One reporter described her as "the most demurely dressed woman at the Roosevelt Hotel for luncheon yesterday. A brown and green sports dress with straight lines and wide belt. A felt hat with a brim and a girlish ribbon tied carelessly around the crown. Not even the hat-ear-flaps on it which are today so voguish. She made the dress but she did not wear orchids on it." Nor did she avoid stockings, as had been her custom a year before. She was accused of trying to copy Mary Pickford's style. Her friends denied this. Joan was merely developing a style of her own, and it would take time.

Joan was also in search of a style for her film career. She realized that not only was she changing—so were the times. The stockmarket crash had put a damper on the jazz baby, though the executives of Culver City were slow to realize it. They also resisted the onslaught of talking pictures. Irving Thalberg prophesied, "Sound will be a useful adjunct to the film medium, but it will never replace silent motion pictures."

When Americans poured into theaters featuring talkies, Thalberg realized his mistake, and he directed MGM's resources into the new medium. Following the huge success of *Broadway Melody*, he cast most of the studio's star roster in *Hollywood Revue of 1929*. Marie Dressler danced a comic ballet, Norma Shearer and John

Gilbert enacted Romeo and Juliet, Laurel and Hardy played magicians, Marion Davies appeared in a song number. Joan Crawford sang "I've Got a Feeling for You" and tap-danced before a bouncy male quintet. She also joined in the finale, "Singin' in the Rain."

MGM executives were greatly concerned about how such stars as Garbo, Shearer, Haines, Novarro and Gilbert would sound in talkies. Little was said about Joan Crawford. Like other contract players, Joan was instructed to take diction lessons from a man who had once coached Enrico Caruso. She decided he was trying to make her speak unnaturally, and the first lesson was her last. "I worked it out alone," she recalled. "If I were to speak lines, it would be a good idea, I thought, to read aloud to myself, listen carefully to my voice quality and enunciation, and try to learn in that manner. I would lock myself in my room and read newspapers, magazines and books aloud. At my elbow I kept a dictionary. When I came to a word I did not know how to pronounce, I looked it up and repeated it correctly fifteen times."

When she first heard her voice coming from the screen, she exclaimed, "That's a man!" But unlike some stars, whose voices didn't fit their faces, Joan's husky voice was a perfect match for her sultry looks. She was a success from her first appearance in *Untamed*, when she intoned the song lyrics "Languid and plaintive . . . hear the chant of the jungle. . . ." Crawford in sound proved a sensation in theaters, and *Untamed* helped establish the film career of a newcomer from Broadway, Robert Montgomery.

Joan's three films in 1930 continued her success. She played a spoiled society girl out west in *Montana Moon* with Johnny Mack Brown and Ricardo Cortez. In *Our Blushing Brides* she was a shopgirl pursued by a department-store heir, Robert Montgomery. Joan's well-developed sense of survival told her she could escape such empty-headed roles only if she could garner a dramatic role like the ones Irving Thalberg found for Norma Shearer. That chance came when Norma became pregnant with her first child and was unable to star in *Within the Law*, based on the hit play by Bayard Veiller. It was the story of a woman who, released from prison, seeks vengeance on the man who had her falsely convicted. Early in her film career Joan's ideal had been Pauline Frederick, and she yearned to emulate the great emotional actress. She pleaded with Thalberg for a chance to show what she could do, and the dubious Thalberg agreed to cast her in *Within the Law*. Joan was determined to shatter her frivolous screen image. She would play the prison sequences without a trace of makeup, her hair unkempt, a loose prison smock around her.

She started the film in a state of terror, fearful that she would fail in her first real challenge. She found no support from Sam Wood, who directed in a perfunctory manner and made no comment on her performance. She searched the faces of the cameramen and soundmen for their reactions, but they either looked blank or gazed away. Finally she gazed upward at an electrician handling lights on the overhead parallels. He nodded and said, "Good girl, Joan." It was her first indication that she was succeeding.

Audiences and critics agreed when the film was released as *Paid*. Said *Photoplay*: "Just wait until you see Joan Crawford in this powerful dramatic role. The story is absorbing and Joan is simply grand." *Variety* agreed: "Histrionically she impresses us as about ready to stand up under any directorial assignment."

The screen career of Douglas Fairbanks Jr. was also progressing, though not at the same pace as his wife's. First National had signed him to a term contract, and he starred in such trivial films as *The Careless Age*, *The Forward Pass*, *Party Girls* and *Loose Ankles*. Then Howard Hawks directed him in a superb flying film, *Dawn Patrol*, costarring Richard Barthelmess and Neil Hamilton. Having had stage training, Douglas made the transition to sound with ease, but there was a certain passivity about his acting that sometimes irritated directors. Al Green once snapped at him: "You don't seem to know whether you're John Barrymore or Ronald Colman. Why not try the scene as Doug Junior?" He had none of the determination that Joan exhibited, and although he proved a capable actor, Douglas in fact profited from his father's name. Film assignments were dropped in his lap; he never had to campaign for them. When he wasn't acting, he was just as happy to be painting, sculpturing or writing. He showed a degree of talent as a caricaturist and a short-story writer, and was as pleased by publication of his work in *Vanity Fair* or *Cosmopolitan* as he was with good reviews for a movie performance.

After their first year of marriage at "El Jodo" (they called the Brentwood house after the combination of the their names), tension began to flare. Each was working at a furious pace, and they met briefly only in the morning before he had to motor over the Cahuenga Pass to First National and she had to rush to Culver City.

Both arrived home exhausted after a day on the set. Joan grew tired of poetry readings and grim Sundays at Pickfair, while Douglas wearied of her constant conversation of happenings at the studio. Joan's career was forever on the rise, eliciting a series of pay raises from MGM, but Douglas' career remained unexciting, and although both claimed it didn't matter, the differences in income helped erode the relationship. In 1931 First National paid him $72,791.72, while she earned $145,750 from MGM.

Douglas adored society. Nothing pleased him more than an invitation to San Simeon, where he could hobnob with the rich and influential friends of William Randolph Hearst. Joan survived the weekends only because of the thoughtfulness of her friend from MGM, Marion Davies. When Joan gave Douglas a surprise birthday party at the Hotel Biltmore, he was pleased to find the guest list just right—Constance Bennett and her husband, the Marquis James Henri de la Falaise de la Coudraye, newly acquired from Gloria Swanson; Norma Shearer and Irving Thalberg; Leslie Howard and his wife; Florence Eldridge and Fredric March. The Brentwood house, now rechristened Cielito Lindo, or "perfect little heaven," was the scene for elegant dinner parties with guests whom Douglas knew or would like to know. He cultivated the friendship of Englishmen like Leslie Howard and Laurence Olivier; they and their wives came to Cielito Lindo, as did Barbara Stanwyck and Frank Fay, Ann Harding and Harry Bannister, the Louis Lightons, Dorothy Sebastian and Bill Boyd, Helen Hayes and Charles MacArthur. Joan was growing more at ease as a hostess, but she became uncomfortable and worried if the dinner parties ran late when she had an early call in the morning.

Joan's new life as wife and hostess prompted her old dancing companions to remark that she was "high-hatting" them.

"I have never snubbed anyone in my life," she replied. "I'll admit that I don't have the big hello for everybody the way I used to, but that is because I got tired of having those hellos answered with polite nods. So I decided to be the same way myself."

She admitted that she was "wild and superficial" in her early Hollywood years, but she had succeeded in what she had aimed to accomplish: attract enough attention to get herself out of supporting roles.

"Every experience I had and every mistake I made during my nightclub career has helped, if only to show me the things which I should avoid in the future. Also I learned to know men pretty thoroughly, and very few of them kept my confidences. Perhaps I was at fault, however. Due to an incident in my childhood, I didn't dare trust anyone. As my need of faith grew intolerable, I reached out eagerly to believe and confide in all my various Hollywood acquaintances, with the usual results. Only in the last year have I developed an instinct for differentiating between sincerity and effusive protestations of loyalty undying.

"Yes, I learned a lot about men, all right. But if a woman knows nothing of men, how in heaven's name can she consider herself capable of judging for herself and choosing the one man she can trust implicitly, the man that could satisfy the many vagaries of a woman's heart and soul."

That man for her, she told interviewers in 1931 with diminishing conviction, was Douglas Fairbanks Jr.

8

WILLIAM CLARK GABLE HAD been an actor from the age of twenty-one, when he left home after an argument with his father, who considered acting an occupation for "sissies." He knocked around the Northwest, working as a lumberjack when he couldn't find jobs in plays. Josephine Dillon, fourteen years older and college-trained in drama, took him in hand and polished his crude speech and manners. Together they went to Hollywood, where they married in 1924. Gable was too big and burly in an era when leading men were handsomely romantic; all he could find was work as an extra. He and Josephine drifted apart, and his new sponsor became a rich Houston widow, Maria Franklin Prentis Lucas Langham, eleven years his senior. After a few roles on Broadway, Gable returned to Los Angeles, where his role as Killer Mears in the play *The Last Mile* brought him studio attention. He failed two screen tests because of his protruding ears, then landed a contract at $350 a week at Metro-Goldwyn-Mayer. His first role was as a laundryman in *The Easiest Way*, starring Constance Bennett. His second was as a bootlegger and killer in *Dance, Fools, Dance*, starring Joan Crawford.

"The first time I met him, I was terrified," she recalled. "I kept thinking, *He is a stage actor. He knows how to read lines. I am suffering by comparison. He's laughing at me.* Later Clark confessed that he had similar misgivings about working with me. *She's a star*, he was thinking. *She knows all the ropes in pictures. She's laughing at me.*"

Despite their mutual terror, the Crawford-Gable combination clicked. Their rough, proletarian manners—so contrasted to the Broadway and British actors imported for talkies—fit perfectly into the tempo of America in 1931. Louis B. Mayer, with his uncanny sense of public taste, recognized the electricity of the pair. Crawford had meanwhile starred in *Complete Surrender* as a cabaret dancer who is saved from suicide by a Salvation Army man, Johnny Mack Brown. After a preview audience failed to respond, Mayer ordered a complete remake with Gable in the Salvation Army role. Retitled *Laughing Sinners*, the movie proved a success. Several months later, when Gable and Crawford were reteamed for *Possessed*, he had changed. *A Free Soul* had been released, and his dynamic presence—plus the audience shock at his slapping of Norma Shearer—had promoted him from leading man to important star. He was also married again. Ria Langham became his bride in 1931, and with the marriage came three stepchildren from Ria's previous marriages. Clark was grateful for the financial aid and moral support that Ria had contributed to his flowering career. She seemed to fulfill the need he felt for an older woman to replace the stepmother who had reared him with an indulgent spirit.

Possessed proved to be an important film in the progress of Joan's professional life. It ended forever her period in movies as an empty-headed hedonist with a passion for dance. Now she moved to portrayals of girls on the rise from the lower classes, an apt metaphor with Americans submerged in the Depression. In *Possessed* she played a dissatisfied factory worker who heads for New York and encounters a rich, powerful and married attorney. Gable proved as persuasive in a tuxedo as he had been in a Salvation Army uniform.

Possessed also produced a profound effect on the personal life of Joan Crawford, who had once proclaimed that film stars should not marry because of the temptation caused by romantic scenes. For the first time she was taught the wisdom of her words. She found herself falling irresistibly in love with Clark Gable.

They had much in common. Both sprang from modest beginnings in the Midwest. Both had learned to survive in the face of hunger and rejection. Despite their auras of self-possession, both were terrified that the incredible luck that had befallen them would suddenly disappear. Both had been abandoned by a parent in infancy—Joan through her father's desertion, Clark by his mother's death. They had transferred their devotion to stepparents. Henry Cassin walked out on little Billie; Jennie Dunlap Gable died when Clark was eighteen. Joan was ever in search of a replacement for her father. Clark married two older women and even called his younger wives "Ma."

Clarence Brown, the sagacious and sensitive director of Garbo and Shearer films, worked with Joan for the first time in *Possessed*. He recognized the attachment that was growing between Joan and Clark, and he made use of it in the love scenes. The romance continued off the sound stage as well. Joan and Clark could easily absent themselves from their homes, using the excuse of work at MGM. They took long ocean drives together, talked endlessly of their own insecurities and hopes, and made love. The attraction was understandable. Joan was fascinated by the rough maleness of Clark, so different from the gentle, contemplative Douglas. Clark was overwhelmed by the youthful vibrance of Joan, who contrasted to the motherly women he had married.

The liaison was soon suspected by Douglas and Ria. Douglas made no issue of it; he was busy with his own career—he made six films for Warner Brothers in 1931, including *Little Caesar* and *Union Depot*—and he too was discovering the excitement of extramarital adventures. Actresses and extra girls were readily available for the handsome scion of Hollywood's first family.

Ria recognized from Clark's moodiness and his lengthening absences from home that he was romancing his leading lady. She understood Clark's Dutch stubbornness too well to confront him. She decided to broadcast her status as Mrs. Clark Gable. She asked MGM to schedule a trip to New York for herself and the children, and at numerous stops across the country she gave press interviews about her life with Clark.

Noninterference from Ria and Douglas made the secret meetings of Joan and Clark easier to manage. "Why don't we get divorces so we can marry?" Joan suggested. "Sounds good to me, baby," Clark replied. But before she could press him to a decision, Louis B. Mayer intervened.

The romance of his two stars had been reported to Mayer, and he was furious. Mayer summoned Gable to his office. His affair with Joan Crawford would stop immediately, Mayer decreed. Gable was convinced he was still too new a star to test the will of Louis B. Mayer, whose powers of retribution were legendary; he was said to have ruined the careers of Francis X. Bushman, Erich von Stroheim and others with the swiftness of an Old Testament prophet meting out justice.

Joan asked for Clark in her next film, *Letty Lynton*. "Absolutely not," said Mayer, who told her what he had told Gable: that the romance would stop, or both would be punished. The studio boss didn't specify the punishment, but he left no doubt that he would carry out his threat. He cast Robert Montgomery opposite Joan in *Letty Lynton*. Clarence Brown again directed and was sympathetic to Joan's disappointment. *Letty Lynton* was another melodrama of a socialite caught between the love of two men, redeemed only by Brown's firm direction—and by the innovative costume designs of Adrian.

Gilbert Adrian was born in Naugatuck, Connecticut, studied at the School of Applied and Fine Arts, and designed costumes for the *Music Box Revues* before going to Hollywood as designer for Rudolph Valentino. Cecil B. De Mille hired Adrian—following couturier tradition, he dropped his first name—and when De Mille went to MGM Adrian went along. Louis Mayer believed in hiring the best possible talent in all areas of production, and he recognized Adrian's prolific and imaginative style. Soon Adrian was designing costumes for the leading MGM actresses, and he was accorded his first screen credit for Greta Garbo's gowns in *Love* in 1927, a tribute to his abilities, since costume designers had rarely seen their names on the screen. Adrian himself had the striking features of an actor, and was able to create fashions that were dramatic yet complementary to the script. He had the rare faculty of making each star feel that he was designing exclusively for *her*; none had reason to suspect that Adrian put forth more effort for a rival. He designed gowns to emphasize the mystique and figure of individual stars: Garbo's were daringly stylish, Norma Shearer's had sedate elegance, Jean Harlow's emphasized her sensuality. When Adrian started designing for Joan Crawford in 1929, he discarded the frills and froufrou of her flapper period. The Crawford look became sleek, tailored, sophisticated.

For *Letty Lynton* Adrian excelled himself. He decided to make Joan's broad mannish shoulders an asset, and he emphasized them with padding. Women everywhere adored the style, and padded shoulders swept the fashion world. Edith Head, who has won ten Academy awards for costume design, has called *Letty Lynton* the single most important influence on fashion in film history. Adrian continued designing all of Joan's clothes on the screen, and much of her private wardrobe throughout her tumultuous MGM years.

Irving Thalberg decided to give the sagging Depression box office a jolt of MGM star power. In a remarkable feat of showmanship, he assembled the first "all-star" cast in a dramatic film: Greta Garbo, John Barrymore, Joan Crawford, Wallace Beery, Lionel Barrymore, Lewis Stone and Jean Hersholt. Edmund Goulding would direct the diverse temperaments in the Vicki Baum tale of life inside the Grand Hotel of Berlin. Joan was thrilled to be included in such company at first. Then she read the script. "I don't want to do *Grand Hotel*, Irving," she told Thalberg.

"Are you crazy?" he replied. "It's the best opportunity you've ever had."

Joan agreed, but she felt destined to be the loser amid the movie's stars. Her best scenes were in the bedroom and would surely be cut by the industry's censor. Thalberg had faith in Eddie Goulding's taste; the Hays Office would raise no objection to his handling of those scenes. He accused Joan of acting like a spoiled child and told her emphatically that she would appear in *Grand Hotel*.

Joan complied. At least *Grand Hotel* would place her in proximity with Garbo. Joan had few idols—Garbo was one. Joan revered the Swede's dramatic intensity, her aloof detachment from Hollywood, her air of mystery. In 1931, when Joan was trying to escape her flapper image and develop a new screen style, she had tried to emulate the Garbo mystique. She wore her hair in the same long, straight style, affected slinky dresses, posed languidly, and answered interviewers' questions enigmatically. After several months the phase passed, Joan realizing that she could not succeed as a Midwest version of the divine Garbo.

Joan often recollected how she had uttered a cheery "Good morning" each day as she passed Garbo's dressing room on the way to work. For three years she heard no response. Then one day Joan was in such a hurry that she forgot her usual greeting. She heard Garbo's door open and then the baritone voice intoning, "Alloooooo."

Joan often stood in the shadows at the rear of a Garbo set to observe the great actress at work, and inevitably their paths crossed on studio streets. Joan always hid from view and said in a hushed tone to her companion, "There's Garbo." In the stars' dressing-room building one day, Joan couldn't hide, and she met Garbo on the stairway. The Swede took Joan's face in her hand and said, "What a pity! Our first picture together and we don't work with each other. I am so sorry. You have a marvelous face." In recounting the incident in later years, Joan commented: "If there was ever a time in my life when I might have become a lesbian, that was it."

While Garbo had superb Adrian gowns as the ballerina Grusinskaya, Joan was limited to a pair of frocks as the compliant stenographer, Flaemmchen. As she suspected, her good scenes fell to the censor's ax. Wallace Beery, portraying the brutish Preysing who hires Flaemmchen to take more than dictation, performed his role with total disregard for Joan's needs. When John Barrymore appeared for his scenes with Joan, he was hung over and profane. Only Lionel Barrymore among the performers proved sympathetic to the aspiring Crawford. He had been a director of movies and tests, including Clark Gable's, and he understood the insecurities of most actors. The scenes between Lionel, the timid clerk Kringelein, and Joan are among the best in *Grand Hotel*.

Goulding controlled the disparate temperaments with gentlemanly skill, and was especially proud of how Crawford had progressed since he first directed her in *Sally, Irene and Mary*. Her acting was no longer superficial, and she seemed to penetrate the character of the Berlin stenographer-for-hire. Why not? There was a lot of Billie Cassin in Flaemmchen. *Grand Hotel*, filmed at a cost of $700,000, earned $2,594,000, an enormous amount in 1932, when the average theater ticket cost twenty-three cents. *Grand Hotel* was named best picture of the year by the Academy of Motion Picture Arts and Sciences, and the career of Joan Crawford seemed continued on an upswing.

"Will Joan Crawford's Career Wreck Her Marriage?

"Here is Hollywood's most unusual triangle: Joan Crawford . . . Douglas Fairbanks Jr. . . . and Joan's FUTURE. Young Doug does not have to worry about 'other men'—but what if Joan's ambition carries her on to the heights predicted for her? Will their marriage mean as much to her then? . . . You have already seen what *Letty Lynton* and *Grand Hotel* have done for her. . . . Joan is the most ambitious girl in Hollywood history. Can Joan and Doug weather Joan's ambition?"

The story was by Dorothy Manners, Joan's friend since the tea-dance days. She told of visiting Joan on the set of *Grand Hotel* and finding her far different from the budding star who was once reprimanded by her director, Harry Beaumont, for breaking up other members of the cast with wisecracks.

"Here was a Joan I hardly recognized. There was something almost desperate about her role in *Grand Hotel*. There was a feverish determination not to be swamped by the glamor of Garbo, by the illustriousness of the Barrymores, by the hit-you-in-the-eye personality of Wallace Beery. No longer was Joan hooking rugs on the sidelines, sipping the inevitable chicken broth on her 'diet,' making funny remarks under her breath. The all-important dinner hour came and went without her notice.

"If Doug called (messages she had always taken time to answer promptly and in person), she sent one of the boys or her maid to tell him she would be working late. One day one of the members of the publicity department went to Joan for material on a story about Hollywood marriage, a subject she had formerly delighted in talking about. But this time the idea of the story seemed to irk her.

" 'Our marriage has been so thoroughly hacked over!' she said. 'I think that all I can intelligently talk about right now is this picture . . . this role.' "

Later she would admit, "We were taking separate roads. Neither path was wrong, but marriage is successful only when a man and woman stay on the same road and walk along it, hand in hand."

Instead of joining his wife on Catalina Island during the fiasco of *Rain*, Doug went yachting off Mexico with Robert Montgomery and Laurence Olivier.

Joan felt greatly complimented when Joe Schenck asked his brother Nick, president of MGM and its parent company, Loew's, Incorporated, to lend Joan Crawford for Joe's United Artists production of *Rain*. It was the first famous role she was cast for, and Joan believed she could bring fresh insight to Sadie Thompson. The director was Lewis Milestone, who had won Academy awards for *Two Arabian Knights* and *All Quiet on the Western Front*. Walter Huston was signed to play Davidson, the missionary who "saves" the South Seas whore, only to succumb to her seduction. The rest of the cast was first-rate: William Gargan, Beulah Bondi, Matt Moore, Guy Kibbee, Walter Catlett.

Expectably, her familiar terror overwhelmed her. Billy Haines told her it was folly to attempt Sadie Thompson: "You couldn't find a sharper razor to cut your throat with." He pointed out that Jeanne Eagels on the stage and Gloria Swanson in a silent film had already established the role. Joan was not only fearful of unfavorable comparison; she was frightened of working away from MGM. The studio crews had become like a family to her; she needed their sympathy and support to overcome her feelings of inadequacy as an actress. To be plunged suddenly into a company of strangers was more than she could face. She told Joe Schenck she couldn't make the picture. Schenck used his enormous charm to assuage her fears. He hired one of her favorite cinematographers, Oliver Marsh. Schenck argued that she would create a new and original Sadie Thompson all her own.

Joan was persuaded but not convinced. She remained unsure in the role of Sadie Thompson, and Milestone provided no help. "What I do on the screen is more instinctive than calculated," Joan later remarked. "The first take of any scene of mine is always the best. Since I am not a studied craftsman, rehearsals rob me of spontaneity. Mr. Milestone had worked out every scene in advance, and in detail. We rehearsed interminably. From the first day I knew that the picture would be a failure and that I was dreadful." As Joan had feared, the New York actors seemed aloof and faintly deprecatory, though in reality they were awed by the presence of a genuine movie star. Joan felt no rapport with Walter Huston, who had arrived with his recent bride, Nan Sunderland. The tone for the location was set at the welcoming dinner Milestone hosted for the cast on Catalina Island.

Joan found herself seated between William Gargan, newly arrived from his New York success in *The Animal Kingdom*, and Walter Catlett, the acidic comic of the *Ziegfeld Follies*. Joan started talking about her recent movies to Gargan, who failed to respond. "Miss Crawford," he said, "I've never seen you on the screen in my life."

She turned to Catlett and started talking about her interpretation of Sadie Thompson. Catlett, who had found a supply of bootleg rye on the island, leaned toward Joan and muttered, "Listen, fishcake, when Jeanne Eagels died, *Rain* died with her."

During the filming on Catalina Island Joan remained in her cottage every evening, playing Bing Crosby records over and over until other members of the company could scarcely stand them.

During her emotional scenes, she asked Milestone to erect "niggers"—black-cloth screens which shielded the set from outside view. When the film company returned to MGM for interiors, Joan felt as if she had won a reprieve from Devil's Island.

Rain proved to be the disaster Joan had anticipated. Abel Green in *Variety* pronounced, "The dramatic significance of it all is beyond her range." Others likened her portrayal to that of a high-school girl and observed, "Joan Crawford should wait until she has grown up before attempting a serious role."

She admitted later: "I did it badly. I know it. I would have given anything to recall it. What was the matter with me? Why had I gone so wrong?" Part of the reason, she concluded, was her awareness of the Eagels-Swanson portrayals—"the two ghosts of Sadie Thompson rose up to haunt me." Also she felt it had been a mistake to approach *Rain* as a classic instead of a lusty melodrama.

Time has been kinder to the Crawford portrayal than the critics or Joan herself. Her Sadie Thompson is touching and persuasive, and the trollop's costumes and makeup do not offend the modern viewer; she seems ideally outfitted for the role. Her transformation from whore to penitent and back again is totally convincing, an unappreciated portent of her growth as an actress.

9

JOAN RENTED a cottage at Malibu to recover from the shattering experience of *Rain*. For weeks she read books, wandered the desolate shore, cooked her own meals and remained completely alone, as Billie Cassin had once been. She thought about Doug and how he had changed from the poetry-reading aesthete to the companion of sophisticates. His friends spoke with more clipped accents, but they seemed just as shallow as the playmates she had known at the Montmartre and the Cocoanut Grove.

As would often happen in times of stress in their lives, Joan and Clark Gable were drawn together. Clark himself was bored with his marriage to Ria. His early poverty had left him a parsimonious man, and he was appalled at how fast his wife could spend his money. Joan and Clark even talked of marriage, but once again they encountered the iron rule of Louis Mayer, who was incensed because Joan and Clark had resumed their dangerous romance against his orders. "I am sending you and Doug to Europe," Mayer told Joan. "You will have a second honeymoon and forget all this foolishness with that roughneck Gable."

Joan was willing to comply. Although she felt a strong physical attraction to Clark, she realized that he possessed the same insecurities that she had; certainly he was not the strong father figure that she had sought ever since her abandonment by Daddy Cassin. Louis B. Mayer did fulfill that figure, and although she sometimes questioned whether his decisions were based on her welfare or that of the corporation, she still relied on him as her paternal authority.

Mayor Jimmy Walker sent eight police motorcycles to escort Joan and Doug to the New York pier. The dock beside the SS *Bremen* was mobbed. Fans grabbed at Joan's dress, women planted kisses on Doug's face. Ironically, the crossing was a memorable time for Joan and Doug. Not since the early months of their marriage, four years before, had they spent time alone together, and they strolled the deck arm-in-arm. In the evening they joined their friends Jill Esmond and Laurence Olivier at the captain's table. Noel Coward and Heather Angel greeted the arrivals at Southampton. On the ride to London Joan insisted on sitting in front with the driver so she could get a better view. It was Joan's first visit to a foreign land, and she was entranced by London. Doug woke up to find her staring out at the foggy streets. "I love it . . . I love it," she said. She braved the stares to browse through Piccadilly shops while Doug and Larry Olivier observed the orators in Hyde Park and even conducted a mock debate. Doug was in his glory. Noel Coward arranged for them to see the spectacular *Cavalcade* from the royal box of the Drury Lane Theater. A mob had gathered outside the theater, and Noel and Douglas carried Joan on their shoulders to get inside. The entire audience rose when the couple entered, and Joan dissolved in tears. Coward invited them to a party at his home on Gerald Road, where they met Lady Mountbatten, Lady Brecknock, Lady Ravensdale and the Duke of Kent, who had become acquainted with Doug during a stay at Pickfair. Noel regaled the guests by playing and singing "Mad Dogs and Englishmen" and "Mad About the Boy." Heather Thatcher, the English actress, honored the visitors at a dinner party in her town apartment, inviting the leading figures of the London stage and cinema.

Crawford's terror surfaced again at a program arranged by the MGM publicity department in London. She was to address three thousand working girls, fans of the American star with whom they identified most. She had prepared a speech about her pleasure at being in England, and she rehearsed it for Doug in their Savoy suite. But the girls started clamoring, "Our Joan! Our Joan!" and all she could manage was a faint "Bless you."

MGM and Warner Brothers began cabling messages for the two stars to return. They went on to Paris.

The channel crossing was choppy, and Joan became violently ill.

She and Doug sought a quieter life in Paris, and they stayed outside the city at the estate of a friend of Doug's. Still, the French reporters found the location and asked a series of polite but persistent questions.

Joan avoided the Paris salons, buying only two hats and gifts of perfume for Claudette Colbert, Ria Gable and Betty Montgomery. She and Doug went to a theater showing *Possessed*—titled *Fascination* in France—and they howled at the dubbed French voice that spoke her dialogue. Both sat for portraits by the celebrated painter Beltrán y Masses. In his romantic way, Doug had hoped that he could rekindle their love by introducing Joan to the Parisian milieu he had known as an art student. He showed her the places he had frequented on the Left Bank and the Île St.-Louis, and she was charmed. He proposed a dinner at his favorite restaurant atop Montmartre; he retained warm memories of the meals he had enjoyed in his youth. But when Doug and Joan arrived, they found the place jammed with American tourists who crowded around to ask for autographs.

The second "honeymoon" ended on that note. Without expressing it, both realized that the intimacy they had cherished four years before had now vanished. Their marriage had become public property, and they had nothing to share in private. Both had matured: Douglas from an unsure young man languishing in his father's shadow to an accomplished actor with a reputation of his own; Joan from an immature, frightened contract player to a mature, frightened box-office star. They had become strangers.

Both Joan and Doug returned to Hollywood with the unspoken realization that their marriage was over. But how to end it? Oddly, it was Douglas Fairbanks Sr. who gave Joan the courage. She telephoned him at Pickfair.

"Uncle Doug, could I talk to you?" she asked wistfully.

"Sure thing, Billie," he replied. "You mean alone, not on the telephone."

"If I could."

"Okay, lunch tomorrow at the Derby. One o'clock."

When her father-in-law arrived at the Brown Derby, Joan was shocked by his appearance. There was more gray in his mustache, less spring in his step, his voice lacked his usual jauntiness. Joan disclosed her sorrow over how she and young Doug had drifted apart: He wanted always to make new social conquests; meeting people frightened her. He couldn't understand why she wanted to stay home and study her roles; to him acting was child's play. They no longer shared the same joys.

"Billie, I understand," said her father-in-law. "This happens to people, even when they have been deeply in love. Painful as it is, the only thing to do is make a clean break and start your lives anew." He didn't add that he had come to the conclusion that his own marriage was over, although Mary was not yet aware of it.

Uncle Doug settled Joan's mind. The only question that remained was how to end the marriage. Would she confront Douglas with his own transparent infidelities? No, that would only arouse his accusations about her affair with Gable. She and Douglas had never exchanged acrimony, and she wanted none now. It was better, she believed, to make the break on a public-relations level, no matter how hurt Douglas might be. She telephoned Katherine Albert in New York. Katherine had been a press agent at MGM when Joan arrived in 1925. A warm, perceptive woman, Katherine recognized the talent and drive in the frightened, overweight girl from the Shubert chorus. She counseled Joan, bolstered her courage, convinced her not to chew gum or laugh so loud. When Joan became a star and began making regular publicity trips to New York, Katherine acted as devil's advocate, tossing questions that Joan would be receiving from reporters. They remained close friends after Katherine left MGM to become a free-lance writer. She had married another MGM publicist-turned-writer, Dale Eunson, and had moved to New York. Joan invited her to come to California for a visit. "Katherine, I'm going to divorce Douglas," Joan announced in her bedroom one night.

"Are you sure that's what you want to do?" Katherine asked, astonished.

"I'm sure. And I want you to have the story exclusively."

"But you know I work for *Modern Screen*, Joan. I couldn't get it in print for thirty days. You can't keep it a secret that long. Not in this town."

"I think I can. You know how well I keep secrets."

"Yes, I do. Tell me, does Doug know?"

"No. Only you. And that's how it will remain until *Modern Screen* prints your story."

Joan remained true to her word. For almost thirty days she kept the news from everyone, including Douglas. *Modern Screen* might have had a remarkable scoop except for a lawsuit against Fairbanks. A man named Dietz claimed that the actor had stolen "the love, and affection, comfort and assistance" of his wife. He also claimed that Fairbanks and his agent, Mike Levee, had kept him against his will in a hotel room for four hours, and he asked $60,000 for both charges.

Dietz dropped the charges, but Louella Parsons learned of the suit and wrote a sympathetic article defending Doug and Joan for the Hearst press. Before filing it, she telephoned Joan for a quote.

"I wish you would not print anything like that right now," Joan replied quietly. "If you will wait, I will have another story for you."

Parsons sensed a scoop and hurried to the Bristol Avenue house. Joan blurted out the fact that she had handed Katherine Albert the divorce story and planned to make a general release when *Modern Screen* hit the stands five days later. A sympathetic story about Doug's lawsuit would be awkward. Parsons wasted no time. She borrowed Joan's typewriter and quickly wrote the story of the divorce, which she telephoned to the Los Angeles *Examiner*.

After Mrs. Parsons left, Joan telephoned Mike Levee, who was her agent as well as Fairbanks'. "I'm divorcing Douglas. It will be in the papers tonight. I want all of his clothes out of the house—right away!"

Levee pondered what to do. If he broke the news immediately to Doug at Warner Brothers, Doug might not be able to continue work. The agent sent his chauffeur to collect Doug's clothing. Late in the day Levee went to Burbank to visit his client.

"Let's have a Scotch," Levee suggested.

Doug agreed. Three Scotches later, Levee remarked, "I hate to tell you this, Doug, but Joan is divorcing you."

Fairbanks roared with laughter. "Is that the reason for the long face, Mike? Is that why you plied me with Scotch?"

"You mean you know?"

"Of course. Louella called me for a comment hours ago."

Both Joan and Doug told reporters the alienation-of-affections suit had no bearing on the split, and both claimed no other party was involved. "I am going to send her flowers, call her up every day and send her telegrams when I can't get her on the phone," he added. "We are still in love."

On May 13, 1933, Joan filed suit for an interlocutory decree of divorce. "He would sulk for days at a time and refuse to speak to me," she testified. "Oh, I was unable to sleep because of it! . . . Whenever I spent the day working at the studio, he would ask where I had been at various times, where I had taken luncheon, and what I had done. All the time he knew I was at work, too." Her husband was unbearably jealous, she added, "and he began to make uncomplimentary remarks about my friends. He was so unreasonable!" In fact, her doctor had advised a three-month rest to restore her well-being. The divorce was granted.

Joan's divorce from Doug removed one of the barriers to a marriage with Clark Gable. All that remained was for him to divorce Ria. He hesitated. He claimed he didn't want to hurt Ria or the children. Also, a divorce settlement would cause him to part with a large chunk of his money, and Ria was his convenient excuse to the parade of women with whom he had brief encounters. The extent of his conquests was indicated one day in a publicity office when he was surveying a photograph that included all the female MGM stars. "What a wonderful display of beautiful women," he said admiringly, "and I've had every one of them."

Joan and Clark continued to be friends and confidants over the years, with one interruption. In 1936 he eagerly undertook *Parnell*, a historical drama of the Irish statesman, a role which Gable believed would prove his talent for serious drama. Joan read the script and considered it boring and pretentious. She refused to play the role of the married woman whose love wrecked Parnell's career; Myrna Loy took the part. Gable was furious with Joan, and even more so when *Parnell* proved a failure. Because of his anger, Joan also refused to make *Saratoga* with Clark, and the ailing Jean Harlow assumed the role. Relations between Joan and Clark remained suspended for three years. Then in 1940 they were reunited in *Strange Cargo*. They were reconciled, but he was now married to Carole Lombard and there was no possibility of renewing the romance. When Lombard died in a 1942 plane crash, Joan wrote Gable: "If you would like to stop by and have a quiet dinner, I'll be home rather late tonight and all this week." He accepted the invitation. Every evening after finishing work on *Somewhere I'll Find You*, he drove to Bristol Avenue and poured out his sorrow over drinks.

Gradually Gable came to terms with his loss, and he enlisted in the Army Air Corps. Until his death in 1960 he and Joan remained close friends, and during periods between marriages they resumed their relationship as lovers. In later years she romanticized about Gable, suggesting that he was her one great love. Perhaps he was, during two or three years when both were intoxicated with being new movie stars and were thrilled by the fantasy of a romance outside their own marriages. But Joan always suspected that Clark was more interested in momentary conquests and wanted to avoid entanglements. Once Adela Rogers St. John asked him why he patronized the prostitutes of a well-known brothel when he could have any woman in Hollywood. "Because I can always send those girls home," he explained.

In later years Joan often made assertions of Gable's quality as a lover. In a television interview with David Frost during the late 1960's she was asked to name her favorite leading man. "Clark Gable, of course," she replied. "Why Gable?" "Because he had balls." The remark was made on tape, which was edited for broadcast.

In unguarded moments of candor during her late drinking years, Joan admitted that Gable was not the lover he was reported to be. In fact, his lovemaking was rather brief and unsatisfactory. Sometimes he used ploys to discourage sex. One night after a few drinks, he said, "So I'm supposed to be the King, the virile, romantic star! Well, what do you think of this?" He removed his false teeth and suddenly Joan saw a wizened old man.

10

WHATEVER JOAN CRAWFORD DID, she did in extremes. As Billie Cassin, she had learned how to sew as a necessity; as a movie star she knitted, crocheted and hooked rugs furiously. "I have nervous hands; I need to keep them busy," she explained about the sweaters, skirts, blankets, rugs, socks and booties she assembled.

She took extraordinary care of her body, which she realized was a prime asset in her career. Every morning she ran for a mile, the chauffeur following her and then driving her the rest of the way to the studio. She swam every day and played tennis and badminton. Before she was married Joan always slept on a screened porch, no matter what the weather, and she took only cold showers. She had massages regularly to maintain her muscle tone.

She smoked cigarettes, because it gave her hands something to do and because everyone did it in Hollywood. She didn't drink, however, because she had known too many drunken "stepfathers," fraternity boys and friends. She served drinks to her guests, but she herself declined even an after-dinner sherry and claimed that until she was thirty-five she did not touch liquor at all—later she made up for her youthful abstinence. She was extreme in her phobias. She claimed that her claustrophobia stemmed from when she was five and her brother, Hal, locked her in a closet as a prank. She abhorred elevators and would climb ten flights of stairs to avoid them. She never entered an airplane until she was middle-aged.

Joan Crawford

The reason for her obsession with cleanliness was undoubtedly the many years spent in the cockroach-ridden apartment behind the laundry, and scrubbing greasy school kitchens and dirty toilets. A psychiatrist might say that Joan was trying to wash away her past as Billie Cassin, and she continued to scrub floors until the end of her life. Many a visitor to her Bristol Avenue villa would arrive to find Joan cleaning on her hands and knees with a scouring brush and a pail of soapy water. Household help came and went because they could not maintain Joan's stringent code of cleanliness.

A friend once dropped in at Joan's house and found her in the midst of cleaning. "Can I help?" she asked.

"Sure," said Joan. "You can clean the bottom side of the dining table."

"The *bottom* side? What for?"

"Someone might drop a napkin and look up at the bottom side. I'd be embarrassed if it were dirty."

During one manic period Joan washed her hands dozens of times each day and changed her clothes almost hourly. She removed all bathtubs from her house, reasoning that it was unsanitary to sit in one's bathwater. She rarely ate in the MGM commissary, preferring to lunch alone in her dressing room. When her meal arrived, she ordered the maid to rewash the glasses, plates and silverware.

Joan was also subject to extremes in her screen appearance— until criticized by her directors or fans. During the early 1930's she affected heavy makeup, believing that the fast-living women she was portraying would exaggerate their features. "Was I wrong?" she wrote in the *Saturday Evening Post*. "Well, you ought to read the bushels of letters razzing me for going too far in lipstick. I was astonished at the attack, but I saw that my objecting friends— although many letters agreed with me and liked the large mouth— were right, and I used less color thereafter."

Her gardenia period lasted for three or four years. "Gardenias are my symbol for romance and poignant memories," she told columnist Jimmy Fidler. "During my first schoolgirl romance I wandered with my youthful sweetheart through a beautiful yard in which we came upon a gardenia tree. The fragrance of the blossoms combined with the beauty of the occasion and the happiness of love to give me a heart-stilling thrill. Yes, gardenias bring memories— memories of that night and other occasions; memories that are rich and real and most of them beautiful. I cannot talk about them.

Lucille Fay LeSueur, Age 5

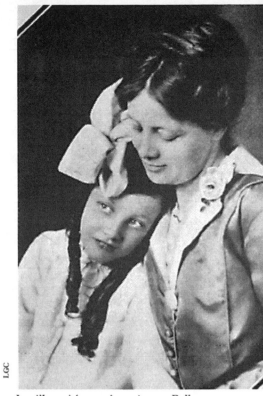

Lucille with mother, Anna Bell Johnson LeSueur

Lucille with brother Hal

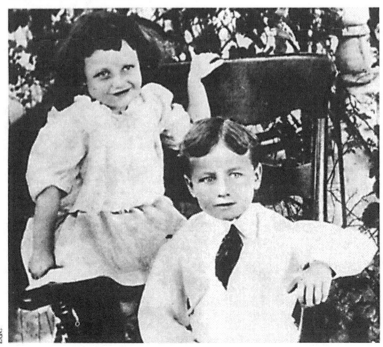

LGC

LGC

The Thirteen Wampas Stars for 1926
Left to right: top row: Mary Astor, Dolores Costello, Fay Wray, Marcelline Day, Mary Brian; *middle row:* Janet Gaynor, Sally O'Neil, Vera Reynolds, Edna Marion; *bottom row:* Joan Crawford, Dolores Del Rio, Joyce Compton, Sally Long

Paris (1926)

An MGM "Action" Publicity Shot

LGC

LGC

Rose Marie (1928)

The Unknown (1927) with Lon Chaney

Winners of the Wilderness (1927)

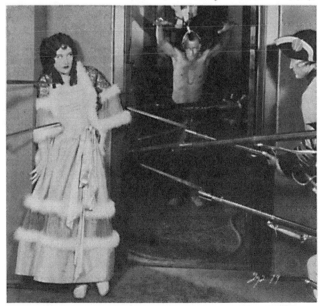

Across to Singapore (1928) with Ramon Novarro

Four Walls (1928) with John Gilbert

Our Dancing Daughters (1928). This role catapulted her from playing obligatory romantic roles to Stardom.

Douglas Fairbanks, Sr., and Jr.

Joan married Douglas Fairbanks, Jr., June 3, 1929

Doug, Joan, friend William Haines, and Robert Young

Our Modern Maidens (1929)

Paid (1930) with Polly Moran and Marie Prevost

Dance Fools Dance (1930) with Clark Gable

Joan and her mother

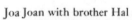
Joa Joan with brother Hal

Grand Hotel (1932) with Wallace Beery

Grand Hotel (1932) with Lionel and John

Joan with Adrian and costume sketch for *Letty Lynton* (1932). His notion to pad the shoulders of her costumes revolutionized American fashion.

Letty Lynton with Nils Asther

Rain (1932) with Walter Huston

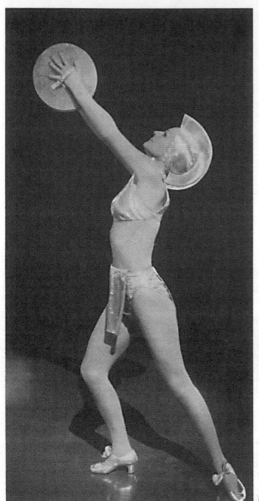

Dancing Lady

On the set of *Dancing Lady* (1933) with
Franchot Tone

Dancing Lady with Fred Astaire

HURRELL/LGC

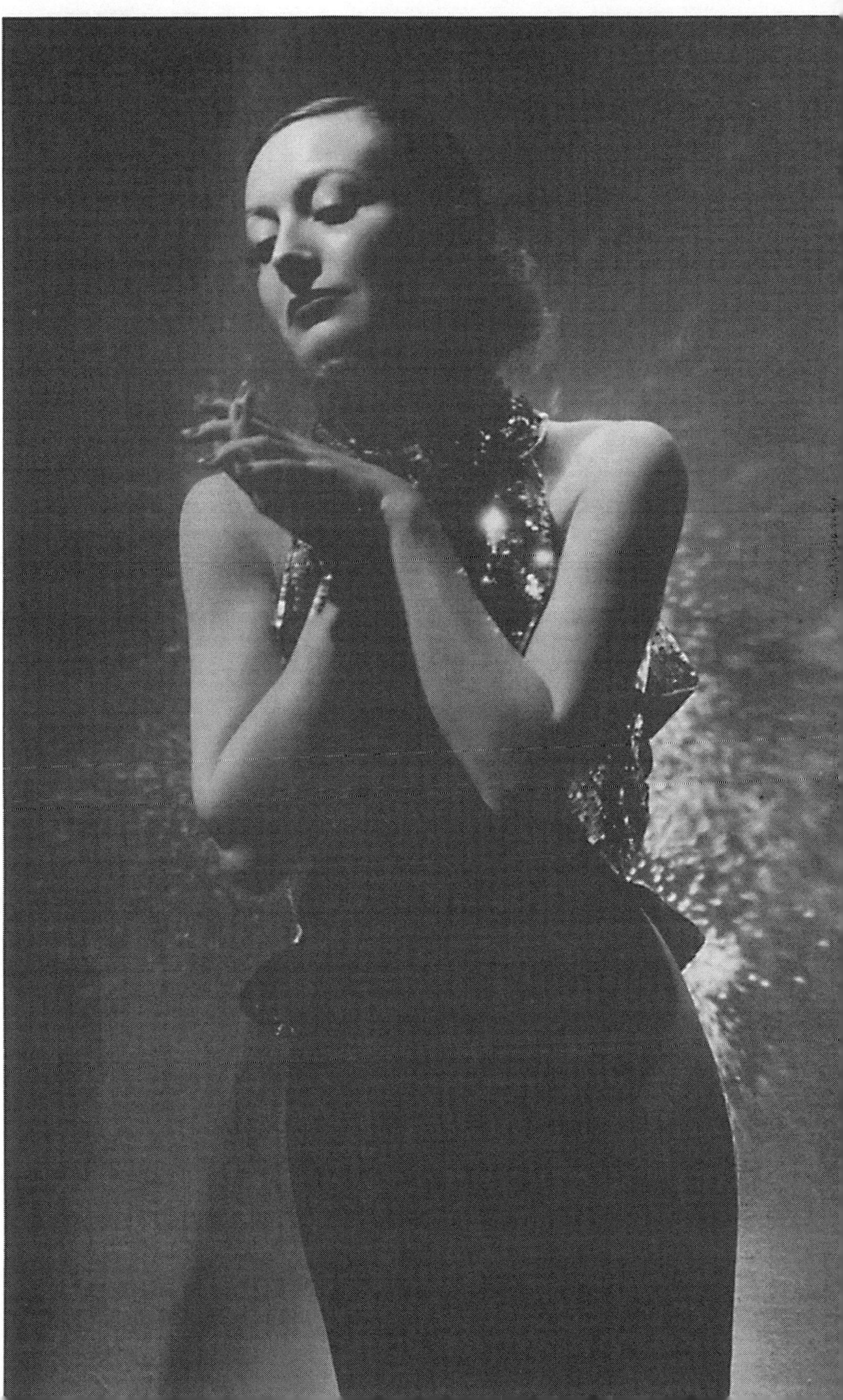

Forsaking All Others (1934) with Gable

On the set of *Chained* (1934) with director Clarence Brown and Clark Gable

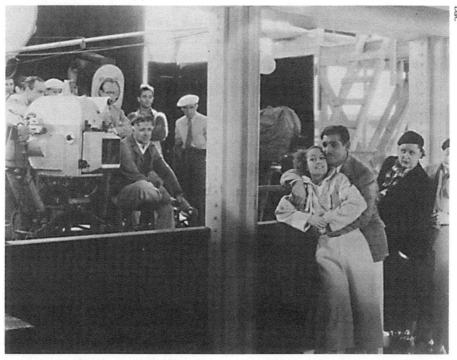

Joan married Franchot Tone, October 11, 1935

The newlyweds doing a radio broadcast in New York

On the set of *Mannequin* (1938) with Spencer Tracy and producer Joseph L. Mankiewicz

The Women (1939) with Rosalind Russell (top) and Norma Shearer

The Gorgeous Hussy (1936) with James Stewart and Robert Taylor

Memories are cherished secrets that we keep deep in our hearts. If we tell them, they cease to be memories.

"I feel lonely and lost unless the odor of gardenias is constantly around me. Nights, beside my bed rests a bowl in which are two or three natant gardenias which permeate my room with their faint perfume. Perhaps I am silly to have such an idea, but I actually believe that the flowers lull me into a peaceful sleep and pleasant dreams." On Mother's Day, Joan sent bouquets of flowers to mothers of her friends, always ordering gardenias to be interwoven on the basket handles. On every social occasion Joan carried a gardenia in her hand; she couldn't wear the flower as a corsage because it blackened when attached to her body. Most of the books in her library contained a pressed gardenia, and she always included one in books she sent to friends. She took sunbaths with a gardenia in her hand, and never dined without one beside her plate. A studio worker, Paul Schrebnick, often asked for the gardenia in Joan's hand at the end of the day. When he died in a traffic accident, she sent a blanket of flowers for the coffin. "Paul" was spelled out in gardenias.

In the 1930's Joan discovered Christian Science. During that period in Hollywood, Christian Science had been embraced by many leading figures, and it was not uncommon to find *Science and Health with the Key to the Scriptures* resting beside movie scripts. Joan did not discuss her new religion in public; to the end of her life she adhered to Louis Mayer's ukase that stars should never talk about politics or religion lest they alienate a segment of the public. "Christian Science fit Joan's philosophy to perfection," Dorothy Manners said of her. "Joan was a very positive person. She was also a very healthy person. She never had colds, she never complained of headaches. She acted as though such ailments didn't exist."

She was possessive in her friendships. She considered herself totally loyal to her friends and demanded the same in return. She read in the newspaper that Dorothy Manners had been one of the handful of guests at the wedding of Jean Harlow and Hal Rossen. "What were you doing there?" Joan demanded.

"I was invited by Jean," Dorothy replied.

"Well, you can't be her friend and mine, too."

"Why not?"

"Because you can't."

97

Joan remained adamant. She demanded total, undiluted loyalty from her friends. Harlow represented a threat to her at MGM. Regretfully, Dorothy abandoned her friendship with Harlow.

Joan strove to excel in everything she did. She was ever aware of competition from new stars at MGM, and when Mayer signed Jeanette MacDonald to a contract, Joan decided to train her voice so that she would also be considered for singing roles. She sought help from Rosa Ponselle, the Metropolitan Opera diva, who lived across the street. She did not like to be criticized. Sally Blane remained a friend from her Lucille LeSueur days and often discovered that Joan did not enjoy candor. As starlets they sometimes drove to the beach, Joan singing loudly. "You're off-key," Sally remarked. When Joan was studying voice with Rosa Ponselle, she gave a Sunday recital at her home. Joan attempted lieder and arias to the acclaim of her guests. Sally was furious because of their obsequious fawning. "They lied to you," Sally told Joan. "You still sing off-key." Joan wouldn't talk to her for a month.

Although fiercely competitive with Shearer, Harlow, Mac-Donald and others who might be considered for desirable roles, she could be considerate and helpful with actresses on the rise, remembering how green and lost she had been in her early days in Culver City. When Betty Furness appeared on the lot as a starlet, Joan befriended her and came out of her dressing room to greet Betty on the set. Joan heard reports that Jean Muir, a promising actress at Warner Brothers, seemed to be destroying her career by erratic behavior. She invited Miss Muir to dinner and told her the lessons she had learned in her years at Metro-Goldwyn-Mayer. "Play in as many pictures as you can," Joan counseled. "Rely on the director to a certain point, then depend on yourself. Have confidence in yourself. Don't be discouraged by these overnight stars who seemingly have not worked for their stardom. They don't last. Hollywood gives you back what you give. All you need is the ability to do hard work."

Gail Patrick was a hopeful young actress who had admired the way Joan Crawford always photographed so handsomely. She told her admiration to a fan-magazine writer, Jerry Asher, who mentioned it to Joan. "Tell her to come to MGM tomorrow afternoon," she said. "I'm having a photo session with George Hurrell. She can watch—and learn." The young actress looked on in awe as Joan posed for hundreds of still photographs, explaining meanwhile how to get the best effects with makeup and clothes. Joan urged that Gail Patrick be tested for a role in *No More Ladies*, and Joan donated the services of her makeup man and hairdresser, and borrowed a gown from Adrian. When Gail won the role, Joan declined her thanks. "There was a time when I would have been grateful if anyone had helped me," she said.

Joan's greatest beneficence began in 1926, when she consulted Dr. William Branch for a minor ailment. Both were on the verge of successful careers, and Joan remarked confidently that when she became a big star, she intended to share her good fortune with others. Eight years later, Joan was a star and Branch a successful physician. She reminded him of her promise, and together they devised a program. He would donate his time and services, and she would pay the hospital bills for needy cases that Dr. Branch believed were worthy. Rooms 351 and 353 of Hollywood Presbyterian Hospital were permanently maintained so that newspapermen, extras, aging stars, gaffers and grips could be given operations and treatment they couldn't otherwise afford. Many recipients never knew that Joan Crawford paid for their operations, and she was upset when news of the Crawford-Branch clinic was printed. But she continued her support for many years.

As soon as she started earning her big salaries, Joan began her policy of gifts to fellow workers. Each member of cast and crew inevitably was given a handsome and valuable gift at the end of a movie. During a film together, Joan noticed that Robert Young carried a shabby kit for his makeup (during the early 1930's film actors followed the stage tradition of applying their own makeup). Joan presented Young with a bag of imitation alligator outfitted with a complete set of makeup.

When Joan encountered a book she found inspiring, she ordered a hundred copies and sent them to friends. One of her favorites was *The Prophet* by Kahlil Gibran.

While Joan was demanding in her friendships, she was also intensely loyal. Katherine Albert and Dorothy Manners were rewarded time after time with exclusive stories they could sell to magazines. At a time when William Haines was considered a pariah in Hollywood, Joan refused to abandon him. Haines was not a victim of talkies, as some historians have reported; his MGM career continued until 1935. It ended when he made the mistake of inciting Louis B. Mayer's moral outrage by refusing to end his romance with a young man, and Mayer fired him from MGM. Haines never made a secret of his homosexuality and lived openly with his lover, Jimmy Shields. Most of Hollywood's homes were closed to Haines, but not Joan Crawford's. He and Jimmy were invited to every party and every Sunday gathering. "They're the happiest married couple in Hollywood," Joan remarked. When Billy Haines went into business as an interior decorator, "Cranberry" was his first customer, and later he decorated her New York apartment. He and Shields lived together until Haines's death in 1973. Six months later, the heartbroken Shields took his own life.

Jerry Asher was a Los Angeles boy who loved Joan Crawford as much as he disliked being a Jew and hated the high-pitched effeminate voice that stigmatized him. She got him a job in the MGM mail room and sent him to her vocal coach until his voice was corrected. He advanced to the publicity department, then became a fan-magazine writer, producing dozens of articles about Joan Crawford. She included Jerry in most of her parties, and his bright, cynical wit contributed to the entertainment.

Harry Mines was a Los Angeles newspaper reporter and reviewer with a passion for Joan Crawford. A writer mentioned Mines to Joan, and he received a telephone call.

"This is Joan Crawford."

"Oh, sure!"

"No, this *is* Joan Crawford. I would like you to come to dinner Sunday night."

Mines became a regular visitor at Bristol Avenue. As she did with many others, Joan sought to change his life. He was interested only in theater and film; she gave him books to read. When she tired of meeting him for previews in Westwood Village, she insisted that he learn to drive. Knowing how much he admired Alfred Lunt and Lynn Fontanne, she made him co-host of a party for the visiting stars. He also idolized Noel Coward. One day Joan told Mines on the telephone, "I've got a present for you. Come at four."

When he arrived, she said, "Your present isn't here yet. Why don't you start a fire in the den?" Mines was doing so when he heard the den door open. It was Noel Coward.

Leonard Spigelgas grew up adoring Joan Crawford in the theaters of Brooklyn. Even when he went to Hollywood as a screenwriter at RKO, he never dreamed of meeting her. Then one day in

1933 his collaborator on a film, Lynn Riggs, announced, "Miss Crawford needs another man for dinner tonight. I told her you would do. Black tie."

It was an evening of firsts for Leonard Spigelgas. Never had he worn a tuxedo to a private home before. Never had he seen so many gorgeous people. Joan Crawford exceeded his boyhood vision of her—superlatively dressed, warm and gracious to her guests, especially the dazzled young man from Brooklyn. The guests were seated in the formal dining room, Miss Crawford assuming the head of the table like a young viscountess. Spigelgas spread the embroidered napkin on his lap and stared down in terror at what the butler had placed before him. It was green, bulbous, with small prickly spines at the top. Did Californians eat cactus as an hors d'oeuvre? The hostess recognized his perplexity. Without being noticed by the other guests, she demonstrated how Spigelgas should gently remove each leaf, dip it in the melted butter, nibble on the end, then discard the leaf onto a plate. Spigelgas followed the instructions carefully, and Miss Crawford nodded her approval.

Another crisis occurred when Spigelgas reached the end of the leaves. Miss Crawford's expressive eyes indicated for him to again study her movements. She held the middle of the remaining plant with a fork, then deftly trimmed it with a knife until the cap lifted off. Then she cut the bottom in quarters, dipped a piece in the melted butter and ate it. He did the same, to her smiling response. And so Leonard Spigelgas ate his first artichoke.

Afterward Miss Crawford led the party to the playroom for more lively conversation.

"Anyone for a swim?" she asked.

Spigelgas was astonished. He had known swimming only between the Fourth of July and Labor Day, and never at night. But several of the others accepted their hostess's invitation, and he agreed. She gave him a suit and pointed him toward the changing room.

He emerged and grew self-conscious among the tanned, muscular bodies. Then Miss Crawford appeared, wearing only a bathing cap and the bottom of a swimsuit. "Dive in!" she shouted, leaping into the water. Another first for Leonard Spigelgas.

Howard Hawks was always on the lookout for good new writers, and he found one in a Mississippian named William Faulkner.

Hawks thought Faulkner's short story "Turn About" would make a good movie; he was especially interested because it concerned fliers in World War I. Hawks had been an army pilot in the war and had directed *The Dawn Patrol*. He and Faulkner worked out a treatment, which Thalberg approved. When the script was completed, Eddie Mannix, one of the MGM executives, asked Hawks, "Who are you casting in the picture?"

"I want Gary Cooper as the aviator, and Robert Young and Franchot Tone as the two young men."

"Who's the girl?"

Hawks looked at the chunky Irishman with surprise. "There's no girl in the picture," the director said.

"There is now. Joan Crawford. The studio stands to lose a half-million dollars if we don't put her to work. She's in your picture. Go down to the commissary and tell her how happy you are."

Hawks had known Joan socially, having directed Doug in *The Dawn Patrol*. He found her in the commissary and told her what Mannix had said. Her eyes brimmed as she realized the cavalier attitude studio executives displayed toward her career. "Are they kidding me, Howard?" she asked hopefully.

"No, they're not. You or me, either. You've got a contract, and they'll make it stick. Now, you can either make it fun, or it can be a horror. You decide which one."

She was silent for a moment. "I'll try to make it nice for you, Howard."

Faulkner was equally surprised by the studio's decision. "Ah don't seem to remember a girl in the story," he drawled. "That's the picture business, Bill," Hawks replied.

Faulkner dutifully rewrote the script, adding a sister to the British naval officer, played by Robert Young. Joan kept her word with Hawks. Her behavior was impeccable, and every day she pinned a gardenia to the director's lapel. The addition of the romantic interest upset the balance of the film, which was released as *Today We Live*, and it was not a commercial success. Joan considered the experience a complete loss—except for the fact that it provided her introduction to Franchot Tone.

Joan had never met anyone quite like him. He was a patrician both in appearance and manner, yet he also possessed a deep concern for social reform.

Franchot was a year older than Joan, born on February 27, 1905, in Niagara Falls. His father was president of the Carborundum Company. Franchot traveled with his parents all over the world, attended Miss Otis's School, then a boys' academy, Hill School, from which he was dismissed "for being a subtle influence for disorder throughout the fall term." His instinct for rebellion began early. With a half-year of high school remaining, Franchot entered Cornell University, where his brother had attended and retained some influence. He joined his brother's fraternity, Alpha Delta Phi, and the drama club, and spent a summer studying in France. He breezed through Cornell in three years, Phi Beta Kappa.

To his father's disapproval, Franchot declined a career at Carborundum to join a Buffalo stock company at fifteen dollars a week. He moved to Greenwich Village and auditioned for the New Playwrights' Theater, making his Broadway debut with Katharine Cornell in *The Age of Innocence*. Soon he was a leading man for such stars as Lenore Ulric, Sylvia Sidney and Jane Cowl. He left the New Playwrights' Theater to help form the Group Theater, along with such talented, radical-minded personalities as Harold Clurman, Lee Strasberg, Cheryl Crawford, Clifford Odets and Stella Adler.

On September 28, 1931, at the depth of the Depression, the Group Theater presented its first play, *The House of Connelly*, with Franchot Tone and Morris Carnovsky in the leading roles. Franchot later appeared in *1931*, *Night Over Taos* and *Success Story* for the Group. His performance in *Success Story* drew an offer of an MGM contract, and although Franchot had no ambition to become a movie star, he perceived the contract as a means of subsidizing the Group Theater, always in fiscal straits because of its uncompromising standards. He intended to endure a year at MGM and return to his comrades in the Group with his booty, and he never lost the attitude that films were somewhat beneath an actor's dignity. Tone's first film at MGM was *Gabriel Over the White House*, with Walter Huston and Karen Morley. His second was *Today We Live*.

Joan and Franchot were drawn to each other immediately. He claimed later that he fell in love with her the moment they met on the set. He had been bored with his life in Hollywood and was not prepared to meet such a vital, exciting woman; he had expected Joan Crawford to be a dull, manufactured movie star. She knew vaguely of his Broadway reputation and was expecting the same disdain she had experienced from other New York actors. Instead, he seemed sensitive and involved. She was intrigued with him and invited him to tea. Serving from a set of rare antique English silver, Joan played the lady, a role which she believed would impress the attractive young actor of Eastern wealth. Indeed, his manner was polished, but he put her completely at ease with his down-to-earth conversation. He was interested in her Hollywood world, not merely for the glamor that it offered; he was fascinated with the power structure of immigrant strong men who ruled the industry, also with the immense influence that movies could exert on the nation's social attitudes. Joan enjoyed the sound of his warm, lyrical voice, even if she did not understand all he said. She was determined to learn more about Franchot Tone.

Joan wasn't ready for another romance. She told Jerry Asher: "I do not believe that I will marry again. I tried it once and failed. Possibly the day will come when I will say, 'Oh, all right, I'll try it again.' Right now, I doubt that."

Her confidant Jerry Asher described her during this period: "Work would have been a blessing to her in those months but no story was in readiness, so her days were crowded with reading, sewing and lying in the sun. Often in those days I talked to her for hours at a time while she lay in the garden sunbathing. She would insist that she was happy again. Then without warning she would lapse into one of her terrible spells of depression. She was going through the bitter lesson of getting acquainted with her new self while she waited for the old wound to heal."

Finally the blessing of work returned. Mayer was concerned about the attrition to Joan's career by *Rain* and *Today We Live*, and he told her, "You and Clark were fine in *Possessed*. Suppose we team you again." Mayer's son-in-law, David O. Selznick, had newly arrived at MGM as a threat to Thalberg, from whom Mayer was becoming estranged. Selznick enjoyed complete access to the MGM contract list and he cast Marie Dressler, John and Lionel Barrymore, Jean Harlow, Wallace Beery, Lee Tracy, Edmund Lowe and Billie Burke in *Dinner at Eight*. For *Dancing Lady* Selznick cast Joan Crawford, Clark Gable, Franchot Tone, May Robson, Winnie Lightner, Ted Healy, the Three Stooges, Robert Benchley, and in specialty numbers. Fred Astaire and Nelson Eddy. Joan was delighted with the prospect of dancing with Astaire, and she filled the Beverly Wilshire Hotel suite of Fred and his bride, Phyllis, with bouquets of flowers. Joan was so eager for *Dancing*

Lady to succeed that she ignored a broken ankle to complete her dances with Astaire. (She had done the same thing in *Paris*, when she continued with a broken ankle for fear she might lose the part.) Despite its hackneyed plot, *Dancing Lady* was a big success. Audiences delighted in its entertainment and the renewal of the Crawford-Gable combination.

Franchot was again cast with Joan in *Sadie McKee*, and now they were observed holding hands between scenes. It was another of the Crawford formula pictures except for the sure touch of Clarence Brown.

Brown directed her next in *Chained*, again with Gable. Joan had been photographed by a series of gifted cinematographers, including Oliver Marsh, William Daniels and Charles Rosher. *Chained* was the first of her eight films with George Folsey.

Folsey was photographing a shipboard scene in which Crawford sipped a ritual glass of sherry while her lover, Otto Kruger, was doing the same in his New York office. Joan wore an Adrian gown with white lace collar. During preparations for the scene, a single small spotlight shone down on her from high above the stage. "Look at that light on her!" Folsey said to his assistant. "It's remarkable."

The soft light suffused the Crawford face with a luminescence that highlighted all her best features, especially her eyes. Folsey ordered a key light (which simulates the source of light in a scene— sun, candle, gas) of 500 watts with a plain diffuser covered with a light coating of oil. He placed the camera high to accentuate the upper part of the head and create a heart-shaped effect. He was careful to allow nothing to be highlighted in the background; all attention should be focused on the face. "Look up; keep your head high," Folsey instructed Joan, realizing that such an attitude would show off her cheekbones.

Studio executives were jubilant when they viewed rushes of the close-up. Joan was ecstatic. She had never looked so good on the screen, and she wanted to learn how Folsey had done it. She observed how Folsey often masked the forehead to direct the light at her eyes, and how he threw a shadow on her chin and neck, sometimes by placing leaves at the bottom of the key light.

MGM attracted Joe Mankiewicz in 1933. He was chunky, blue-eyed, with a quick intelligence. He graduated at nineteen from

Columbia University and set out for Berlin, where his professor father hoped he would study literature. Instead, Joe studied movies, translating titles for UFA, stringing for *Variety* and reporting for the Chicago *Tribune*. He followed his brother Herman to Hollywood in 1929 and demonstrated his worth by writing titles for six Paramount silent features in eight weeks. When talkies began, Joe's sharp wit made him an ideal dialogue writer for W. C. Fields, Jack Oakie, Skeets Gallagher and other Paramount players. At MGM he was assigned to the production unit of Bernard H. Hyman. One of Joe's first scripts was *Forsaking All Others*, based on an original story by Edward Barry Roberts and Frank Cavett. Screenwriters always fashioned scripts with definite stars in mind, and Joe was told to write *Forsaking All Others* for Loretta Young, George Brent and Joel McCrea. When the script was completed, producer Hyman changed his mind.

"We're going to use Joan Crawford, Clark Gable and Robert Montgomery," he announced. "I want you to go to Miss Crawford's house on Bristol Avenue and read the script to her."

The proposal filled Joe with terror. He had been accustomed to dealing with lowbrow comics at Paramount; never had he presented his material to a glamorous star.

"Can't I just send the script to her?" he inquired.

"No, she likes to have it read to her," said Hyman.

Joe drove to Brentwood and parked his modest car in the courtyard before the gleaming white house. The butler admitted him inside and escorted him to the drawing room, which resembled nothing less than a drawing room in a movie set. Gardenias were in every corner, and the scent was heavy and intoxicating. Crawford entered in flowing chiffon. She offered her hand and bade Joe take a seat on the sofa.

The reading was at first faltering. She listened raptly, giggled at amusing lines, laughed at funny ones. Joe felt encouraged, and the reading became more enthusiastic. He came to a line for Robert Montgomery: "I could build a fire by rubbing two boy scouts together."

Miss Crawford threw up her arms in unbridled glee. As she did, a scarlet fingernail flew off her hand and landed on the white carpet. Mankiewicz was startled; he had never seen a false fingernail before.

"Go on, go on," she urged him, and he continued reading the script between anxious glances at the red object on the rug. Finally he finished, and she kissed him on the cheek. "It's quite marvelous, Joe dear," she said.

It was the beginning of her most successful collaboration. For the next nine years Joe Mankiewicz helped fashion Joan Crawford movies as writer, producer and script doctor, providing nine films that helped maintain her status as a top box-office star.

With the success of *Forsaking All Others*, Joe Mankiewicz was assigned to write another Crawford vehicle, *I Live My Life*. He was then promoted to producer of the Crawford films, Louis Mayer explaining, "You're the only one on the lot who knows what to do with her." That was true. Other producers still dismissed Crawford as "that chorus girl brought out here by Harry Rapf." Mankiewicz understood her appeal: "She is not demonstrably a proficient actress, nor is she identifiably a sexpot. But she is on a level that lower-middle-class audiences can identify with."

When reviewers attacked her for playing the shopgirl in Adrian gowns and spacious apartments, Mankiewicz consoled her.

"Joan, forget those snobs. We're not making pictures for them; they get in on passes, anyway. Just remember the shopgirl, who sees you in a fantasized version of her own life. She doesn't want to see you in a housedress with armpit stains. She wants you dressed by Adrian, as she would like to be."

The Gorgeous Hussy gave Joan her first costume picture and her largest array of leading men—Robert Taylor, Melvyn Douglas, Franchot Tone and James Stewart, as well as Lionel Barrymore as Andrew Jackson. But although gorgeous, Peggy O'Neal proved to be no hussy, and audiences were disappointed. The film's failure permitted producers to gloat, "Crawford can't make a costume picture." And she never did again.

Mankiewicz continued the Crawford string with six more films. Nearly always the scripts were based on unpublished plays, magazine short stories or novels that the studio had bought years before and forgotten. Mankiewicz had to search through piles of manuscripts for the material, then labor with screenwriters to fashion a workable script. Never did the studio purchase hit plays or best-selling novels for Crawford; such vehicles were reserved for Garbo, Shearer and other stars of MGM's "prestige" films.

As a writer and observer of the human comedy, Mankiewicz found Joan a fascinating study. He admired the devotion with which she played Joan Crawford—"she woke up like a movie star, she went to the john like a movie star. She had a special outfit for answering the fan mail. She put on another outfit to have lunch." Mankiewicz recognized that she was always role-playing, assuming a new identity as each situation changed. He grew to recognize her attitudes when she entered his office. If she arrived in a stylish dress, jewels and sables, he rose from his desk with a courtly "Joan, darling," kissed her on the cheek and asked his secretary to bring some sherry for Miss Crawford. If she swaggered into his office in slacks, he whacked her on the behind and said with a wink, "Gettin' much, kid?" One night Mankiewicz was invited to dinner at Joan's house. Black tie, of course, although only he, Joan and Franchot occupied the long dinner table. Gardenias were everywhere and the menu was printed. When the butler arrived with the dinner wine, Joan inquired, "Are you sure this is room temperature?" The line struck a reminiscent tone in Mankiewicz's ear. Then he remembered where he had heard it: in a recent Joan Crawford movie.

Learning that F. Scott Fitzgerald had been assigned to work on a script for her, Joan Crawford fixed her gaze on his bleary eyes and commanded: "Write hard, Mr. Fitzgerald, write hard!" The Knute Rockne-like injunction did not please Fitzgerald, nor did the assignment. He was barely enduring his purgatory at MGM, moving despondently from one failed script to another. As he remarked in a letter to his friend Gerald Murphy: ". . . I am writing a picture called *Infidelity* for Joan Crawford. Writing for her is difficult. She can't change her emotions in the middle of a scene without going through a sort of Jekyll and Hyde contortion of the face, so that when one wants to indicate that she is going from joy to sorrow, one must cut away and then cut back. Also, you can never give her such a stage direction as 'telling a lie,' because if you did, she would practically give a representation of Benedict Arnold selling West Point to the British. . . ."

Infidelity was doomed from the start. Two years before, Hunt Stromberg had produced *Wife vs. Secretary*, in which secretary Jean Harlow threatened the marriage of Clark Gable and wife Myrna Loy. The film had evoked the wrath of the industry's censor, Joseph Breen, who insisted that Harlow's apartment be cut down in size, lest it appear that she was augmenting her secretarial salary by means of favors to the boss. The success of *Wife vs. Secretary* prompted Stromberg to assign a similar plot to Fitzgerald. Joe Breen was on his guard.

Needing to succeed at MGM because of the financial burden of his wife Zelda's mental treatment, Fitzgerald plunged into a study of Joan Crawford. He no longer harbored his admiration for her as "the best example of the flapper," one of the "young things with a talent for living." Now he recognized her shortcomings as an actress.

Day after day Fitzgerald scrutinized the Crawford films, sitting alone in an underground projection room in the Thalberg Building. During a screening of *Chained*, he penciled notes: "Why do her lips have to be glistening wet? . . . Don't like her smiling to herself— or such hammy gestures that most actresses get away with. . . . Cynical accepting smile has gotten a little tired. . . . Bad acting to following the stage direction 'as an afterthought. . . .' She cannot fake her bluff, or pretend to." During the ranch scenes in Argentina, she seemed better to Fitzgerald: "Her smile brighter in outdoor situation than in drawing rooms. . . . Outdoor girl better. . . . Hearty laughter rather good. . . . A sad smile not bad, but the serious expression best. . . . Absolutely necessary that she feel her lines. Must be serious from first. So much better when she is serious. Must have direct, consuming purpose in mind at all points of the story—never anything vague or blurred. Must be driven."

Fitzgerald plunged himself into the writing of *Infidelity*, excited with the notion of escaping the verbosity of films of the 1930's. In a memo to producer Stromberg, he exulted: "Note how we . . . engrave our characters and our situations with practically no dialogue—a completely new technique and one that is not without its air of intrigue and appealing mystery." He fashioned a story of adultery, drawing from an episode in 1924 when Zelda had taken a French aviator as her lover. Convinced that he had composed a masterpiece, Fitzgerald left for the East to visit Zelda and their daughter, Scottie. He returned to Hollywood for the heartbreaking news: *Infidelity* had been shelved. Joe Breen had turned thumbs down. The title itself contained a threat to the American family, which the industry's Catholic-bred censor aimed to defend.

Thirty-five years later at Town Hall in New York, a member of the audience asked Joan Crawford if she had known F. Scott Fitzgerald. "I only remember him coming to my house in California with Helen Hayes and Charlie MacArthur, and all he did was stand in my kitchen near where the liquor was and get very drunk."

11

FOLLOWING THE DIVORCE from Doug Fairbanks, Joan had told her confidant Jerry Asher: "I'll never marry again as long as I live. There is no such thing as honesty or true love. If anyone ever catches me believing in anything, I hope they give me a good sock in the jaw." Like most things she told to interviewers, she believed it at the time. During 1935 she appeared at Hollywood gatherings with Ricardo Cortez, Alexander Kirkland, Gene Raymond and others, steadfastly refusing to devote herself to a single man. But gradually she was succumbing to the persuasions of Franchot Tone. He was charmingly insistent, lavishing on her not only flowers but also rare books and works of art. He avoided the film-colony parties and escorted her to plays and concerts, dining in quiet restaurants.

She paid visits to his beach house, making sure that she wasn't seen; she lay on the floor of her chauffeured limousine, covered with a blanket. Franchot moved from Santa Monica to Brentwood so he could be closer to Joan. At night he built a fire in her den and read Ibsen, Shaw and Shakespeare to her while she hooked a rug, one leg tucked under her. Franchot introduced her to the works of Stanislavsky and to his friends of the Group Theater, who were also making their way to Hollywood. For Crawford it was a new and stimulating world.

Franchot wanted Joan to marry him. She resisted, for she still hadn't recovered from the depression that enveloped her after the failure of her marriage to Doug. She was convinced that a movie actress could not have a successful marriage. Franchot argued, "Just because your marriage failed is no reason to suppose there is anything fundamentally wrong with the institution. How conceited you are to think that!"

Joan was going through another of her characteristic periods of terrifying self-doubt. The black mood could be incited by the simplest of happenings. A thoughtless friend could show her a derisive review of her latest performance. A role she coveted could be handed to Norma Shearer. A director might fail to compliment Joan after a challenging scene. All the phantoms that haunted Billie Cassin returned to plague the adult Joan. She seemed physically ill, but Dr. Branch could detect no ailment. He recommended a complete rest. Again she rented a house at Malibu, where the beach and sun could refresh her. She read mystery novels beside a dune and darkened her skin until the freckles didn't show. She allowed Franchot to visit her, and he elevated her spirit. He had vast reserves of charm that could make her laugh even during her blackest moods.

"Let's go to New York, Joan," he said excitedly one day. "*Men in White* is opening. It's a terrific new play the Group is doing; I sent them some money to help put it on."

"New York?" she said. "But if you and I go there together, the press will have a heyday."

"Not in New York, darling. In Hollywood, yes, but New York is much more sophisticated." Crawford emerged from the Twentieth Century Limited at Grand Central Station to find the largest crowd that ever greeted her arrival in New York. The Joan Crawford Fan Club clamored for attention, while MGM publicity men strove to control the dozens of reporters and photographers.

"Are you engaged to Franchot Tone?"

"Do you plan to get married again, Miss Crawford?"

Joan smiled as the cameras continued flashing. She worried that someone might discover Franchot hiding inside the train.

The crowd hushed to await her answer. A voice called out: "Tell them, 'Time will tell,' Joan." Amid the laughter she turned around and saw a Western Union delivery boy who had made the suggestion. "That's right," Joan said. "Time will tell." More laughter, and the tension was eased.

Franchot was thrilled as he and Joan watched *Men in White* unfold on the stage. It was a culmination of all that he and others had striven for in the Group Theater—strong, socially conscious drama that could revitalize the American theater. "This is where we belong, in the theater," he whispered. "Someday this is where we'll be!"

She was overwhelmed by his enthusiasm and by the power of the Sidney Kingsley play. On the return trip to California by train they formulated plans to build a little theater at Joan's house where they would present classical plays for the entertainment and education of their friends. Joan had bought the lot behind her home and was making plans to reconstruct the compound to fit her new needs and personality.

Franchot continued arguing for marriage. Joan remained undecided, expressing her reluctance both to Franchot and to interviewers.

"I do not want to say that I will or will not marry again," she told the world through Jerry Asher. "At the present time I do not know. There is so much between the thought and taking the fatal step. Franchot Tone and I are very deep friends. But it is so much bigger than that. We have so much respect and admiration for each other. And we want to keep both. Until things are adjusted, we will remain as we are."

Among the things that needed adjusting was Franchot's movie career. Tone was part of the flood of actors who poured into Culver City, and producers didn't know what to do with him. Even though he had played proletarian roles with the Group Theater, his new bosses couldn't picture him as a shirtsleeve guy; his polished manner seemed best suited to white tie and tails. Tone also fell victim to another kind of studio manipulation. Mayer had adopted a bullpen technique to keep his stars under control. If Myrna Loy became difficult and refused a script, Rosalind Russell was warming up to replace her. Each star had a potential replacement, and Robert Montgomery's was Franchot Tone. When Montgomery grew restless under studio control, he was reminded that Tone was available to slip into the Montgomery dinner jacket. Mayer fancied that the Crawford-Tone romance could contribute to the box office, and he approved casting of the pair in four films within two years. Tone had third or fourth billing, and it rankled him that he seemed typed as the "other man" in Joan Crawford movies.

Both Franchot and Joan were delighted when Paramount borrowed him to costar with Gary Cooper in *Lives of a Bengal Lancer*. He was successful in a manly, adventurous role, and Irving Thalberg cast him in *Mutiny on the Bounty* with Clark Gable and Charles Laughton. Tone substituted for Robert Montgomery, who insisted on a three-month summer vacation in his new contract.

With Franchot's movie career ascending, Joan began thinking more seriously about his proposals of marriage. He had already changed her life in profound ways, introducing her to serious artists of the theater and broadening her intellectual horizons. He interested her in the newly formed Screen Actors Guild, and she became one of its early members. He even convinced her to appear on radio.

Joan had turned down all offers to play on radio broadcasts. She was terrified by the thought of performing not only for a studio audience but also for millions of radio listeners. What if she failed? What if her voice froze in her throat and the public failure exposed her timidity and lack of professionalism? When Bing Crosby invited Joan to appear on his musical program, Franchot urged her to accept.

"I can't do it! I can't!" she said.

"Of course you can!" Franchot said. "You love Bing's singing. He's the easiest man in the world to work with. You'll be playing yourself. What could be simpler?"

"Play Joan Crawford? That would be the worst thing of all. At least if I played a role, I could be excused for not being enough of an actress. But if I failed as Joan Crawford . . ."

"Darling, you're not going to fail."

"It's easy for you to say. You've faced audiences. I never have. I'm scared to death."

"Joan, I'll be there. I'll get you through it. You're an actress. This is another challenge you can meet, just as you've met other challenges. You can do it, Joan. Trust me."

Joan agreed to trust him. For a month she agonized over what she would wear, how she would read the lines, how to keep her nerves under control. She was so shaky at rehearsals that a bar was placed before her microphone so she could hold onto something. Her script pages were mounted on cardboard so the paper wouldn't rattle. Franchot remained ever-present to bolster her morale, and Dr. William Branch stood nearby in case she needed medical attention. But with the help of Bing's consummate ease, Joan made it through the broadcast. Now Franchot insisted that playing a role on radio would be easier for her. That would be her next challenge.

Joan came to the decision to marry Franchot Tone after a glowing evening with Alfred Lunt and Lynn Fontanne. The warm, enduring relationship of the two stars, both off the stage and on, provided a hopeful model for Joan and Franchot to aspire to. Joan envisioned a similar life for herself and Franchot. Like Lunt and Fontanne on the stage, Tone and Crawford in films would establish a pattern of ever-ascending attainment. Their careers would be interlinked, like their lives. The prospect held enormous appeal for Joan. It meant that she could give up her solitary quest for achievement. She would have someone she loved at her side always. No more the lonely battles.

Radio appearances in New York provided the occasion for the marriage. Joan had agreed to repeat her role in *Paid* on *Lux Radio Theater*, and Franchot was scheduled to appear in *East Meets West* for *Cavalcade of America*. By marrying in the East they could escape the Hollywood hoopla, and Joan could meet Franchot's family.

After Joan and Franchot arrived in New York, they disclosed their plans to Nick Schenck. The president of Loew's, MGM's parent company, called a friend from his days of operating Palisades Park. His friend, Herbert W. Jenkins, was now mayor of Englewood Cliffs, New Jersey, and he arranged for a marriage license to be delivered to his home. In the mayor's parlor on October 11, 1935, Joan Crawford married Franchot Tone, with Nick Schenck and another MGM executive as witnesses. Joan went to her radio rehearsal that afternoon with a glove covering her wedding band.

Characteristically, Joan considered the press. She had promised an exclusive on the wedding to Walter Winchell. She endeavored to play square with reporters, and she telephoned him the news. "Walter, I want you to hold the release until your Sunday-night broadcast," Joan said.

"Good God, Joan, this is Friday!" replied Winchell. "This is hot stuff. It won't keep for three days."

"That's the chance you'll have to take. Promise?"

"I promise," Winchell agreed reluctantly.

Enjoying their delicious secret, Joan and Franchot went out on the town, dancing until early morning in the smart clubs—Franchot was not a good dancer, but he was learning. In the hours before dawn, fans and reporters no longer pursued them, and Joan and Franchot were free to act like a couple of love-struck kids in the big city.

The Sunday dawn was beginning to outline the skyscrapers of Manhattan as the newlyweds headed back to the Waldorf-Astoria Hotel. On Sixth Avenue Franchot told the taxi driver, "Stop the car." He had spotted a decrepit old man selling newspapers on a deserted corner. Franchot and Joan got out of the cab and invited the man to dance. His rheumy eyes lighted up, and together the three figures twirled around and around in the gathering dawn.

The Winchell broadcast brought a phalanx of newsmen to the Waldorf, and the newlyweds were besieged by reporters on train stops across the country and upon their arrival in Los Angeles. When Joan reported to the studio, she was told that Franchot would appear in her next film. His role amounted to twenty-six lines.

Joan's wedding night was marred by a telephone call from a stranger who announced that he possessed a pornographic movie featuring Joan Crawford. Rumors of such a film had followed her for years, and she had received other such telephone calls. This time she told the caller to take his proposition to Louis Mayer or J. Robert Rubin, the MGM attorney. Both men viewed the stag reel and declared that the sex-starved nymph was *not* Joan Crawford.

The rumors pursued Joan Crawford until her death, and the question "Did she make the blue movie?" remains unanswered.

The best evidence indicates that she did not. The title of the alleged reel is generally reported as *The Casting Couch.* The minimal plot concerns an aspiring actress who applies for a movie role. The casting agent asks her to test for the role, and the testing includes a variety of sexual acts.

Arthur Knight, the film historian who has long surveyed sex in the movies for *Playboy* magazine, estimates that *The Casting Couch* was made in 1918 or 1919, a time when Joan Crawford was still a schoolgirl in Kansas City. Knight adds: "*Playboy* pays a lot of money to acquire pornographic films; you'd think that if a Joan Crawford stag reel existed, one would have been offered for sale. None has. Furthermore, I spent a week at the Kinsey Institute in

Bloomington, Indiana, which has probably the largest collection of pornographic movies. I saw none with Joan Crawford. I don't believe such a film exists." But the rumors refuse to die. Scores of people in Hollywood believe that Joan Crawford, or Louis Mayer, or both, purchased the existing copies for a huge sum. The most appealing legend is that one copy escaped and fell into the hands of a decadent Austrian count, who screens it over and over again in his alpine castle.

At first it didn't disturb Franchot to move into Joan's house, the same one she had shared with Douglas Fairbanks Jr. Nor was he concerned—at first—that her fame and salary exceeded his. In the year they were married, MGM paid her $241,483, while Franchot was earning $1,000 a week. They were in love, they were married, and together they would ascend the heights of Art. They took a box at the Hollywood Bowl and listened raptly to the Symphonies Under the Stars; they studied opera together and for dinner guests played the entire score of *Gotterdammerung* on the phonograph while Franchot read the libretto. Joan pored through Franchot's copy of Stanislavsky's *An Actor Prepares*, writing comments profusely in the margins. He introduced her to the poetry of Edna St. Vincent Millay, and Joan was entranced. "This woman is writing *me*," she exclaimed.

After the day's work at the studio, they sat before the den fire and she played Juliet to his Romeo, Eliza to his Higgins. If they could not costar at MGM, radio offered them equal status, and they made semiannual appearances on *Lux Radio Theater*. At first Joan had her customary qualms. Franchot remained firm.

"The only way to overcome fear is to pull its teeth!" he insisted.

Joan agreed to perform the Virgin Queen to Franchot's Essex in Maxwell Anderson's *Elizabeth the Queen*. She recalled: "When I stepped onto the stage my knees and elbows were water. My voice was ebbing out of the soles of my feet. But when I began to read, I forgot myself. I felt very proud when I was told I had given a good performance. It represented a real conquest."

Franchot retained guilt feelings about having deserted the Group Theater for a career of playing sophisticates at Metro-Goldwyn-Mayer, and he maintained contact with his former comrades. Many had also come to Hollywood, and every Sunday Franchot and Joan entertained the émigrés for drinks, dinner and a movie.

Despite her perplexity over their political beliefs, Joan felt an artistic kinship with the Group Theater members. When Howard Clurman urged Franchot to return to the Group and did not include Joan in the suggestion, she was greatly offended. So much so that she did not appear at the Group gatherings at her own house for a few weeks.

Crawford was not sympathetic to complaints made by the newcomers about the studio system. When Stella Adler grumbled about having to wake up at dawn to go to work, Joan replied, "For what they pay us, it's more than worth it."

"For what they pay *you*," Adler replied.

The Tones provided equal time for Joan's Hollywood friends, with regular Saturday dinners that often included the Fred Astaires, the Fred MacMurrays, Barbara Stanwyck and Frank Fay, Helen Hayes and Charles MacArthur, the Gary Coopers, Sam and Frances Goldwyn, playwright Lynn Riggs, the Irving Berlins, Joan Bennett and Gene Markey, the Ray Millands, Sally Blane and Norman Foster, the George Murphys, Bill Haines and Jimmy Shields, Richard Cromwell, Jerry Asher.

The onetime scullery maid of Rockingham Academy shared with her fans her menu for a typical dinner party:

Fruit appetizer of fresh pineapple and strawberries topped with mint ice; almond soup; roast squab stuffed with onion and orange slices; wild rice and green peas; salad of French endive, watercress, lettuce and chickory, with plain French dressing; crepes suzette, served with flaming brandy.

Not only did Joan Crawford share her dinner menus with the women of Depression America. She also took them shopping with her.

Liza Wilson wrote in *Photoplay* an account of a shopping trip with Joan to buy a hat at I. Magnin's in Beverly Hills for her cocktail party in honor of Leopold Stokowski.

"Before an hour had elapsed, Joan had hats, dresses, pajamas, hosiery, lingerie, slippers, perfume, powder bags and even gadgets. Joan is the most amazing shopper. The slightly mad type. . . . When she finds a hat she likes, she immediately has it copied in a dozen or more colors. She buys expensive straws and brings them back year after year to be reblocked. She prefers simple tailored suits and vagabond hats, but of course, if the *Occasion* demands a picture hat, she wears a picture hat. Her Stokowski party hat was one of the loveliest I have ever seen her wear. It was an enormous floppy blue straw, worn on the back of her head *sans* crown and showing the top of her head.

"Joan hates waiting for anything; she's the impatient sort, so she rarely has the shop deliver things to her home. She simply stacks them up as she buys them, and insists on carting them herself out to her big black Cadillac waiting in front of the store. . . .

"Joan is both a source of joy and horror to the salesgirls. They worship her as a big movie star, and they love her as one girl to another (Joan always chats and gossips with them). But when it comes to doing over their sacred Hattie Carnegies, Chanels and John Fredericks that Joan buys, it pains them to the heart. No one is ever allowed to fit Joan. She does her own fittings. She takes charge of the pins and tucks the dress in here and flares it there and ups the hem and downs the neckline and all they can do is sit helplessly by and say, 'Yes, Miss Crawford. . . .'

"Another of Joan's annoying little habits is waiting on herself. She never misses a chance to dart behind the counter and pick out exactly what she wants without any of the chi-chi of having it sold to her. And, to the floorwalker's horror, often she disappears, when no one is looking, into the holy of holies—the stockroom.

"Through all this shopping orgy (even when a customer, not recognizing her behind the counter, asks to see something in washable gloves), Joan keeps in a gay, rollicking humor. The one and only way to make her furious is to try to sell her something that looks like what the cat dragged in."

For a time during her marriage to Franchot, Joan slackened her ardent pursuit of publicity. She had been convinced that a major reason for the failure of her marriage to Douglas was their willingness to share their life together with the reporters of Hollywood. She didn't want to repeat the mistake in her second marriage, and Franchot, who had little regard for journalists, supported her in this.

"I've come to the conclusion that Garbo and Hepburn are right," she told Ed Sullivan of the New York *Daily News*. "Run away from the newspapermen and photographers, thumb your nose at them. Because the best a celebrity can get from the ladies and gentlemen of the press—most of them—is the worst of it. They misquote you, they annoy you to death, and if you try to be 'regular,' they step all over you." She told of rising at six A.M. for a train interview with a reporter at Harmon, New York. She told him about how difficult it was for her to sleep on a train, and he quoted her as saying: "I find it almost impossible to sleep in a Pullman berth—alone."

Joan said to Sullivan: "The other day in your column you wrote a letter to Franchot and myself. You said that I shouldn't forget that the same newspapermen who were pestering us for our honeymoon plans were the writers who had built me up from an unknown chorus girl to a movie star."

"Yes, I wrote that, and I meant it," Sullivan responded.

"Well, you're all wrong," Joan insisted. "When I read that in your column I thought to myself that I'd like to have you in California to show you my scrapbooks. I'd show you thousands of newspaper clippings, and most of them are *raps* and *digs*. There's no reason why I should go out of my way to do anything for the press. They've done little enough for me. I've worked damned hard to get where I am and I've had little help from the press." She started crying.

"I didn't know you were so sensitive," the former sportswriter said feebly.

"What difference does it make whether I'm sensitive or not?"

"But you shouldn't take things so seriously. When I wrote that in my column, I didn't write it with malice."

"I know. I've cried and cried, time and again, over some story in the paper or in the screen magazines, and then I've pulled myself together and I've said, 'Forget it, Joan. Don't take any of them seriously.' But half an hour after I've made my fine resolution, I've sent the maid out to buy the latest screen magazines to read what some other writer has to say about me. It's crazy, but we can't all be sensible, can we?"

Joan finally admitted she could never pull a Garbo: "If a posse of newspapermen and women were chasing me, the temptation to yell, 'Yoo-hoo! Here I am!' would be too much for my sense of humor. Greta can avoid the press, and I think she's magnificent, really, but I couldn't, dammit."

She was right. Publicity was too much a part of her need to be a success, to be loved. Painful though they might be in certain respects, she continued her semiannual pilgrimages to New York.

Not only was it the center of the publishing world, but it was also the nation's largest movie market and the heartland of the Joan Crawford cult. Working girls adored her, copied her fashions, imitated her makeup and hairstyles.

The Crawford advent to Manhattan was scrupulously planned and executed by the New York publicity department of MGM. Newspapers, photo services, syndicates and magazines were notified of the exact time of arrival at Grand Central Station, and interviews were scheduled at ninety-minute intervals throughout the day. Joan approached each one with total freshness, never repeating a quote.

Her publicity acumen was noted by Milton Weiss, a young publicist for MGM. He had scheduled a shopping trip to Macy's, with Joan to be accompanied by a young reporter on the *Journal*, Dorothy Kilgallen. The main floor was buzzing with excitement when Joan Crawford arrived, but she sensed that an added element was needed for an exciting story. "Find out what floor the china department is on," she whispered to Weiss. He did, and Joan led Kilgallen and the growing entourage of fans into the racks of china. The resulting bedlam gave Kilgallen her story.

Joan's visits to New York were often timed to coincide with the opening of her movies. When *The Gorgeous Hussy* was making its appearance at the Capitol, she asked if she could attend on the first day. The operator of the Capitol, Major Edward Bowes, replied, "Yes, if you don't come as Joan Crawford." He realized what a mob scene would result if she didn't appear incognito. Katherine Albert, Joan's close friend and publicist, was assigned to pick her up at the hotel. Joan appeared as Major Bowes had decreed—hair pinned up, no makeup, a nondescript dress. "We'd better leave," Katherine suggested.

Joan looked troubled. "Just a minute," she said. She disappeared into the bedroom and returned a few minutes later with makeup on her face. Katherine tried to hurry her out the door, but Joan went back and changed to a glamorous dress. Again she hesitated, removed the pins and shook out her hair. Then she selected an Adrian jacket with the wide shoulders and pinned a gardenia on it. "Okay, let's go," Joan said. The Capitol was a mob scene that day.

For another opening at the Capitol, Joan was persuaded to make an appearance onstage. The headliner of the stage show was Milton Berle, and he devised an exchange of jokes. He and Joan rehearsed the routine, and she became letter-perfect in her delivery.

"And here she is, the star of the movie you just saw and loved," Berle announced to the Capitol audience. "Ladies and gentlemen— Joan Crawford!"

A shrill cry filled the theater as Joan strode onstage. The ovation continued for minutes, until Berle finally achieved silence.

"Welcome to New York, Miss Crawford, I'll bet you're glad to be here?" Berle began. He looked at Joan and saw terror in her huge eyes.

She turned away from the audience and through clenched teeth said, "I'm stuck. I can't remember a word. Get me offstage. Hurry!"

"Honey, just stick with me," the comedian whispered. "I'll do it all."

He put a supporting arm around her shoulder and said into the microphone: "I can see you're tired out from talking all the way through the movie. . . . I want to tell you, you're the kind of girl I'd like to take home to Mother . . . if Mother wasn't home. . . ." After a barrage of jokes he led her offstage to enormous applause.

Not only was the press informed of Miss Crawford's activities in New York. The Joan Crawford Fan Clubs were supplied with an hour-by-hour schedule. Once a friend asked if she wouldn't prefer privacy during her visits to New York.

"Listen, honey, those fans put me where I am," Joan replied. "If they want to know my whereabouts at any given time, they damn well better be told. If it wasn't for them, I'd be back in Kansas City."

12

Life MAGAZINE IN 1937 PROCLAIMED Joan Crawford the First Queen of the Movies. The reasoning stemmed from her position as seventh in *Motion Picture Herald*'s 1936 poll of theater owners, who were asked to name the stars who made the most money for them. Joan Crawford had appeared among the top ten since the poll had begun in 1932, when she was number three. In 1936 she was preceded by four men (Clark Gable, Robert Taylor, Joe E. Brown, Dick Powell), a child (Shirley Temple) and a musical team (Fred Astaire and Ginger Rogers). "It is an axiom in Hollywood that movie favorites are usually created by women," said *Life*. "Joan Crawford's public is predominately female, predominately lowbrow. A former shopgirl herself, she has risen to stardom as the Shopgirl's Dream." Within a year the Shopgirl's Dream would find herself dropped from the list of moneymaking stars and in serious career trouble.

The disappointment of *The Gorgeous Hussy* was followed by other well-cast but uninspired films: *Love on the Run*, *The Last of Mrs. Cheney*, *The Bride Wore Red*. Dorothy Arzner directed *The Bride Wore Red*, and Joan looked forward to working with a woman director, but by the end of filming, Crawford and Arzner communicated only through written messages carried by the studio publicist, Maxine Thomas.

Mannequin returned Crawford to the role of working girl. For the first time she costarred with Spencer Tracy, and the combination was electric, before the camera and otherwise.

Joan had never worked with an actor like Tracy. All of her other costars, even Clark Gable, seemed to *work* at acting; they required conscious effort to release their male inhibitions and assume emotions that they would repress in their private lives. Not Tracy. In rehearsal he seemed to walk through the scene, as if it were some child's game unworthy of his attention. But as soon as the camera started to roll, he *became* the character. If the scene required a display of temper, his emotions flared in an instant.

With her own native intelligence about acting, Joan realized she could not perform full-throttle against Tracy's underplaying. Under Frank Borzage's sensitive direction, she lowered her level of energy, approached her scenes obliquely instead of head-on. Even Tracy noticed the difference. "This dame's catching on," he remarked.

He played games with her, making incongruous gestures to break her up in the most dramatic scenes. At first he succeeded, and Borzage grumbled because she burst into laughter at the peak of emotion. She disciplined herself to concentrate on the scene despite Tracy's impish gestures. It was an important lesson in concentration.

"Ya got spunk, kid," Tracy conceded.

"You ain't so bad yourself, Slug," Joan replied. She called him Slug because of the pugilistic stance he took when clowning on the set.

Joan was intrigued by the bluff Irishman. She had tired of striving to promote Franchot's career at MGM—*The Bride Wore Red* was the last of their seven films together. Franchot was relieving his boredom and frustration in alcohol, and that was something Joan could not tolerate. Spence drank, too, but his drinking seemed to fit his rough nature.

During the filming of *Mannequin*, Joan contracted pneumonia. Her code did not permit her to be absent from production—she had even kept working with broken ankles—and she tried to continue. Dr. Branch decreed a rest, and she reluctantly remained in bed at home. When her fever subsided, Dr. Branch invited her to get some fresh air at the Riviera Club, where he played polo. Among his fellow players was Spencer Tracy.

Tracy helped Joan overcome her terror of horses. Soon she had acquired two ponies of her own and was swinging a polo mallet in practice matches. She enjoyed the rugged exercise—and the easy camaraderie with Tracy. No matter that he remained firmly locked in a Catholic marriage. Tracy himself wanted no further complication in his already tumultuous life. He had been amused by Joan's buoyant energy, but it soon bored him.

Joan and Spencer were scheduled to costar in an abbreviated version of *Mannequin* on *Lux Radio Theater*. She displayed her customary nervousness during rehearsal, stumbling over her lines again and again. "For crissake, Joan, can't you read the lines?" Tracy blurted. "I thought you were supposed to be a pro." Joan burst into tears and fled from the studio. She threw herself into her car and, sobbing, sped out Sunset Boulevard to her home. She brooded about Tracy's lack of feeling for almost a day. Then Joan realized that she had been merely a diversion for him, one of many. She decided to give him no further opportunity to hurt her. The Crawford-Tracy affair was over.

Mannequin turned out to be more of the same—Crawford as a Delancey Street working girl torn between her chiseler husband (Alan Curtis) and a shipping magnate (Tracy). Audiences and critics alike felt a shuddering sense of *déjà vu*. So did theater owners. After being proclaimed First Queen of the Movies, Joan Crawford found herself dropped from the list of top-ten moneymaking stars in 1937.

In 1938 came a shattering blow. Harry Brandt, owner of a small chain of movie houses, wrote an article in the *Independent Film Journal* with the title "Box Office Poison." He claimed that theater owners were losing money with films featuring stars who lacked popular appeal.

"Among these players whose dramatic ability is unquestioned, but whose box-office draw is nil, can be numbered Mae West, Edward Arnold, Greta Garbo, Joan Crawford, Katharine Hepburn and many, many others," declared Brandt.

It was a thoughtless attack on performers who had given movies stature and would continue to do so—most of those Brandt mentioned continued on to greater success. Some of the victims were amused. Hepburn and Dietrich met on a train to New York and argued over their preeminence.

"I insist that I am the biggest box-office poison," said Hepburn, "and I've got the figures to prove it."

"No, darling, *I* am the winner, and I don't need figures," Dietrich replied. "Paramount paid me a huge amount of money *not* to make my next picture."

Joan Crawford could not take the attack lightly. How could she have gone from "Queen" to "Poison" in one brief year? As always, she took her worries to Papa Mayer. "Now, Joan, don't you concern yourself," the studio chief counseled. "The public loves you, and they will always love you. And I love you. You know that, don't you? I will always take care of my little Joan. You are just like a daughter to me." It was a standard Mayer routine, but no matter how many times she heard it, Joan was always heartened, even though, as she later told Joe Mankiewicz, "Somehow his hand always touched my right tit whenever he said the word 'daughter.' "

Joan's contract expired in 1938, and Mayer did not hesitate to use his "daughter's" depressed position to the studio's advantage. He offered her a contract of only one year, three pictures at $150,000 apiece, a rise from her salary of $125,000 per film. Joan had been at Metro-Goldwyn-Mayer for thirteen years, most of her adult life, and the thought of leaving the security of the studio frightened her. She told her agent, Mike Levee, to seek a longer contract. She would even be willing to cut her price per picture. Mayer then made his final proposal: a five-year contract, three pictures a year at $100,000 apiece. "Take it," Joan instructed her agent.

Crawford had arrived at the unhappy conclusion that nobody was going to look after her career but Crawford. Louis B. Mayer, for all his paternal piety, had shown his lack of concern by offering her a new contract for one year only. Thus, if her popularity continued to slide, MGM could be rid of her with little financial loss.

"No more goddamn shopgirls," she announced. She began looking for a new sophistication befitting the post-Depression times. She had seen Keith Winter's play *The Shining Hour* in New York, and she pestered Mayer to buy it for her. He did, and then she urged him to cast Margaret Sullavan as her romantic rival. Mayer considered her foolhardy; Sullavan was an accomplished, Broadway-trained actress, a striking beauty, and she was younger than Joan. "I don't care," Joan replied. "I need a good picture, and I can use all the help I can get. If Maggie is good in the picture, I'll be the winner."

Indeed, she was not intimidated by Sullavan, who became a personal friend. Frank Borzage maintained a balance between the two actresses in directing their scenes together, and George Folsey was careful to photograph both with equal care. With Robert Young and Melvyn Douglas as male leads, *The Shining Hour* proved the quality film that Joan was seeking. Yet it failed to attract much attention in theaters. The MGM production minds grew desperate. With Jeanette MacDonald and Nelson Eddy feuding, why not co-star Joan Crawford with Eddy in a Sigmund Romberg operetta? After all, she had taken all those opera lessons. Happily, Mayer vetoed the idea. Instead, he convinced her to appear in *The Ice Follies of 1939* as a favor to the producer, Harry Rapf, who had brought her to Hollywood. The film marked a new low point in the Crawford career.

Franchot chafed under his MGM servitude, complaining about being cast as a dissolute playboy. His servitude to Joan Crawford rankled his manhood.

Franchot complained to Katherine Albert: "Every night Joan comes down the stairs all dressed up for dinner, and she expects me to compliment her on how she looks. Every night! My God, if Venus de Milo walked down the stairs every night, I couldn't continue raving about her." His moods blackened, and he began drinking more heavily. Some nights he didn't come home, and when she questioned him, he used his fists. Visiting Joan on a movie set one morning, Clarence Brown noticed that her makeup barely covered bruises. The director sensed what had happened.

"Why, that son of a bitch!" Brown exploded. "I'll beat the hell out of him!"

"No, don't get involved, Clarence," Joan said. "Let me handle it my own way."

Her dreams of an artistic union were disintegrating. The theater she had built, where they had planned to play classical dramas, was never used. They were both too busy at the studio. As with Douglas, Joan believed that her marriage to Franchot might be secure if they had children. Joan suffered two miscarriages, and she was told that childbearing would be impossible for her.

But their marriage might have continued except for an indiscretion on Franchot's part. He never expected that Joan would blunder into his dressing room at a time when he was having an affair with a young extra.

"I suppose this has been a regular occurrence," Joan said angrily.

"Of course," Franchot replied defiantly. "It happens every day. I have to prove to myself that I am still a man, before I go home to you."

A day later, Joan received a telephone call from her longtime friend Dorothy Manners. She was writing magazine stories as well as working as an assistant to Louella Parsons. Dorothy suggested a magazine story about the disparate backgrounds of Joan and Franchot: she a former chorus girl, he a scion of wealth. Joan was silent for a few moments. "I've got a better story for you," Joan suggested.

"What's that?" Dorothy inquired.

"I'm divorcing him."

In March 1939 Joan's lawyer sought an absentee divorce for her in Los Angeles Superior Court. The judge refused, citing news reports that Joan and Franchot had celebrated an "Eve of Divorce" in New York nightclubs the night before.

On April 11 Joan appeared in court and testified that she and Franchot had often quarreled and he once told her: "I am sorry we married. Marriage was a mistake for me. I'm not the marrying kind, and I want my freedom." She added that Franchot had agreed before their marriage that her career would continue. "But shortly after our marriage, when he asked me to go out socially and I refused because I had been working hard and I was tired, he became very angry and went out by himself. He wouldn't tell me where he had been, and he stayed out until all hours."

Divorce was granted, but not before a lecture from the judge: "You say that your husband caused you much nervousness and mental anguish. How does it happen, then, that you were publicized in pictures published around the world as having a friendly dance with him in New York after these divorce proceedings were started?"

Joan stiffened and replied, "I hope that I am intelligent enough to be friendly with my husband."

Joan wanted to be a mother. Most of her friends among Hollywood couples had children, and she envied them. She romanticized about her own childhood, when she had served as surrogate mother to the younger students at St. Agnes and Rockingham Academy, forgetting the drudgery and remembering only the tender moments of bathing the little children and tucking them into bed.

After the breakup with Franchot, Joan decided to adopt a child. She kept the matter a secret to everyone except her lawyer, and made unnoticed trips to the East to meet with adoption agencies. Negotiations were sensitive, not merely because she was a renowned movie star; only thirteen states permitted adoptions by unmarried mothers or fathers, and stringent rules governed such adoptions.

Finally, after months of inquiries she located an agency in Tennessee that was willing to fit her needs. The place was later exposed as a "baby mill," but Joan asked no questions. She was told the life histories of five pregnant young women. One of them intrigued Joan. When the baby was born, it was a blond, blue-eyed girl. In 1939 Joan traveled by train to New York incognito. The baby was delivered at the age of ten days to her, and Joan named her new daughter Christina. "I don't remember so much happiness coming into my life in one small bundle," she announced to the press. A year later she adopted a boy, but made the error of disclosing his place and date of birth. His mother appeared at Joan's door, making threats and demanding money. Her campaign continued, until finally Joan concluded that the boy would be harmed by the tug-of-war. With great sorrow she gave him back to his mother, who sold him to another family.

13

Louis B. Mayer was appalled when Joan Crawford announced she wanted the role of Crystal in *The Women*. He warned her that she would offend her loyal fans by playing a coldhearted bitch. "I'll play Wally Beery's grandmother if it's a good role," she retorted.

She insisted that her career needed the boost of appearing with an all-star cast in Clare Boothe Luce's hit play, and privately she relished a confrontation with Norma Shearer, now devoid of her protector-prince, Irving Thalberg, who had died in 1936.

Mayer disapproved but would not interfere. He told Joan she would have to convince the producer and director, Hunt Stromberg and George Cukor. Stromberg was dubious about casting Crawford as the tough perfume salesgirl who steals Norma Shearer's husband. The cast had been carefully selected—Shearer, Rosalind Russell, Mary Boland, Paulette Goddard, Joan Fontaine, Lucille Watson, Ruth Hussey, Mary Beth Hughes, Virginia Weidler, Virginia Grey, Cora Witherspoon, Marjorie Main, Hedda Hopper—and Stromberg feared the inclusion of Joan Crawford would offset the balance. He argued that it was too small a part for someone of her stature, but that didn't bother her. She realized that the hard-boiled Crystal would be a vital presence amid the host of genteel society women. Stromberg finally agreed to give her the role—if she could convince the director, George Cukor.

Crawford and Cukor had had a previous encounter in 1935,

when he took over the direction of *No More Ladies* from Edward H. Griffith, who was ill with pneumonia. The stage-trained Cukor was contemptuous of motion-picture actresses, and after Joan delivered a long speech to Robert Montgomery, the director said, "Very fine, Miss Crawford. Now, would you please repeat it? You remembered the words; now let's put some meaning into them." Crawford did not revolt under such treatment. She submitted to Cukor's direction, learning to give more menace to her characterization, and she was eager to work with him again on *The Women*. But Cukor was not in good humor, having recently been fired from *Gone With the Wind* (David O. Selznick had listed Joan Crawford among the candidates for Scarlett O'Hara, but he never seriously considered her). Cukor's reaction to Crawford as Crystal was violent, but Joan convinced him of her sincerity in wanting to play the lesser role, and Cukor acquiesced.

With Norma Shearer and Joan Crawford cast in the same film for the first time, their fellow workers at MGM waited for the explosion. It had been building for fourteen years, ever since Joan had made her movie debut doubling as the back of Norma's head. Joan had watched helplessly over the years as Irving Thalberg carefully chose his wife's vehicles, giving Joan Norma's rejects. She often met the Thalbergs socially, but was always treated with an air of condescension, as though the former chorus girl was out of her element. Thalberg's death left Norma more vulnerable, but Louis Mayer remained solicitous of her career, perhaps out of expiation for his having removed Thalberg as head of production at MGM. When Mayer cast Norma with Clark Gable in *Idiot's Delight*, based on Robert Sherwood's hit play, Crawford cried because she didn't get the role of the chorus girl turned mistress of a munitions magnate.

Joan always remained in total control of herself on a movie set; fits of temper were not permitted in her code of behavior. But so deep was the antagonism toward Norma Shearer that on one occasion she lost her composure. It was the only time Joe Mankiewicz ever saw her explode. Edsel Ford and his family, including a youthful Henry Ford II, were visiting the set of *Mannequin*. Both Crawford and Spencer Tracy greeted the Fords with great charm; then she excused herself to make a wardrobe change for the next scene. As she entered her dressing room, Mankiewicz was approached by the worried-looking assistant director.

"Mr. Mankiewicz, we're in for trouble," said the assistant.

"Why is that?" the producer asked.

The assistant explained that Norma Shearer was shooting wardrobe tests on a nearby stage and wanted to borrow William Daniels, who was photographing *Mannequin*. Both Shearer and Crawford, as well as Garbo, valued Daniels as a superb photographer of women.

"What'll I do?" the assistant director asked Mankiewicz.

"There's Crawford's dressing room. Go ask her."

Mankiewicz watched as the man knocked on Joan's door, then disappeared inside. Thirty seconds later the door was flung open, and the assistant emerged hurriedly. Crawford stood in the doorway, wearing only her underwear, her feet planted wide apart. "And you can tell Miss Shearer that *I* didn't get where I am on my ass!" she exclaimed. She slammed the door shut. A few minutes later she emerged from the room in her glamorous costume and rejoined the Ford party as if nothing had happened.

Cukor directed *The Women* with extraordinary skill and cunning, keeping the divergent temperaments in line by continual activity. When the actresses weren't rehearsing or acting in scenes, they were being fitted for costumes or tested with new makeup and hairstyles. Cukor's device worked—until Shearer and Crawford had their scene together. Fortunately, they met in the script only once, when Mary Haines confronts Crystal in a couturier fitting room. The stage was hushed for the meeting of the widowed Queen of Metro-Goldwyn-Mayer and her longtime rival. The rehearsal was polite, and Cukor breathed more easily when he completed the master shot. Then the camera moved in for the close-ups; Miss Shearer's first, of course.

Crawford was prepared to deliver the offstage lines, as she always did for other actors (lazier stars retired to their dressing rooms and allowed the script clerk or director to "feed" the lines). She positioned herself in a chair at the side of the camera and took out her knitting. She was working on an afghan that required large needles.

Norma delivered her lines in front of the camera. Joan answered with her lines, but she never looked at Norma. She continued gazing at her knitting. The needles moved at a furious pace, and they clicked. Loudly. "Joan, darling, I find your knitting distracting," Norma said.

Joan seemed not to hear. The scene continued, and the flashing needles grew louder. The tension mounted, and crew members looked from the irritated Shearer to the oblivious Crawford, then to Cukor, who seemed like an unwilling explorer on the brink of a volcano. Again Norma started the scene, and again Joan's needles distracted her. "Mr. Cukor," Norma said with icy control, "I think that Miss Crawford can go home now and you can give me her lines."

Cukor was furious with Joan. He grabbed her by the elbow and almost dragged her away from the set. "How dare you behave so rudely?" he muttered.

"I'm just paying her back for all the rudeness she and Irving gave me," Joan snapped.

"I will not allow such unprofessional behavior on my set," the director replied. "You are dismissed for the day. And when you come back tomorrow, I want you to apologize to Norma."

Joan was unrepentant. She remembered too well the years of playing second-best to Norma, of being considered cheap and inferior by Irving. Now he was no longer there to protect his dear wife, and Joan could express her feelings without fear of reprisal. With swift strokes she penned her resentment and dispatched a telegram to Norma.

Joan remained defiant on *The Women* set the next day, and Norma was icily aloof. She gave no indication she had received the angry telegram. Under Cukor's watchful direction, the two actresses completed their scene together and parted. They never spoke to each other again.

Mayer had bought the Rachel Crothers play *Susan and God* for Norma Shearer, but she had balked at playing the mother of a fourteen-year-old girl. Crawford had no such concern. She had seen the play performed by Gertrude Lawrence and admired it, and welcomed the chance to appear opposite Fredric March. Joan also wanted to work again with George Cukor, despite the imbroglio of the knitting needles.

Cukor was willing. He saw more in Joan Crawford than did MGM's other directors. He realized her eagerness to succeed, and he drove her hard. *Susan and God* was high comedy of the kind that Crawford had never attempted before, and she happily submitted to Cukor's unrelenting discipline. She developed an unerring and almost supernatural sense of when Cukor disapproved of her work. Once she performed a scene with her back to the camera, and when it was over she said, "You didn't like it." The amazed director asked how she could tell, since she couldn't see his face. "I felt you were interested up to a certain point," she said. "Then you went *Ugh!*"

Susan and God proved a splendid success, and Crawford felt confident enough to take her acting career another step forward. She had seen a Swedish film in which Ingrid Bergman portrayed a woman whose horribly scarred face embitters her into a life of crime. "Are you crazy?" Mayer exploded. "Do you want the public to see you looking ugly? What kind of foolishness is that?" But Joan persisted, and Mayer threw up his hands in dismay. He was growing weary of Joan and her constant demands. "If you want to destroy your career, go ahead," Mayer declared.

Joan applied herself uncompromisingly to the role of Anna Holm. Jack Dawn, who had created makeup for Lon Chaney, devised a horrific mass of scar tissue to apply to the right side of Joan's face. Cukor wanted to infuse her with the psychology of a disfigured woman, and whenever he felt that she was lapsing into her customary attitude as a glamorous star, he gestured to her in imitation of Chaney's hunchback of Notre Dame. She understood.

Cukor also felt that Crawford would rely upon the scar as a melodramatic prop, the way some actors reacted to canes. So he rehearsed her ceaselessly, waiting for her to assume the hopeless fatigue that such disfigurement would engender. "I guess the ham's out of you now," Cukor announced. "We'll take the scene." He was especially concerned about the courtroom scene in which Anna Holm tells her life story. He wanted it to be a grim recital, without a hint of melodrama, and he instructed Crawford to repeat the multiplication table until she achieved the dreary monotone that he was seeking.

Conrad Veidt, who played Anna's evil mentor, was an inspiration to Joan; she had rarely seen such dramatic intensity. Joan believed that *A Woman's Face* would prove a milestone for her career, and the reviews seemed to confirm her hopes. Critics proclaimed that Joan Crawford had established herself as an actress.

14

By 1941, not only had Louis B. Mayer wearied of his veteran female stars—so had the public. Garbo, Shearer and Crawford had been on the screen since silent films, Jeanette MacDonald for a dozen years. Moviegoers sought newer faces and fresh talent, and Mayer supplied them with Judy Garland, Lana Turner, Hedy Lamarr, Kathryn Grayson, Ann Sothern and an actress Mayer had discovered in a London play, Greer Garson. All that remained was for the older stars—now in their mid- or late thirties—to be removed gracefully from the studio payroll. That could be accomplished by giving them bad pictures.

Crawford received three of her worst. She appeared with Robert Taylor, Herbert Marshall and Greer Garson in *When Ladies Meet*, a remake of a 1933 movie. Then she was miscast in a Columbia farce, *They All Kissed the Bride*. The role had been intended for Carole Lombard, and in her honor Joan donated her salary to the Red Cross. Back to MGM for a potboiler, *Reunion in France*, Joan portrayed a giddy Parisian who saves the life of a downed American flier, John Wayne.

"When you start to lose your career in the picture business," William Haines told Joan, "it's like walking on nothing."

Crawford found herself walking on nothing. But she wouldn't give up, as Greta and Norma had done. She had been nurturing the idea of becoming a producer. She believed she could find and develop stories for herself with as much skill as the producers at MGM. She knew as much about the movie business as any of them. "It's an interesting idea, but it wouldn't work," Mayer replied indulgently to her proposal.

To Harry Mines, it seemed like a good idea at the time. He realized that Joan had been bored and lonely since her divorce from Franchot. She had occasionally gone dancing with friends like Cesar Romero, Glenn Ford, Charles Martin, Jean-Pierre Aumont, and she had also had a fling with a rich and powerful businessman of New York; Joan found him fascinating but also quite married. During his rounds as a Hollywood reporter, Mines had made the acquaintance of an actor named Phillip Terry. He was good-looking and personable in a low-key manner, a onetime Stanford football player. "You know Joan Crawford, don't you?" Terry said to Mines at Paramount studio.

"Yes," said the reporter.

"I'd sure love to meet her," said Terry.

"Maybe I can arrange it."

Joan agreed that Mines could bring Phillip Terry to dinner. Terry sat between Joan and Mines on the living-room couch and plied her with questions. One of them was for her telephone number. She was reluctant to give it, so he copied it from the receiver before leaving the house.

The next day he called for a date. She admired his resourcefulness and accepted. He took her out to dinner and they returned to her house and read the script of her new film, *Reunion in France.* She invited him back to dinner, and she was impressed by how comfortable she felt with him. She had admittedly been lonely. Phil Terry appealed to her. He was manly yet gentle. He did not appear to be the kind who would betray her with other women, as Douglas and Franchot had. He was sympathetic with her concern over the decline that had entered her career, and he bolstered her confidence that her talent and energy would restore her position. He was totally supportive at a time when she desperately needed support. Six weeks after their first dinner, Joan telephoned Harry Mines. "I want you to have the news," she announced. "Phil Terry and I are going to get married." Mines convinced her she would get in trouble by not breaking the news through regular channels, so

Joan called Katherine Albert, who gave the exclusive to Louella Parsons.

They had applied for the license in Ventura, seventy miles north of Los Angeles, attracting no attention because of their legal names, Lucille Tone and Frederick Kormann. Just past midnight—to qualify for the three-day wait in California—on July 21, 1942, they were married at the home of her attorney, Neil McCarthy, in Hidden Hills, near the San Fernando Valley. At nine A.M. the same day, Joan appeared on the set of *Reunion in France*. John Wayne recalls: "I knew what kind of a marriage it was going to be when I saw her walk on the set. First came Joan, then her secretary, then her makeup man, then her wardrobe woman, finally Phil Terry, carrying the dog."

Newspaper and magazine writers busily set about to answer a natural question: Who is Phillip Terry?

He had been born Frederick Kormann in San Francisco and traveled the oil fields of Oklahoma and Texas with his father, an oil operator. Working on oil rigs built his physique, and he was a hard-muscled one hundred and seventy-five pounds and six feet one when he enrolled at Stanford University, a prime candidate for Glenn (Pop) Warner's football team. Kormann became interested in theater and took up a friend's advice to study in London, where he quickly acquired an English accent. Hollywood studios were unimpressed with the accent, British actors having flooded the industry. As an Americanized Phillip Terry, the young man became a contract player at MGM in 1937. He played a bit role in *Mannequin*, starring Joan Crawford. After two years at MGM, he moved to Paramount, where he starred in *The Parson of Panamint*. It turned out to be a routine western, and Terry was relegated to supporting roles in *Wake Island* and, on loan to MGM, *Bataan*.

His marriage to Joan Crawford was his first. On the wedding license her age was listed as thirty-four, his twenty-eight. He was actually thirty-three, three years younger than Joan's real age. In an autobiography she wrote for the *Ladies' Home Journal* in late 1942, Joan Crawford concluded: "I feel that I am making real progress in my work. I hope that I have in some measure justified the faith of such friends as Ray Sterling, Doctor Wood, Paul Bern and others. I can look forward without fear, and backward with the satisfaction of knowing that many of my dreams have come true.

"I am Mrs. Phillip Terry. I could not ask for more."

Joan Crawford had pleaded with Louis Mayer to be cast in *Madame Curie* and *Random Harvest*, but Mayer had a new favorite, Greer Garson, who epitomized the female virtues that he revered. Garson starred in the two prestigious films while Crawford was dealt *Above Suspicion*. Neither critics nor audiences could comprehend the labyrinthine plot.

"I want out of my contract," Joan announced to Mayer.

He was shocked. Joan had been with MGM almost as long as he had been himself, longer than any other star. He pleaded with her to stay. Joan argued that the studio's producers had grown tired of her, and the public was doing the same. She needed to get a fresh start, away from MGM, if she were to salvage what was left of her career.

Mayer finally agreed. But Nick Schenck and the business minds of the East wanted to keep Crawford; they could still squeeze dollars from her films, no matter how bad. Mayer persuaded Schenck to release Crawford from her contract.

On a warm late afternoon in 1943, Joan carried her belongings out of her dressing room and piled them in the back of her convertible. She was leaving the studio the same way she had arrived eighteen years before—alone. Nobody arrived to wish her well or to thank her for the years of service to MGM. She didn't expect that. They had always taken her for granted; she could hear them say, "Crawford? Oh, yeah, that chorus girl that Harry Rapf found in a Shubert show." The men who ran the studio remembered her as the overweight dancer who did the Charleston with Michael Cudahy at the Grove. They could never accept her as the accomplished film actress she had become.

She started the motor of the convertible and glided down to the main studio street. Instead of driving out the front entrance beside the Thalberg Building as she usually did, she turned right and drove slowly through the rows of towering stages. Each one held memories for her. Stage 15, where she and Myrna Loy had played chorus girls in 1925. Stage 22, where the romance with Gable had begun. Stage 27, where she had danced with Astaire. She remembered the fatherly reassurance of Clarence Brown before she started each scene, the lessons in acting she learned from Lon Chaney, John Gilbert, Billy Haines, Pauline Frederick, Lionel Barrymore, Spencer Tracy, Conrad Veidt. MGM had been her school, her home, the focus of her life. As a girl she had been wrenched from home to home, from one school to another. For eighteen of her adult years she had cherished the stability of her life at MGM. She waved to the gateman as she drove through the studio exit on Overland Avenue, then remembered with a shudder the paralyzing loneliness of Billie Cassin.

III

*Crawford on Her Own:
1943–1955*

15

WARTIME AUDIENCES WERE SEEKING new female stars, all-American girls who combined vitality with virtue—like Betty Grable, Ann Sheridan and Betty Hutton. Joan Crawford seemed hopelessly tied to the 1930's "woman's picture," which appeared as dated as an NRA poster. Only Jack Warner would take a chance on Crawford. Her name provided the class he wanted to obtain at Warner Brothers. Besides, he could use her as a threat against his number-one dramatic star, Bette Davis, who was always giving him trouble. Warner made an offer: $500,000 for three pictures. Crawford accepted, and was placed on weekly salary.

The studio submitted scripts, but most of them were Bette Davis rejects, and Joan sent them back. Jack Warner proposed casting Crawford opposite James Cagney in *Yankee Doodle Dandy*. "I'm too old," Joan told Warner. "Give it to Joan Leslie." Warner did.

Almost two years passed, and Joan Crawford appeared in only one Warner Brothers film, *Hollywood Canteen*, in which she briefly played herself. Joan actually worked at the Canteen every Monday night, serving sandwiches to soldiers and sailors and writing postcards to their families. Because of her fear of live audiences, she couldn't tour army camps with other stars, but she found ways to help the war effort. She joined the American Women's Voluntary Services and helped organize a day school for children of women toiling in war plants.

Phil Terry signed a contract with RKO after Joan left MGM. The RKO studio chief, Charles Koerner, told Louella Parsons: "I think we have something in Phillip Terry. He is in *Music in Manhattan*, and some say he is a combination of Clark Gable and Cary Grant." Terry was cast in *George White's Scandals* and *Pan-Americana*, and Joan packed him a lunch to take to the studio every day. On some days, out of boredom she accompanied him to the studio. She remained in his dressing room all day, knitting. She and Phil adopted a second child, a boy they called Phillip Jr.—after their divorce he was renamed Christopher. Their social life was far different from the life Crawford had known with Douglas and Franchot. Servants were impossible to keep during the war, so Joan closed up half of the house and did the cooking and cleaning herself. Entertaining was difficult because of food rationing, and Joan rarely gave parties. She planted a victory garden and was as enthusiastic over her tomatoes and squash as if they had been priceless pieces of jewelry.

RKO decided Phil Terry was not a combination Clark Gable and Cary Grant after all, and his option was dropped. For a time he worked in a war plant, and Crawford rose at dawn to see him off to work, waving affectionately from the balcony overlooking the courtyard. In the evening she always greeted him with a kiss and "Phillip darling" before their nightly cocktail: she always called him "Phillip" or "darling" or both, never "Phil." The cocktail was something new for Joan. Before her marriage to Terry she rarely had tasted any drink stronger than champagne, and then only a glass or two, but she found that Phillip was an accomplished bartender. Now she looked forward to the nightly ritual of cocktails. She wasn't acting, and she was bored, utterly bored.

Joan had hired new and high-powered agents for her transition from contract player to independent star. Jules Stein had expanded his Music Corporation of America from booking bands to representing important film stars, and Crawford became an MCA client. Lew Wasserman, the dynamic head of the agency's motion-picture department, searched the other studios for contract possibilities after Joan's departure from Metro-Goldwyn-Mayer. The prospects were not encouraging.

"Am I finished, washed up?" she asked Lew Wasserman.

"Of course you aren't washed up," the agent said in his calm, assured manner.

"But I haven't been on the screen in two years! People are going to forget there ever was a Joan Crawford."

"That will never happen, never. We've just got to find the right vehicle for you, Joan, something that is worthy of you. It will come. Believe me, it will."

Bolstered by Wasserman, she continued to resist Warner's efforts to rush her into a picture. Warner believed he had the ideal subject in a script by Edmund Goulding, *Never Goodbye*. It contained a strong woman's role, and Goulding himself would direct. He had directed Joan in *Paris* and *Grand Hotel* and was considered an uncanny director of women.

Joan had learned to analyze scripts at MGM, and scrutinized them, making notes on the good and bad elements—*Never Goodbye* had too many of the bad, she concluded. Warner exploded at her decision. He fired off a letter telling Joan that Warner Brothers wasn't MGM, that he expected his employees to earn the huge salaries he paid them, that she was acting like a prima donna. Joan drove to the Burbank studio and asked for an appointment with Mr. Warner. He was panic-stricken. "Don't tell her I'm here!" he instructed his assistant. "Tell her I've gone anywhere!" He rushed out the rear exit to his office.

"I'm sorry, but Mr. Warner had to attend a screening, Miss Crawford," his secretary said. "Is there any message I can give him?"

"Yes, you can just tell him that I think he's right: I shouldn't be paid for not working," Joan replied. "So I want to be taken off salary until we can find a picture for me to do."

Jack Warner was flabbergasted. Suspending actors was a way of life to him, like telling jokes in the executive dining room. No actor had ever asked to be taken off salary. "That broad must be crazy," Warner concluded. Crawford's judgment was vindicated in the end; the Goulding project was never filmed.

When James M. Cain published *Mildred Pierce* in 1941 the movie studios viewed it as fine material for a film, but the Breen Office made it clear that Cain's mixture of infidelity and murder was unsuitable material for family audiences, and interest in the novel vanished. Warner Brothers took a chance and bought the film rights; if properly laundered, *Mildred Pierce* might prove a vehicle for Bette Davis. Miss Davis declined. After several scripts had failed to meet the Breen Office standards, Jack Warner told Jerry Wald, "See if you can do something with *Mildred Pierce.*" Wald was willing to undertake anything. He was a hustler who had risen from New York radio columnist to screenwriter to producer, with a determination that inspired Budd Schulberg to write *What Makes Sammy Run?* At Warner Brothers he had been successful in producing such war films as *Objective, Burma!*, *Destination Tokyo*, *Action in the North Atlantic* and *Pride of the Marines,* and he found himself typed as a maker of "men's movies." *Mildred Pierce* seemed like a good chance to demonstrate his facility with a woman's picture.

Jerry Wald met Joan Crawford when Lew Wasserman brought her around in a tour of producers' offices. Wald was understandably awed by the star, having seen all her films. Crawford quickly put him at ease and impressed him with her eagerness to make a film that veered from the glamorous image she had acquired at Metro-Goldwyn-Mayer. Wald assigned Ranald MacDougall to write a script of *Mildred Pierce* for her. MacDougall had been a radio writer, and he had an acute ear for dialogue. His script retained the grittiness of the Cain novel while skirting the censorable passages.

"I love it, I love it!" Joan told Wald over the telephone on the night she read the script. "It's exactly what I've been waiting for." For an hour they discussed casting, clothes, cameramen and every aspect of filming. The enthusiastic Wald told the news to J. L. Warner the next morning, and the studio boss was delighted to have two burdens off his shoulders: Joan Crawford and *Mildred Pierce.* "I want Mike Curtiz to direct," Warner said.

Wald was pleased. Michael Curtiz had become Warner Brothers' most prestigious director, especially with the 1942 success of *Casablanca.* Although the Hungarian's handling of the English language was notorious ("Bring on the empty horses!"), he had displayed a remarkable talent for dealing with the American idiom in such films as *Four Daughters*, *Angels with Dirty Faces*, *Yankee Doodle Dandy* and *Roughly Speaking.* He had directed Bette Davis and Olivia de Havilland, and seemed ideal for Joan Crawford and *Mildred Pierce.*

"Me direct that temperamental bitch! Not on your goddamn life!" Curtiz ranted at Wald. "She comes over here with her high-hat airs and her goddamn shoulder pads! I won't work with her. She's through, washed up. Why should I waste my time directing a has-been?"

Wald indicated to Joan in gentler terms that he was having trouble convincing Curtiz to direct her. "Okay, then, I'll make a test for him," said Crawford, a large concession from an actress who was a star when Mihaly Kertesz was directing low-budget movies in Budapest. Curtiz warily undertook the test with Crawford, but when he looked at the footage in a projection room, he cried. "Okay, I work with her," he agreed. "But she better know who's boss!" Joan astonished Curtiz and Warner by volunteering to appear in screen tests for other members of the cast, tedious work that was usually performed by contract players. Joan welcomed the chore. Except for the brief appearance in *Hollywood Canteen*, she had not acted before a camera in two years. She was working at a new studio with none of the crew members who had adored and protected her over the years, and the tests gave her the feel of the Warners operation, which was more brisk and informal than MGM's.

Wald assembled an accomplished cast: Bruce Bennett as Mildred's ineffectual husband, Zachary Scott as the caddish playboy, Eve Arden as Mildred's faithful friend, Jack Carson as Bennett's cynical partner, Ann Blyth as the selfish daughter.

Ann Blyth was one of thirty young actresses who tested for the role of Veda. The studio was reluctant to give her a test, since she was under contract to Universal. Curtiz was unimpressed by the sixteen-year-old girl, who seemed too sweet to play the bitchy Veda. Joan took the young actress into her dressing room and practiced her lines over and over again. The scene was enough to convince the studio to cast Ann Blyth, even though Universal would profit from her success.

The first days of filming *Mildred Pierce* were catastrophic. Curtiz raged over Crawford's lip makeup and elaborate hairstyle. When a dress designer arrived on the set with Joan in one of the costumes he had designed, the director was sitting on a camera boom ten feet above the floor. Curtiz glared down and bellowed at the designer: "No, you son of a bitch, I told you *no shoulder pads!*"

When Joan reappeared in another frock, Curtiz again exploded. "You and your damned Adrian shoulder pads! This stinks!" He began tearing the dress.

"Mr. Curtiz, I happened to buy this dress at Sears, Roebuck," she replied tearfully. "There are no shoulder pads." She was hurt and confused. She had worked with directors who seemed insensitive to her need for reassurance—Lewis Milestone, Woody Van

Dyke, Sam Wood; even then she treated them with the respect she always accorded to father figures of authority. But Curtiz was abusive and unreachable. He frightened her.

The cameraman, Ernest Haller, quarreled with Joan over lighting and complained to Wald, "I can't photograph her."

But suddenly it started to work. Curtiz realized Crawford was not trying to proclaim her star status; she only wanted a good picture, which she desperately needed. Haller compromised between the realistic cinematic style of Warner Brothers and the glamorous appearance that Joan needed. The crew recognized that Joan worked as hard as anyone on the set and talked to them in their own language.

Jerry Wald sensed that something extraordinary was happening and telephoned Henry Rogers, Joan Crawford's press agent.

"Why don't you start a campaign for Joan to win the Oscar?" Wald suggested.

"But, Jerry, the picture is just starting," Rogers replied.

"So?"

"So how would I go about it?"

"It's simple. Call up Hedda Hopper and tell her, 'Joan Crawford is giving such a strong performance on *Mildred Pierce* that her fellow workers are already predicting she'll win the Oscar fot it.' "

"Jerry, you're full of shit."

"Possibly. But it might work. What have you got to lose?"

During his daily conversation with Hopper, Rogers made the "confidential" report to the columnist. Two days later she wrote in the Los Angeles *Times:* "Insiders say that Joan Crawford is delivering such a terrific performance on *Mildred Pierce* that she's a cinch for the Academy award."

Wald to Rogers: "See—it's working!" Without consulting his client, the publicist continued his campaign. A half-dozen columnists reported the Oscar prediction for Joan Crawford.

Jerry Wald telephoned Henry Rogers at midnight: "I think we've got it made. I just got back from a party where I talked to Hal Wallis. He told me, 'It looks like Joan Crawford has a good chance to win the Oscar. I don't know where I heard it. I may have read it somewhere.' "

When *Mildred Pierce* completed filming, Crawford and Curtiz were speaking to each other in terms of endearment. At the end-of-shooting party she presented him with an oversized set of Adrian shoulder pads. The director addressed the whole company: "When I agreed to direct Miss Crawford, I felt she was going to be stubborn as a mule and I made up my mind to be plenty hard on her. Now that I have learned how sweet she is and how professional and talented she is, I take back even thinking those things about her."

With the opening of *Mildred Pierce* in October 1945, reviewers joined the bandwagon. The New York *Times* called Crawford's performance "sincere and effective." The *Herald Tribune* agreed: "Intense and restrained . . . she plays with studied under-emphasis." James Agee in *The Nation* termed it Crawford's best performance. Even author James M. Cain approved. He sent Joan a leather-bound copy of *Mildred Pierce* with the inscription: "To Joan Crawford, who brought Mildred to life as I had always hoped she would be and who has my lifelong gratitude."

Her career had been restored. Now Joan faced the problem of tidying up her personal life.

Joan's friends were baffled over her marriage to Phillip Terry. They were amused by the fervency of their affection. At dinner parties the butler sometimes carried notes of endearment between Joan and Phil at the end of each course. Yet there was something disturbingly mechanical about the marriage. A visitor to the Bristol Avenue house once noted the daily schedule Joan issued to members of the staff. Time was allotted for manicure, facial, massage, dictation, play with children, as well as a siesta for Mr. and Mrs. Terry. Even the sex was scheduled.

While Joan luxuriated in the resurgence of her career, Phil's was languishing. Paramount hired him to play Ray Milland's brother in *The Lost Weekend*, the big Academy award winner in the year Joan won hers, and the studio cast him in another success, *To Each His Own*, but again his performance was overshadowed by an award-winning star, Olivia de Havilland. Joan tried to accord Phil the husband's role of giving orders to the household and acting as host, but she was too accustomed to directing her life according to her own exacting wishes. As with Douglas and Franchot, she and Phil lived in *her* house, and when they went to New York, they stayed in *her* East River apartment.

When Joan and Phil returned from the triumphant premiere of *Mildred Pierce* in New York, her good friend Ruth Waterbury wrote: "At home all the laughter and caresses and enthusiasms they had shared were gone. They weren't even quarreling. They simply sat in those large, beautiful rooms and said not a word. Theirs wasn't the silence of contentment. It was the wounding silence of two people who had nothing to say to each other. We all know couples who live through years like that, but such people are not actors—to whom drama is the breath of life."

The decision to divorce came at a party given by Claudette Colbert and her husband, Joel Pressman. The happiness of the host and hostess, said Ruth Waterbury, compelled the Terrys to part: "They spurned a half-loaf of affection; they wanted a great loaf or nothing."

As was the custom, the news was issued by Louella Parsons. Her two rivals, Hedda Hopper and Sheilah Graham, were incensed by the exclusive, and began taking potshots at Crawford. Despite the crossfire, Joan Crawford appeared at the annual Christmas luncheon of the Hollywood Women's Press Club to receive her Golden Apple award as the most cooperative actress of 1945.

The marriage lasted the customary Crawford span of four years. On April 25, 1946, Joan testified in Los Angeles Superior Court: "For the first year and a half of our marriage I was never allowed to entertain or go out of the house at night. Consequently I lost many valuable contacts in the motion-picture field."

She added that she read between two hundred and three hundred scripts a year and "he would tell me I was wrong about a script many times when I felt I was right. I turned down script after script because of his criticisms." It was hard to maintain her mental and physical balance, and during the first year of the marriage she lost seventeen pounds.

Outside the courtroom, Joan told reporters, "I'll never go through this again." Did that mean she would never again listen to "The Wedding March" from *Lohengrin?*

She smiled. "Maybe that's the trouble. I never had any music at my weddings."

16

CRAWFORD NEVER ENJOYED being Crawford more than now. She was once again on top, and she had done it entirely on her own, with no assistance from Papa Mayer. She was the town's best comeback story, and Hollywood loved a comeback almost as much as a fall from grace. Scripts arrived at Bristol Avenue every day from producers who had always been "on location" when she called them before. Columnists who considered her a has-been now eagerly sought interviews. She accepted them all. Publicity was a necessary adjunct to her career, and she approached each interview as seriously as she did a movie scene. She was an interviewer's joy. None would leave her without a new, publishable story, and she was always prepared with fresh observations, no matter how controversial, no matter how trivial.

"With *Mildred Pierce* released, I kept hearing that all I would do would be drab roles. All I want are acting roles, Louella, and if they're dressy, okay—and if they are old ladies, okay, or if they are good girls or bad girls. I don't care, so long as they have character. . . ."

"The rest of the world may think the life of a Hollywood bachelor girl is the greatest ever, but I get lonesome sometimes. . . ."

"When I was at Metro I had to live up to a mold the minute I entered the studio. Now I am free. I don't have to be anything at all, except myself at my best, whatever that may turn out to be.

Finally I've overcome my self-consciousness, which was a long, private battle. Now I dare to be my true self with everyone. I no longer want to change. . . ."

"With each marriage, I believed sincerely that this was *it*, forever and forever. Call me a Gullible-Annie, an incurable romantic or whatever—but I entered each marriage with the same sincerity, the same hopes and prayers. And the end of each was the same. . . ."

"Bags and shoes are my weaknesses. Chewing gum is my vice, and knitting is my avocation. . . ."

"I want the kind of love I haven't had. I want the kind of marriage I haven't had. 'What is love? How do you define it?' I answer, 'Love is faith, compatibility—mentally, spiritually, physically— and a divine, mutual sense of humor.' . . ."

"Do you know, I never had a sense of humor? But I think I am beginning to develop one. Just in the last two years. . . ."

The Crawford fans couldn't get enough. They eagerly accepted every piece of information about Joan and passed it on: her favorite foods were salads, cereals and rhubarb. She wore a size-four shoe, she took at least four showers a day, her bed was on a sleeping porch, and she slept in short nightgowns with long sleeves, satin and monogrammed. She called herself Elephant Annie because she never forgot. She loved perfume, her favorite being Jungle Gardenia. Her favorite color was green.

The Crawford fans were more loyal than those of any other star. Joan nurtured them, pleased them, humored them. Many had been devoted to her since the 1920's. Even in the dark days after leaving MGM, she maintained personal correspondence with fifteen hundred of her hard-core fans, writing to them about members of their families and other matters.

The Joan Crawford Club News was mimeographed and mailed monthly from New York. Each issue contained a letter from Joan Crawford herself. In September 1946 she wrote:

"Don't you think we have the nicest club newspaper in the whole world? I am always so excited when I see it in the mail, and it's always full of wonderful surprises for me. . . . Martha Kay's article on the Academy-award presentations was accurate beyond words. I think she has ink in her veins because she is going to make a wonderful reporter. . . ."

With the wartime austerity and Phillip Terry gone, Joan began entertaining at Bristol Avenue. The formal dinners were always followed by the running of a movie in the playroom, and Joan enjoyed playing the grand hostess, although the role sometimes bewildered the servants. One evening at the dining table she asked the butler, "Would you please bring me a serviette?" Minutes went by and no napkin. She repeated the request, to no avail. Finally she said, "I asked you to bring me a serviette."

"Miss Crawford," the butler replied helplessly, "Ah don't know what in the world you're talkin' about."

She became more at ease. One night the butler asked Cedric Hardwicke and Roland Young if they would like anything.

"Yes, I would like a mink coat," replied Hardwicke. "It's chilly in the garden."

"And I would like a silver fox," added Young.

The butler reported this to Joan, and she instructed him to get them. The two English actors wore her furs for the remainder of the evening.

Now that she had decided she would never marry again, Joan felt more at ease in her relationships with men. She liked them to be tall and handsome, complementing her own glamorous appearance.

"Nice manners are the quickest way to intrigue me," she told an interviewer. "When I'm out on a date I want my escort to light my cigarette. I could open the car door myself, but I won't. I sit there until he does." At dinner she expected her date to unfold her "serviette" and place it in her lap. As her friend William Haines said, "To be Joan Crawford's boyfriend, a man must be a combination bull and butler." The man most willing to perform these functions in the immediate postwar years was Greg Bautzer.

Greg Bautzer had been on his own from the age of twelve, and had grown up in the tough waterfront town of San Pedro. He worked his way through the University of Southern California Law School, and after flying with the navy in the war, he opened a law practice with Bentley Ryan. Tall and muscular, his handsome face tanned from hours of surfing and tennis, Bautzer became a popular escort for glamorous stars.

In 1947 Bautzer accompanied a client, trade-paper publisher William R. Wilkerson, to Las Vegas for the purchase of property on which to build the Flamingo Hotel. Wilkerson introduced the attorney to his longtime friend Joan Crawford.

While Wilkerson gambled, Bautzer asked Joan why she was in Las Vegas. "I'm here to complete the adoption of two baby girls," she said.

"You don't gamble?"

"No, I only believe in sure things."

When Bautzer returned to Los Angeles, he asked Joan to Wilkerson's nightclub, the Trocadero, on Sunday night, when stars like Judy Garland and Red Skelton joined the informal entertainment. Bautzer enjoyed the excitement of escorting Joan Crawford, and she found him to be a superb dancer, an attentive date who did not compete with her for attention. It was an ideal match.

They began dating often. Bautzer learned to satisfy her unique requirements. He knew to follow two paces behind when she made her entrance at a party or café—any closer and he would receive an elbow in the ribs. He carried her knitting bag and sometimes her poodle. He placed the "serviette" in her lap, and didn't mind when his friends taunted him as Greg the Geek. He was infatuated with Joan and was willing to play the role she demanded of an escort—in public.

Bautzer took a special interest in Christopher, who seemed to be crying out for male companionship. The lawyer spent Sundays at the Crawford house, swimming and throwing a baseball with the boy. One day Joan stormed out of the house.

"Christopher, how many times have I told you *not* to throw the ball with your left hand?" she demanded. "Use your right hand!"

The boy was crestfallen. "But Greg says I throw better with my left hand," he said.

"And how many times have I told you to say 'Uncle Greg'?" Joan demanded.

"I'm sorry, Mother. 'Uncle Greg.' "

Bautzer intervened. "I told him to call me 'Greg.' I'm not his uncle."

Joan swung toward Bautzer and yelled, "Well, *I'm* his mother, and I said for him to call you 'Uncle Greg.' And you're not to tell him to throw with his left hand when I distinctly said for him to throw with his right."

Greg gazed at her furious face and said, "You're right, Joan. He's your child, and I shouldn't be countermanding your instructions."

"Then you're sorry?" she asked.

"Yes, I'm sorry," Greg replied.

"Are you really sorry?"

"I *said* I was sorry."

"If you're really sorry, you'll kneel in front of me."

He gazed at her with astonishment. "You're kidding!" he said.

"No, I'm not kidding. If you were truly sorry, you'd kneel. Franchot always did."

"I don't believe you."

"He most certainly did, and he was proud to do so!"

"Well, I sure as hell am not going to kneel, so you can forget about it right now."

She stormed back into the house, and Greg resumed the game of catch with the boy. Years later Bautzer asked Franchot Tone if Joan had told the truth. "Sure; I didn't mind," Tone replied.

As the Bautzer-Crawford romance became more intense, so did their clash of wills. Both possessed strong tempers, and when provoked Joan was capable of throwing whatever was handy at the moment, from a highball glass to—on one memorable occasion—a leg of lamb.

Joan arrived for a meeting with her publicist, Henry Rogers, in a state of high excitement. "That son of a bitch, I hate him and I love him," she ranted.

"Who are you talking about?" Rogers asked.

"Greg, of course. Who do you think I'm talking about?"

"I wasn't sure. What happened this time?"

"Yesterday I had a terrific fight with him, and I threw him out of the house. I told him I never wanted to see him again. I wouldn't answer the phone all day, because I knew he was calling me. Then last night I was in bed when I heard footsteps across the gravel in the courtyard. Then a pounding on the door. I was terrified. Then I heard a rustling in the rose vines. Someone was climbing up the trellis. I heard him say 'Ouch!' and then I realized it was Greg. He got up to the porch, broke the glass and opened the door. God, it was beautiful!"

The battles and the reconciliations continued over a period of four years. After one furious encounter, both decided never to see each other again. But neither wanted Hollywood to know. "Now, I'm giving a big dinner party Saturday night," Joan said to Henry Rogers' wife, Rosalind. "Greg has to be there."

"But why do you want him there if you have split up?" Mrs. Rogers inquired.

"Because if he's *not* there, everyone in town will know about it. So tell him he'd better come."

Greg dutifully appeared for the Saturday-night dinner, mingling amiably with the other guests while steering clear of the hostess. He was seated next to Rosalind Rogers at dinner, and together they discussed his difficulties with Joan, speaking in quiet tones so they wouldn't be overheard. They failed to notice the outraged looks being hurled from the head of the table.

At two o'clock that morning Henry and Rosalind Rogers were awakened by a rapping at their door. The caller was a Western Union delivery man with a three-page telegram to Rosalind from Joan Crawford: "I don't understand your actions. . . . How could you be so crass as to try to take Greg away from me? . . . How could you do such a thing in my own home? . . . You call yourself a friend, and then you turn on me. . . . I want nothing further to do with Henry Rogers. . . . Our professional relationship has ended as of this moment. . . ."

"She's gone crazy!" said the infuriated Rosalind.

"I'll have to call her," Henry said.

"No, don't call her," said his wife. "Just wait and see what happens." They waited three days. Then Joan telephoned Rosalind. "Roz, darling, I just heard the most delicious news," said Joan. The matter of the two-A.M. telegram was never mentioned, then or ever.

The Crawford-Bautzer romance seemed to follow the four-year cycle of her marriages, and by the end of that time both seemed battle-weary. The finale came one night after a party at the home of Louis B. Mayer. Joan and Greg remained cordial throughout the evening, but for one brief moment he left her to greet a young actress.

"Lovely party, wasn't it?" she remarked as she drove his car west on Sunset Boulevard toward Brentwood, passing the UCLA campus.

"Yes, it was very nice," Greg replied. "I had a good time. Did you?"

"Yes. It was nice to see L.B. looking so well."

The car continued past the west gate of Bel Air, climbed the hill beyond and started descending. "Greg, darling, the right-rear tire feels as though it's getting flat," she said. "Would you mind getting out and having a look at it?"

She drove to the curb and he opened the right-hand door. As he was gazing down at the right-rear tire, Crawford gunned the motor and sped off on Sunset with a screech of rubber.

"What the—" Greg watched the speeding car disappear over the next hill. He looked at his watch. One-thirty. No taxis available at that hour, and no public telephone anywhere. He turned up his tuxedo collar against the early-morning chill and started tramping the three miles to his suite at the Bel Air Hotel. The romance was over.

Jerry Wald was preparing *Humoresque*, a remake of a 1920 film, with John Garfield as a violinist whose career is threatened by an affair with a wealthy, destructively selfish woman. Crawford heard about the role and told Wald she wanted to play it. "It's not the major role," the producer warned her.

"I don't care; it's a delicious part," Joan answered.

Planned as a modest film, *Humoresque* burgeoned into a major production, with Adrian designing Crawford's gowns and Isaac Stern recording Garfield's violin playing. The iconoclastic Garfield had misgivings about playing opposite Crawford, and he viewed her skeptically when they met for the first time on the film set.

"So you're Joan Crawford, the big movie star! Glad to meet ya," he said mockingly. She smiled and held out her hand. Instead of taking it, he gave her a playful pinch on the breast.

"Why, you insolent son of a . . ." She stopped herself and then began to smile again. "You know," she said in a voice an octave lower, "I think we're going to get along just fine."

The filming went smoothly, but Joan was more temperamental than she had been on *Mildred Pierce*. When she didn't get the key light she wanted in close-ups, she suddenly developed a headache. She would not appear for work during her menstrual period, reasoning that she didn't photograph as well. When her publicist, Henry Rogers, was barred from the studio, she met him in the parking lot, thus stopping production. The barring of Henry Rogers was quickly lifted.

With the success of *Mildred Pierce* and *Humoresque*, Lew Wasserman pressed for a new Crawford contract. Jack Warner agreed to pay her $200,000 a picture on a seven-year contract.

Possessed bore no relation to the 1931 movie of the same title that Joan made with Clark Gable. She was cast in the 1947 Warners film as a schizophrenic who is driven to murder out of unrequited love for Van Heflin. Joan read through dozens of books on mental disease, interviewed psychiatrists and spent six weeks visiting mental hospitals to prepare for the role.

The director of *Possessed* was Curtis Bernhardt, who had gained a reputation for directing women. He had just worked with Bette Davis in *A Stolen Life*, and he absentmindedly called Joan "Bette." When he did it the third time, Joan threw her purse at him. Ever since Crawford had arrived on the Burbank lot, a feud between her and Davis had been expected. For a decade Davis had been the undisputed queen of Warners, but now her reign was threatened by an invader who managed to win an Oscar in her first film at the studio. "Bette Davis and I haven't feuded at all," Joan told an interviewer. "We were strangers when I came to Warners. We're getting acquainted as our time permits. She's actually been charming to me." Curtis Bernhardt astounded the commissary crowd one noon by arriving with both Crawford and Davis. He sat between the two stars and all three conducted an animated conversation throughout the lunch. The incident put an end to the rumors, for a while.

Darryl Zanuck wanted Joan to star in a film at Twentieth Century-Fox, *Daisy Kenyon*. "I'll do it," Joan agreed, "if I can have Henry Fonda and Dana Andrews." That wasn't easy. Both were independent-minded actors, and both realized that their roles in *Daisy Kenyon* were mere window-dressing for the female star. The plot echoed the Crawford films of MGM—a successful career woman caught between a back-street liaison with a married lawyer (Andrews) and her true love (Fonda).

Fonda was surprisingly compliant. *Daisy Kenyon* would mark the end of his Fox contract, which he eagerly sought. Andrews was agreeable until he read the script; he tried to decline, but when his attorney warned him he would be liable for the salaries of Crawford and Fonda, Andrews acquiesced.

Both actors were startled to find the *Daisy Kenyon* set at a cool fifty-eight degrees in accordance with Miss Crawford's contract. After three days, Fonda appeared wearing a raccoon coat. Joan was amused, and she presented both of her costars with suits of long underwear. The temperature remained the same.

Joan returned to Warner Brothers for the lurid *Flamingo Road* with Sydney Greenstreet, Zachary Scott and David Brian, then played herself in a walk-on for *It's a Great Feeling*. Another Wald melodrama, *The Damned Don't Cry*, followed, with Vincent Sherman directing. Like Nicholas Ray, Robert Aldrich, Ranald MacDougall and other directors during her postwar career, he was also a romance.

She requested Sherman as her director for *Harriet Craig*, a third film based on George Kelly's play *Craig's Wife*. It was Joan's first film at Columbia, and her introduction to the byzantine politics of the studio boss, Harry Cohn. He operated on a divide-and-conquer policy, distrusting too close an association between his producers and stars.

He telephoned Joan in her dressing room: "I don't understand it, Joan."

"What is it, Harry?" she asked.

"Why doesn't Bill Dozier like you?" Dozier was producing *Craig's Wife*.

"But he *does* like me," Joan answered sweetly. "In fact, he's here with me now. Why don't you ask him?"

Cohn sputtered. "Naw, I was just kidding."

As her second film career thrived, Joan Crawford played the publicity game with consummate skill. The fan-magazine photographers were her special pets. She sent them gifts, gave them dinner parties, remembered the names of their wives and children. When she found them waiting outside a private party, she asked the host, "Why don't you let the boys inside for half an hour? Your guests won't mind—hell, we're in the business to get our pictures taken. And it'll be a nice break for the boys." Joan was always available for home layouts—playing badminton, diving in the pool, dressing the children for school.

The photographers, of course, protected Joan. They realized that she preferred full-face shots, so they avoided photographing her in profile. They always overexposed their film so her face would look its best, without freckles or blemishes. The photographers looked the other way if they found Joan with an escort she didn't want publicized with her. For a time she dated Brian Donlevy, and while she enjoyed his company, she didn't feel he was the kind of boyfriend who fit her image.

With the help of her publicity office, Rogers and Cowan, and with such studio publicists as Johnny Mitchell and Harry Friedman, Joan kept her name and face in the gossip columns.

The Burrelle clipping service named her the Most Publicized Woman in History, and the Los Angeles Downtown Business Men's Association selected her America's Most Glamorous Mother. The American Bachelor Congress, "a fraternal organization of unattached social figures and sportsmen," dubbed her the Most Eligible Bachelorette in America. The Community Chest selected her as the Red Feather Woman of America.

Joan kept in the news in other ways. A woman sued for invasion of privacy, claiming her mental treatments had been observed by Joan as research for *Possessed*. A waiter returned a $50,000 diamond brooch Joan had lost in Slapsy Maxie's nightclub. Joan was named Most Cooperative Star by the Hollywood Women's Press Club. Joan in the hospital with influenza. Joan's $400,000 was top salary at Warner Brothers. And so on.

Joan's romantic interludes kept her in the columns. Columnists reported her dates with younger actors like Rock Hudson and George Nader, and reacted with astonishment when she started appearing with a cowboy actor, Don "Red" Barry. She was overwhelmed when he sent her a white mink coat, a diamond necklace and a jeweled vanity case. The romance ended when the furrier and jeweler claimed the gifts, which had not been paid for.

She needed male company, both as complement to her status as movie queen and for fulfillment of her need to be loved and appreciated. Sex was a necessary but functional aspect of her life. After her dinner guests had departed, she said to her male friend of the moment, "Come on," and led him upstairs to the bedroom, undressing on the way.

She often went to big Hollywood parties alone. The other guests began to recognize the pattern. Joan always arrived late, just before dinner was served. Shortly after dinner was over, she announced she had to go home—because of an early call, or to check on the children. She asked one of the unattached males if he would mind accompanying her home. At the William Goetzes' house one night, her escort on the departure was William Paley. At a *Redbook*-magazine awards dinner at the Bel Air Hotel, Glenn Ford performed the role.

At a dinner party given by the David Selznicks, Joan was preparing her early departure and trying to outmaneuver Sam Spiegel, who had volunteered to escort her. She finally asked an Air Force major who was the date of Olivia de Havilland. "He came back later—much later," Miss de Havilland recalled.

With the onset of middle age, Joan Crawford seemed to be lapsing into increasingly eccentric behavior. Friends noticed it in her treatment of the children. Fellow workers discovered it in her attitudes at the studio. She still prided herself in being "one of the boys" and showed her earthy side by nailing a semi-chamberpot to her dressing-room door—"for my half-assed friends." But for the first time she seemed threatened by younger actresses in her films.

It started on *Goodbye, My Fancy*. Janice Rule was making her film debut after impressive performances in television and the New York theater. She was strikingly beautiful as well as talented, a natural target for attention from the movie crew and visiting press. Crawford noticed, of course; nothing on her movie sets escaped her gaze. She smoldered for days, then began making snide comments whenever Miss Rule, with her lack of film experience, ruined scenes by failing to "hit her marks"—walk to the position where she would be in the camera's focus. "You're wasting a lot of time and money," Crawford snapped at the young actress. The browbeating made Miss Rule more nervous, and she failed in one take after another.

"Miss Rule," Crawford told her, "you'd better enjoy making films while you can. I doubt that you'll be with us long."

Joan claimed that she hadn't started drinking until she was thirty-five. Now she was making up for it. One cocktail before dinner led to two, sometimes three. The drinking as well as her smoking was in contradiction to the tenets of Christian Science, to which she remained devoted; she sent her own children to Christian Science Sunday school. But her contradictions went unexplained.

Why did she often borrow five dollars from a new acquaintance on a movie set, later paying it back? Was it to show that she was a real woman and not just a rich movie star? Was it to establish a personal and responsible relationship with the individual?

If she cared so much about her appearance, why did she greet her dates in a slip and with no makeup? Did she want him to know there was a real person behind the glamor? Did she want him to help pick her dress and watch her make up, so he could share the experience of creating Joan Crawford?

Whatever were her motivations, Joan's actions became increasingly eccentric and unpredictable.

Josh Logan was preparing to direct a new play by Norman Krasna, *Kind Sir*. Someone suggested Joan Crawford for the female lead, and it seemed a showmanly idea: a charismatic movie star in her stage debut. Surprisingly, she was enthusiastic about the proposal. She found the play delightful, and she asked to read the woman's role from a stage.

Logan and Krasna excitedly arranged for a theater. They sat out front while Joan delivered the playwright's dialogue with brilliant aplomb. At the end of the three acts, the two men were ecstatic and asked Joan to sign a contract.

"Oh, no, never," Joan replied. "I just wanted to know whether or not I could do it, for my own satisfaction. I could never play a long run on a stage. I'd be bored to death. But thank you for letting me make the experiment."

Joan had a new date, a businessman from Chicago who was overwhelmed and somewhat nervous about escorting Joan Crawford to dinner for the first time. So he asked his friend Tony Owen and his wife, Donna Reed, if they would join them for dinner. Miss Reed happily consented. She had greatly admired Miss Crawford and had been the recipient of several Crawford congratulatory notes, though the two actresses had never met; Miss Reed arrived at MGM shortly after Joan left.

The Owens and their friend were to meet Joan at her dressing room on the Universal lot; she was living there during the filming of *Female on the Beach*. They planned to dine at the Sportsman's Lodge, two miles west of the studio, so Joan could retire early for the early-morning call.

When the three arrived at the dressing room, Joan was dressed in elegant style. She greeted the visitors warmly, and the two women exchanged compliments.

"Oh, dear, the dogs have tinkled on the carpet," said Joan, glancing down. "Excuse me a minute." She went to the kitchen and emerged with a towel and a bottle of soda water. On her hands and knees she poured the soda on the stain until the carpet foamed, then dabbed with the towel. "Well, that's done," she said, shaking a reproving finger at the poodles. She washed her hands in the kitchen and returned with a cheery "Shall we go?"

They went outside, and Joan announced she would drive her own car and the Owens could follow. "We'll take the freeway," she declared.

"Don't you think we should go on Ventura Boulevard?" Owen reasoned. "The Sportsman's Lodge is only a couple of miles away."

"No, the freeway is better," Joan replied. Before Owen could protest, she and her escort got into her car and headed out the studio gate. She turned left on Lankersheim Boulevard, passed under the bridge of the Hollywood Freeway, and drove up the on-ramp.

"My God, she's going east," exclaimed Owen. "The Sportsman's Lodge is west." He sounded his horn, but her car was already on the freeway and angling into the fast lane.

"We've got to catch her," said Donna, but it was impossible. The Crawford car was speeding along at seventy miles an hour, past the Hollywood Bowl, through Hollywood, hurtling along toward downtown Los Angeles.

"She'll be in Palm Springs if I don't stop her," said Owen, gunning the car motor. Finally in the Silver Lake district he managed to overtake the Crawford car and gesture desperately that the restaurant was in the opposite direction. She nodded, swerved to the right-hand lane, took an off-ramp and returned to the freeway in the westerly direction. She continued speeding along.

"How on earth can she get out of this situation?" Donna mused. "What can she possibly say?"

"I can't imagine," said Owen.

Joan stepped out of her car in front of the Sportsman's Lodge and said brightly, "Didn't I tell you—the freeway's great!"

"Come in my dressing room and we'll talk," Joan Crawford instructed the press agent newly assigned to her movie. Claude was a diffident, unassuming man, unlike most press agents. It was his first meeting with Crawford, and he was eager to learn her desires about publicity and to fulfill them to the best of his ability.

Claude followed her to the inner room. She seemed preoccupied with picking a dress out of the closet, but she continued talking.

"Now, I don't mind press visitors at any time," she said, hanging the dress she selected on a hook. "I'll see them all—Harrison, Army, Vernon, Bob, Skinny, Aline, Neil."

"Even Sheilah."

"Even Sheilah," said Joan, unbuttoning her blouse. "All I ask is that you let me know the morning of the visit. If they have an angle, let me know what it is. Otherwise I'll think of something myself." She unzipped her skirt and pulled it down. "As you know, my contract gives me approval of all publicity copy and stills. You don't have to show me all the releases you write, just the ones that contain my quotes. I'll initial the copy and I'm sure the legal department will want the originals for their files."

To Claude's total astonishment, she removed her slip, brassiere and underpants and stood before the mirror looking for blemishes. She continued talking.

"Now, on the photographs, you can just submit the contact sheets. I'll take them home with me and return them the next day with my kills; I promise not to keep them longer." She began putting on a fresh set of underwear. "I know you'll probably want to develop a campaign to sell this picture. When you get it worked out, let me know what it is and I'll do everything I can to help."

She wiggled into the dress, pulled up the zipper and straightened her hair. "I just know we're going to have a wonderful time working together on this picture, Claude," she said, angling her head for him to kiss her cheek. "Bless you." She strode breezily out of the room.

Katherine Albert and Dale Eunson had been among Joan's closest friends since the beginning of her Hollywood years. Joan was devoted to them, admired their close and productive partnership. Each time Joan became enmeshed in a new romance, she told Katherine, "At last I've found my Dale."

Joan listened to Katherine's sage advice, and followed it. Joan, in turn, told Katherine all her secrets. Katherine, employing her excellent taste and judgment, wrote selectively about those secrets in magazine stories. Katherine joked, "Every two years I write about 'The New Joan Crawford.' "

Friends learned to detect when Joan was about to terminate a marriage or a romance. During a party Joan would say to Katherine, "Come into the bedroom, I want to talk to you." Joan would tell of her decision to drop the unwary male and ask advice on how to do it.

When Joan ended a lengthy romance with Charles Martin, a writer and director, she asked Katherine to perform a mission: get back the expensive watch Joan had given to Martin. Katherine did. "Give it to Dale; I don't want it," Joan told her.

In 1934 Katherine and Dale became parents of their only child, a daughter. She was named Joan, and her godmother, Joan Crawford, showered her with gifts and attention. When the girl was fourteen, Samuel Goldwyn gave her an acting contract and starred her in the title role of *Roseanna McCoy*. She acquired a new name, Joan Evans.

She seemed headed for a bright career, and no one was prouder than Joan Crawford. The girl's parents were also pleased, although they regretted their daughter's loss of a normal girlhood.

But Katherine and Dale grew alarmed when Joan became seriously attached to a young man, Kirby Weatherly. The girl announced she wanted to marry, and her parents objected. Not that they found Weatherly unacceptable; they felt Joan should enjoy more of her youth before settling down to marriage. She was eighteen, and her parents' arguments had no effect.

Katherine telephoned Joan Crawford and told her the situation. "Will you try to talk some sense into her? She'll listen to you."

"Of course, darling," Crawford replied. "I'll ask Joan and Kirby to come to my house tonight."

At midnight the telephone rang at the Eunsons' house. Dale heard Joan Crawford's buoyant voice: "Joan and Kirby have just been married at my house!"

Katherine came on the telephone and excoriated Crawford for her betrayal. When the heartbroken mother hung up the receiver she told her husband, "I'll never speak to her again."

The marriage of Kirby and Joan Weatherly proved successful, but Katherine never relented in her vow.

Along with other major stars of Hollywood, Joan was invited to a ball Louis B. Mayer was giving in honor of Henry Ford II in 1949. Having no current romance to escort her, she asked the producer of *Harriet Craig*, William Dozier. He was between his marriages to Joan Fontaine and Ann Rutherford, and he readily agreed.

When he arrived at Bristol Avenue, the maid told him that Miss Crawford was awaiting him in her bedroom. Dozier found Joan fully dressed—except for jewelry. "Oh, Bill, I can't decide what to wear; please help me," she said. Dozier helped her pick out an emerald necklace, and she poured drinks. Before leaving, she tucked a half-pint of Canadian Club in her velvet purse.

As soon as they arrived at the Trianon Room of the Beverly Wilshire Hotel, they saw Greg Bautzer with Ginger Rogers. Dozier felt a sudden sensation of impending doom.

Joan and Dozier sat at the table hosted by Harry Cohn, and she was vivacious, perhaps overly so. Joan asked Dozier to dance, and he marveled at how smooth and effortless it was to dance with her. He felt her back stiffen, however, when Greg and Ginger were gliding by in a tight embrace, smiling amorously and whispering into each other's ears.

Later Nate Spingold, a Columbia executive, asked Joan to dance. Dozier noticed an old friend, Barbara Stanwyck, at a table nearby and went to ask her to dance. When he returned to the table, Spingold told him Joan had left the party. "Oh, God," Dozier sighed, "her old disappearing act."

He waited until she had time to reach home, then he telephoned. Joan was sobbing.

"Oh, Bill, I thought that you, of all people, would be different," she said.

"What do you mean?" he asked.

"I thought when you took someone to a party, you'd *stay* with her."

"Joan, for heaven's sake, I danced with Barbara while you were dancing with Nate. What's wrong with that?"

"I don't know. I just had to get out of there."

"I know you're upset. I'll come out there and we'll talk."

"Oh, Bill, would you?" But when he arrived, the maid told him Miss Crawford had retired. He threw a handful of gravel at the bedroom window and left.

When Dozier arrived at his Columbia-studio office in the morning, he found it filled with bouquets of flowers. On his desk was a note: "Dear Bill, Please forgive a poor, frightened little girl. Love, Joan."

17

WHY DID Joan Crawford adopt children? Did she do so for the maternal pleasure of watching children grow and out of a desire to give unfortunates a better life? Did she need children to assuage her loneliness after her failed marriages? Did she believe children were a necessary adjunct to a movie star's life? Was she motivated by the miseries of her own childhood?

Although her motivation was undoubtedly not merely for publicity, she did not hesitate to use the children as part of her public image. They were the most photographed of Hollywood children, appearing with their mother at premieres, ice-show openings and other events where photographers would be present.

Once Crawford arrived for an interview with Louella Parsons impeccably attired in a dark blue tailored dress and carrying a tiny white poodle in a small green coat with the initials C.C. embroidered on it. Mrs. Parsons asked about the initials.

Said Joan: "All my children have a C, you know—Christina, Christopher, Cathy and Cynthia—so we thought the dog should be called Cliquot to carry out the C idea." Cathy and Cindy had arrived as infants in 1947. Joan later referred to them as twins, although they were born more than a month apart and looked nothing alike.

All three girls had been adopted while Joan was single, and she became an advocate in liberalizing adoption laws, especially in California. In 1950 she told me in an Associated Press interview: "Adoption laws are keeping children from finding good homes. Most people have to go out of California to adopt children. That means lawyers' fees here, and in the other state, plane fare, nurse's salary and so forth. The expense discourages most prospective parents. Under California law, I couldn't adopt a child, because single persons are not allowed to. I think that is wrong. There are a lot of single men and women who would like to have children and could give them good homes." And Joan discussed the children in interview after interview:

"Some people have wondered at my plunging into the responsibility of bringing up one boy and three girls, and I will admit it is a responsibility. But it is a self-sought one: they are all adopted.

"I started with Christina. She is eight, a sensitive child with very blue eyes and very blond hair. She is a serious child, thinks a lot, has a decided will of her own. It is not easy to discipline her, but I am forced to, when she insists on doing things her own way. I find punishing her by hurting her dignity is very effective. She is the eldest in the family and likes to feel she is looked up to, especially by Christopher. And when she behaves well, she is. So when she deliberately disobeys an order I have given her, I send her to bed before Christopher. She is crushed, because she feels she has lost face in his estimation.

"Her brother, Christopher, is a chubby, cuddly boy of five—always laughing—and has a way with him that makes it hard not to spoil him. But that is one thing I am determined not to do. It is much harder to make him do things for himself than to do them for him, but I insist that he dress himself, pick up his clothes and keep his toys neat. Happy-go-lucky Christopher would much rather leave things behind and coax everyone to wait on him. His little conscience is clear; he sleeps with a smile, such a contented smile.

"The two youngest are so young—they are just babies. Cynthia is ten months and Cathy eight. But they have their definite personalities. Cynthia (we call her Cindy) is all energy, kicking her little feet so gaily and always making an effort to stand and walk. I think she will be a dancer; she makes such definite motions. Cathy is a quiet little thing. She lies peacefully in her crib and looks and looks. . . . I often wonder what babies see, very little I am told. But when they get such a faraway look, you think perhaps they are seeing all sorts of wonderful things.

"When I look ahead, then I visualize a life that will have great interest for me, the unfolding of the four characters; in bringing them up it will help me to discipline myself."

Those are key words: "not easy to discipline her . . . punishing her by hurting her dignity . . . hard not to spoil him . . . one thing I am determined not to do . . . discipline."

It was perhaps natural that Crawford, the most disciplined of movie stars, sought to have the most disciplined of children, especially when she had to assume the roles of both father and mother. Joan accepted the responsibilities, some of her friends believed, with a vengeance. One of her friends sadly remarked: "I'm sure that Joan loved those children. But something, probably out of her own miserable childhood, drove her to discipline them unreasonably. Very often the battered child grows up to become an abusive parent." The private picture of Joan Crawford as mother proved far different from what appeared in the movie magazines.

Christina was five and not especially beautiful, except for her flowing blond hair. When complimenting her, visitors always mentioned her lovely hair. The girl was at the mirror one day, combing her hair over and over again. "Mommy, dearest, don't you think I have beautiful hair?" she said. "I will not have a daughter who is vain," Joan replied, and sheared Christina's hair with a pair of scissors.

Once an actor sat at the bar of Joan's playrooom, conversing with the hostess about events in the studios. After twenty minutes Joan remarked, "Shall we let Christopher out now?"

"What?" the actor asked.

Joan walked across the room and opened a closet door. Young Christopher came out, blinking at the sunlight. "He has been a naughty boy," Joan explained, "but I think he has learned his lesson."

Christina was having a birthday party. Many other movie stars' children were invited, and Joan had ordered a clown and a pony ride. On the morning of the party, Christina in her excitement talked back to her mother. It was too late to call off the party, and so Christina watched it from the window of her bedroom.

At the end of a dinner party, Joan asked the women guests, "Would you like to see the children's clothes?" She led them upstairs to the bedrooms and proudly displayed the racks of pastel dresses, all starched and freshly ironed. When she went into Christopher's room, she opened the boy's closets. One of her guests, Betty Furness, was astonished to see that Christopher was tied to the four corners of the bed. "Oh, he kicks off the covers, and he sucks his thumb," Joan explained. "I'm teaching him not to."

Guests at Joan's house learned to endure the ritual in which the children appeared and made their farewells to the visitors. Christopher was required to bow, and the girls curtsied as they went around the room saying "Good night, Uncle Clark, good night Aunt Barbara," etc. If the girls failed to curtsy correctly, they were required to repeat the procedure. The final obeisance was saved for their mother, and it was always, "Good night, Mommy dearest, I love you."

When the boy was six, Joan saved his discipline until her dinner guests had assembled. She reminded Christopher of his infraction that day, pulled down his pants and spanked his bare behind.

Visitors to the Crawford home were continually appalled by Joan's treatment of her children. A close friend recalled seeing Joan take Christopher's chin in her hand, saying, "Isn't he a beautiful boy?" She held the boy's face so tightly and for so long that his face turned deep red.

The same friend was waiting for Joan in the den one day when she heard a sound behind the door. She found Christina there, quivering in fright. "Tina, what are you doing?" the friend asked. "I didn't clean up my room before going to school, and I don't want Mommy to find me," the girl explained.

Christina idolized Judy Garland, whom Joan had befriended at MGM (the two stars once met on personal appearances in New York, and Joan discarded Judy's entire wardrobe and bought her dresses Joan considered more suitable). Judy often attended the Sunday-afternoon parties at the Crawford house, and Christina followed her around, wide-eyed. Joan sometimes encouraged her talented guests to perform, and on one occasion Judy Garland was asked to sing. Because she had not done her household chores to her mother's satisfaction that morning, Christina was sent to her room before the concert began.

One day Joan heard Christopher squealing in pain. She rushed to the sobbing boy and said, "What is the matter, dearest?" He pointed to his terrified sister and said, "Tina shut my hand in the door."

"I didn't mean to," Christina said desperately.

"Of course you didn't *mean to*, but you were thoughtless and careless," said her mother. "How would you like it if someone did that to you?" She grabbed Christina by the arm and pressed the door against her hand until the girl screamed in agony.

At Christmas, packages mounted around the Crawford tree. Being young, the four children were consumed with curiosity, and they peeked inside the gaily wrapped boxes. Their mother found out, and she ordered that all presents for the children be put away. The presents would have to be earned, one by one, through additional household chores.

James MacArthur came to Hollywood in 1950 when his mother, Helen Hayes, returned to the screen in *My Son John*. They were entertained on a Sunday afternoon at the home of Helen's old friend Joan Crawford. James was invited to spend a weekend with Christopher, who was three years younger.

The two boys were preparing for sleep in Christopher's room when the maid entered and began strapping Christopher to his bed. Young MacArthur was astonished. "Is this the way they treat children in Hollywood?" he mused. "And will I be next?" The maid left the room without applying the same treatment to the guest.

"How can you let them do that to you?" James inquired in the darkness.

"Don't worry about it," Christopher replied, executing a Houdini-like escape from his bonds.

There were other tales told by housekeepers and governesses who periodically left the Crawford employ. Of how Joan, after an evening of drinking, would terrify the children by bursting into their bedrooms and tearing apart their closets in a rage over their failures to meet her standards of neatness. Of relentless beatings, particularly of Christina and Christopher, over insignificant offenses.

Joan would countenance no criticism about the upbringing of her children. One night she was escorted to an awards dinner by her director Curtis Bernhardt. He drove to her house and observed the ritual "Good night, Uncle Curtis" with curtsies and bows.

Bernhardt and Joan rode to the dinner in a studio limousine. As they drove along Wilshire Boulevard, the director remarked, "You know, Joan, you treat those children like monkeys. You make them bow and curtsy just like trained animals in a circus act. Why don't you let them be themselves?"

"Out!" she ordered.

"What?"

"Get out of the car! Don't tell me how to raise my children!"

Bernhardt stepped out on the sidewalk. After the limousine had proceeded a few feet, she allowed him to reenter. But she wouldn't hear another word about her children.

Not even her closest friends could temper her attitude. Cesar Romero once remarked, "My God, Joan, why don't you ease up? They're only kids."

It was the only time she was angry with him. " 'They're only kids'! Well, I was a kid once, and I didn't have a damn thing. Those kids are going to appreciate everything they get."

She made the girls learn how to cook and sew, and Christopher had to help with the household chores along with them. If they misbehaved, their toys were taken away and had to be earned again by special duties. Olivia de Havilland once observed Joan and her children at the desert resort of La Quinta: "Joan came marching out to the pool in a white bathing suit and spent the morning teaching the children to dive in the water and swim the length of the pool. She cracked out the commands like a drillmaster, or a master training a German shepherd."

Christopher seemed to suffer the most. Robert Preston was a next-door neighbor for eight years. Often when he drove out his driveway in the early morning on his way to the studio, he found Christopher standing at the curb. It was too early for his school bus, but the boy seemed to station himself there for a talk with his neighbor, such was his need for male companionship.

The boy tried to fulfill his mother's demands, but it appeared impossible. In the limousine en route to a movie premiere, Joan kept admonishing Chris to sit up straight, brush his hair, and so on. Christopher suddenly became ill and vomited. Joan was furious.

When he was nine, he ran away. He was absent for four hours while Joan was at CBS to audition for a radio series. The police were notified and Christopher was found playing with two other boys several blocks away.

Reporters were present when Christopher returned to his mother.

"Hello, son," she said with a smile, inviting him to join her on a couch.

"Hello, Mummy," he replied.

"Do you realize what you've done? How many people you've upset and hurt? And over what?"

Christopher admitted that he had been angry because he could not have chocolate syrup on his ice cream.

"Chocolate syrup, indeed!" said his mother. "You're lucky to have ice cream. You may choose your punishment. What would you do if our positions were reversed and I ran away because I couldn't have chocolate syrup?"

The boy gulped as his eyes brimmed. "I wouldn't allow you privileges," he said.

"So be it. Just go upstairs, son. I'll be up shortly with the hairbrush. I'm going to tan your hide, and you'll take it like a man." Later she remarked to reporters, "He's not going to sit on his bottom for a good many days."

It was not the end of Christopher's attempts to escape. When he was twelve, he was picked up by police as he was on his way to ship out to sea as a cabin boy. Four times he tried to run away from a military academy at Altadena, northeast of Los Angeles. Each time he was returned.

Christina, being the oldest child and the most like Joan herself, received the greatest punishment. The girl complained about the girlish dresses her mother made her wear to school, even though Christina towered over her fellow students. She continued to attend classes in short gingham outfits that drew ridicule from her contemporaries, making Christina more withdrawn and shy. She began saving her meager allowance to buy inexpensive dresses that were more in style, making sure that her mother never saw them.

Once Christina made the mistake of appearing in pedal pushers, which were then stylish. Joan stripped them off and gave them to the Goodwill.

Joan had sent her children to the public school in Brentwood, but she found it failed to provide the discipline she had known as a child. When Christina was ten, Joan sent her to the private Chadwick School in Rolling Hills, south of Los Angeles. The girl was thrilled to be in an atmosphere where teachers and administrators were genuinely concerned with their students, and where the other children, many of them lonely and from broken homes, were open to friendship. As Joan in her forties faced greater career problems and tired of her role as disciplinarian-mother, she enrolled Christopher and later the "twins" at Chadwick School.

On weekends at home, the arguments between Christina and her mother continued, especially over the girl's desire to dress in the style of others her age. The weekend visits became less frequent. When Christina came home for the summer of 1953, the encounters with her mother were so acrimonious that Joan sent her back to school two weeks later. Christopher, who was eleven, followed soon thereafter.

The two Crawford children were the only students at Chadwick School that summer, and their mother refused to support them. Commander Joseph Chadwick and his wife, Margaret, took the pair into their home, assigning them chores for their keep. "Living with the Chadwicks was my first taste of normal family life," Christina later recalled.

At Thanksgiving, Christina was scheduled to spend the holiday with her mother. When Joan learned the girl had not prepared her Christmas-card list as she had been ordered, Joan became incensed and ordered Christina to remain at school. Joan became angrier when the Chadwicks suggested that Christina might better stay with them in view of the turmoil at home.

Three days later, a station wagon appeared at Chadwick School to claim Christina. Inside were a chauffeur, Crawford's secretary and a private detective. They took Christina away from the only secure environment she had ever known, to a mountaintop convent, Flintridge Sacred Heart Academy. Christopher was sent to a military school, and the two younger girls to a Catholic grammar school.

Joan told the nuns of Sacred Heart that there had been some "difficulty" with Christina at her previous school and she was not to be allowed to leave on weekends or vacations. Christina endured two lonely years in the convent, achieving the highest honors of a non-Catholic student. At graduation time she was forbidden to attend the celebration party. She was the only student with no member of her family at the graduation. Joan later remarked: "She wanted to be on her own, so I let her."

Problems with the children would continue throughout Joan's life. Said her longtime friend Dorothy Manners: "Joan was generous and kind, but her one blind spot was her children. She dressed the poor boy in velvet, and made all of the children bow and scrape.

She felt in her heart that she was doing the right thing. Her reasoning was: I got where I was because I am a disciplined person. *I am disciplined*. Therefore she tried to discipline her children. She believed that undisciplined people were unhappy."

Adela Rogers St. John offered another observation: "I don't think that Joan really *liked* children. Some women don't, you know."

None of her friends' analyses can explain adequately Joan's unthinking and sometimes horrid treatment of her children. She could be an overwhelmingly kind and generous person in other respects; for instance, her endowment of hospital rooms and medical care for Hollywood's needy. Her gift-giving was prodigious, and not always did she seek favor from the recipient. Why, then, would she treat her children so cruelly? The answer must lie in her own Dickensian childhood. The beatings she received from the hands of her mother and the principal of Rockingham Academy were transferred to Tina, Chris, Cindy and Cathy. It was an instinctive, unreasoning reaction to the injustice that had been inflicted on her.

Helen Hayes, who had known Joan for almost half a century, remarked sadly, "Joan tried to be all things to all people. I just wish she hadn't tried to be a mother."

18

IT WAS part of Joan Crawford's code that *she* had to be the one to end a marriage or a romance; she would have been shattered if a man left her. The same with studios. The last years at MGM had been corrosive for her because she felt she was no longer needed. Now she felt the same thing happening at Warner Brothers.

The scripts were becoming fewer and less attractive. *Goodbye, My Fancy* had been a provocative stage vehicle for Madeleine Carroll, but its political sting was removed in the Warners film. The result was a tepid triangle with Joan, Robert Young and Frank Lovejoy.

When *Goodbye, My Fancy* failed to attract customers, Jack Warner sent Joan the script of a rancid melodrama, *This Woman Is Dangerous*. It was a familiar technique to avoid paying stars—submit scripts they had to refuse. He also proposed *This Woman Is Dangerous* for Dennis Morgan, whose salary had inflated during the wartime dearth of leading men. To Jack Warner's dismay, both Crawford and Morgan agreed to appear in the film, but meanwhile Crawford instructed Lew Wasserman to get her out of the Warner Brothers contract. The agent argued that she would be throwing away as much as $800,000.

"I don't care," she replied. "I can't stand to be anywhere I'm not wanted." Jack Warner was happy to terminate the contract, and Crawford's agents at MCA realized that she needed to reestablish herself as a box-office attraction. The solution was *Sudden Fear*.

The suspense story by Edna Sherry was owned by an independent producer, Joseph Kaufman. Five scripts were written and none satisfied Crawford or himself. Kaufman sought the help of David Miller, who had directed *Billy the Kid* with Robert Taylor and *Flying Tigers* with John Wayne.

Miller discarded the five scripts and returned to the original story. The key, he told the producer, came in a paragraph describing how the woman playwright, newly married to an ambitious actor, hears a recording in which her husband and his former sweetheart are plotting to murder her. Kaufman was elated. He proposed making a deal with Miller immediately. "No, I want to get Miss Crawford's reaction first," said the director. They telephoned Joan, who was delighted with the script solution. Miller asked: "Is it good enough for you to waive script approval?"

She paused. "Yes," she said slowly.

"What happens if you and I can't agree?" Miller asked.

"Simple. We'll have Joe arbitrate."

"No, that won't work. I want to be in a position to tell you, 'Go fuck yourself!' "

Kaufman's face turned white, but Joan laughed heartily at the other end of the wire. "How are you going to put that in the contract?" she asked.

"It doesn't have to be in the contract——as long as I have your agreement."

"You have it."

Crawford had capitulated on script control, but she retained her say on casting. Predictably, she wanted Clark Gable to play the actor who is fired by the playwright, later woos and menaces her. Kaufman resisted, not only because the budget couldn't afford Gable, but because the casting would destroy credibility.

David Miller explained the casting problem over dinner with Sam Weisbord and Joe Schoenfeld of the William Morris Agency. The director explained that he needed an actor who was not too well known, but who had enough physical presence to match Crawford, with a combination of charm and underlying menace.

"Then you want Jack Palance," said Schoenfeld.

Absolutely, Miller agreed. But how would he sell the idea to Crawford? He called her and asked if he could come to dinner and bring a film to show. She happily assented. He arrived with the cans of film, the children paid their respects, and dinner was served in the grand tradition. Joan carried a bottle of champagne into the playroom and drank from it as the film unreeled. It was *Panic in the Streets*, with Elia Kazan directing Richard Widmark, Paul Douglas, Barbara Bel Geddes, Zero Mostel and Jack Palance. "A very good movie," Joan said.

A week later Miller again asked if he could come to dinner and bring a movie. The same ceremony with the children, the elegant dinner, champagne in the playroom. Joan was surprised when Miller again ran *Panic in the Streets*. "You must have a reason," she mused afterward. "I know—you want Richard Widmark as Lester Blaine."

"No, I don't," the director replied.

"But you're running this picture twice for a reason," she said suspiciously. "What's your game?"

"Okay, Joan, I'll tell you. I want to cast Jack Palance."

Her face darkened. "Get out!" she cried. The surprised Miller found himself being pushed out of the playroom while she pursued him mercilessly, shoving him down the hall, flinging open the front 'door and pushing him outside. She slammed the door.

He was in bed when the telephone rang. Joan was sobbing. "You don't love me," she wept. "You don't respect me. How could you ever suggest that I accept such a leading man? Don't you realize that I have played opposite the biggest stars in films? Gable, Tracy, Taylor, Cooper!"

"I agree, Joan. But please don't say no until I've had a chance to reason with you. Will you let me run the film again?"

"I guess so. But I don't want you using your arguments on me."

They watched *Panic in the Streets* a third time the following night. She stopped the film after the third reel and said, "Let's go to the bar."

She poured drinks and said, "I want you to level with me. Why do you want me to play opposite this man?"

"It's difficult for me to tell you," Miller replied.

"You must." Then her voice fell to the alto tone that demanded an answer: *"That's what I want."*

Miller began: "In your last few pictures, Joan, you've played not only the female lead but the male lead as well. That won't work in this picture. We need suspense for the audience. Hitchcock will take a girl like Joan Fontaine, who is as delicate as Dresden china, and dress her in a tweed suit with a bun in her hair to make her even more vulnerable."

Her eyes began to brim. "You mean I'm not a woman."

Miller kissed her on the cheek to stop the tears. "I'm not talking about here and now. I'm talking about what happens before the camera."

"I'm sorry," she said softly.

"I'm sorry," he said.

"All right, I'll take Jack Palance."

The casting of Palance proved ideal for the suspense of *Sudden Fear*, but his off-screen relationship to Joan was turbulent. Palance was understandably nervous about his first starring role and apprehensive about playing opposite the legendary Crawford. He remained aloof and unresponsive, something Crawford was not accustomed to in a leading man. Also, it was her first contact with a new breed of actor that was emerging from the Actors Studio in New York. Led by Marlon Brando, the young performers were beginning to overturn previous theories of screen acting, and Crawford was confused and disturbed by Palance's moodiness and peculiar techniques, such as racing around the studio stage to incite his emotion.

Miller was directing a close-up of Crawford while Palance stood off-camera delivering his lines. Joan had always managed her close-ups in one or two takes. Miller was surprised when she required five. He took her away from the camera and asked, "What's the matter?" Irritated, she said, "I wish you would tell him that when he's not on-camera he should act as though he is!"

One crucial scene required Joan to climb a ladder in order to hide the phonograph record containing the incriminating conversation. Joan was to lose her balance and drop the record, shattering it on the floor. After the sixth take, Miller wasn't satisfied.

"What the hell do you want?" she demanded.

"It's too planned," he said. "You're telling the audience what you're going to do."

"Then show me!"

The director climbed the ladder and almost fell off as he demonstrated the movement. "All right, I'm ready," she said, and the next take was perfect. She strode triumphantly toward her dressing room.

"Absolutely sensational, Sarah!" said Miller.

"Sarah who?"

"Sarah Bernhardt."

Crawford beamed.

For a bedroom scene Miller wanted Joan to appear bare-shouldered under the sheets, as though she were sleeping naked. "No, I want to wear a nightgown, and I've got eight of them I want to test," Joan announced.

"Joan, are you kidding?" he protested. "All the audience will see is the shoulder straps. I don't have time to test nightgowns. I want to finish with this set tonight. I promised the studio that another company could use it tomorrow."

"That's what I want!" she shouted in her alto voice.

The director told his assistant to direct the tests, and Miller remained in the cutting room until they were completed.

Joan telephoned Miller that evening. "You want to say to me 'Go fuck yourself.' Right?"

"Right."

"I'm sorry. I apologize. It will never happen again."

Sudden Fear was completed at a cost of $720,000, not counting Joan's salary of $200,000. That amount was placed in escrow with the proviso that she could either collect it or else take a forty-percent interest in the film's profits. She decided to take the percentage, and it was one of the few wise business decisions she made. *Sudden Fear* was a big success, giving Joan her third Oscar nomination. (The second was for *Possessed*.)

At the *Photoplay* awards dinner given at the Beverly Hills Hotel in February 1953, Crawford had every reason to be pleased. Her arrival at the Crystal Room had evoked a sensation from her most loyal friends, the fan-magazine photographers, while stars and producers stopped by her table to comment on how stunning she looked and to promise that they would vote for her in the Oscar race. *Sudden Fear* had begun a whole new career for her, she was told. "You were great!" exclaimed Hedda Hopper. "Class will tell!"

Midway through dinner Joan heard a rustle of activity outside the Crystal Room. The flashes in the foyer indicated someone important was making a very late entrance. Crawford, along with the three hundred and fifty other guests in the room, turned to see who it was.

There was Marilyn Monroe hobbling to the top of the stairs, leaning on the arm of columnist Sidney Skolsky. She wore a gold lamé gown into which she had been sewn at Twentieth Century-Fox studio, the metallic cloth clinging tightly to the ample hips, the neckline descending between the famous Monroe breasts. So tight was the skirt that she could take only a few steps at a time, and this prolonged her journey down the stairs and across the dance floor to the Fox table. Her ripe, luscious Rubenesque body and the theatricality of her entrance overwhelmed the onlookers, and they roared in admiration. Grown men put fingers to their lips to emit shrill whistles, while Jerry Lewis, the master of ceremonies for the awards program, leaped upon the head table and imitated an animal in heat. A score of columnists penciled hurried notes. Demure and wide-eyed, Marilyn eased slowly into her chair, fearful that the gown would tear.

Joan Crawford watched the charade in silent fury. How dare the little blonde turn the awards dinner into a burlesque show, strutting through the crowd like a stripper on the runway! Crawford's outrage went deeper. Marilyn Monroe was twenty-seven and in full, lush beauty. Joan Crawford was twenty years older and required more and more makeup to retain her looks. In one brief moment Marilyn seemed to sweep aside Hollywood's past, that segment of history of which Crawford was so much a part. Marilyn was the new Hollywood, sexually liberated, unbound by tradition, instantly famous. She hadn't served an apprenticeship, as Joan had, striving to improve herself as an actress and a person, struggling for better roles.

Three days later I interviewed Crawford in the Polo Lounge of the Beverly Hills Hotel. Her publicist, Henry Rogers, had suggested the topics: a proposed television series and Joan's nomination for the Oscar. The series sounded amorphous, and Joan minimized her chances of winning the award, predicting it would go to Shirley Booth for *Come Back, Little Sheba* or Leslie Caron for *Lili.*

"What did you think of Marilyn Monroe at the *Photoplay* dinner?" I asked.

Crawford's eyes shone fiercely. "It was the most shocking display of bad taste I've ever seen," she began. The words of scorn poured out as Henry Rogers shifted uncomfortably in his chair.

"Look—there's nothing wrong with my tits, but I don't go around throwing them in people's faces," Joan said. When she concluded, her anger seemed exorcised and she was calm. She remarked in parting, "I know you've got a good story. But when you quote me, for God's sake, go easy."

At Fox I read the quotes to Marilyn to determine if she wanted to reply. She flushed and started to answer angrily, then responded, "No comment." I released the story:

> HOLLYWOOD, March 2 (AP)—Joan Crawford today aimed this curt message to Marilyn Monroe: stop believing your own publicity. . . .
>
> "It was like a burlesque show," said the horrified Miss Crawford, who was present at the affair. "The audience yelled and shouted, and Jerry Lewis got up on the table and whistled. But those of us in the industry just shuddered.
>
> "Certainly her picture isn't doing business, and I'll tell you why. Sex plays a tremendously important part in every person's life. People are interested in it, intrigued with it. But they don't like to see it flaunted in their faces.
>
> "Kids don't like her. Sex plays a growingly important part in their lives, too; and they don't like to see it exploited.
>
> "And don't forget the women. They're the ones who pick out the movie entertainment for the family. They won't pick anything that won't be suitable for their husbands and children. . . .
>
> "The publicity has gone too far, and apparently Miss Monroe is making the mistake of believing her publicity. Someone should make her see the light. She should be told that the public likes provocative feminine personalities; but it also likes to know that underneath it all the actresses are ladies. . . ."

Reaction was immediate. Newspaper readers were startled to see one glamorous star attacking another. Particularly when the attacker was Joan Crawford. Marilyn Monroe was at a stage in her career when everything she did created news, and the Crawford tirade added to the whirl of controversy surrounding her.

Hollywood chose up sides. Louella Parsons, Walter Winchell and other columnists sprang to Marilyn's defense. Critics insisted that Joan was jealous of Monroe's youthful beauty, which was true. Betty Grable, costarring with Marilyn in *How to Marry a Millionaire*, came to her defense, and Fox publicity chief Harry Brand excoriated Crawford for the attack. But his boss Darryl Zanuck wrote her: "Don't apologize to Marilyn. It was good for her."

Marilyn told Louella Parsons she had cried all night after the interview appeared. Marilyn added she was especially hurt because the attack came from Crawford: "I've always admired her for being such a wonderful mother—for taking four children and giving them a fine home. Who better than I knows what that means to homeless little ones?" When Louella encountered Crawford at a party she demanded, "Why did you tear Marilyn apart publicly? If you thought she needed your help, why didn't you give it to her in private?" Joan lied harmlessly: she thought her remarks about Marilyn had been off the record.

My next meeting with Joan was in the lobby of the Pantages Theater at the Academy awards. While complaining about the furor, she started leading me toward the ladies' room. "I can't go in there!" I protested. "Stay here; I've got to tinkle," she said. When she returned, I pointed out that I had followed her instructions and had eliminated her more damaging remarks. She admitted I had.

Marilyn maintained her cool "no-comment" attitude, and I wrote that both actresses seemed upset with me. The comment elicited a telegram: "DESPITE ALL THE TROUBLE I GOT INTO OVER THE STORY, I STILL LOVE YOU. JOAN CRAWFORD."

The brouhaha benefited both stars. Monroe realized the need to soften the sexy buildup, and she went on to her greater success. And Joan delighted in finding herself in a controversy, especially when she could suddenly play the role of defender of traditional American values. She was following the normal middle-age trend to conservatism. She had been apolitical in her youth, became acquainted with—though did not embrace—Franchot's radical politics during her second marriage. Following her Christian Science beliefs in fixed values, she rejected the social change that inevitably followed the war years. She was totally without prejudice, but she took no interest in the rising sentiment for black equality. America had been good to her; she had become rich and famous beyond Billie Cassin's most extravagant dreams. She saw no reason to change a country that had proved so beneficent.

19

Sudden Fear HAD RESTORED Joan Crawford's self-confidence. Rare for her, she became overly confident, and thus lost the chance to star in *From Here to Eternity*. Overriding the objections of Fred Zinnemann, Harry Cohn had cast Crawford as Karen Holmes, the faithless wife of an army officer. Joan objected to the wardrobe and insisted on her own designer, Sheila O'Brien. Cohn would not be dictated to by Crawford. "Fuck her," he said, and cast Deborah Kerr as Karen Holmes.

Sheila O'Brien was a new member of the Crawford team. She had worked in the MGM wardrobe department during Joan's tenure at the studio, and later began making dresses for her. After Adrian did his work for Crawford in *Possessed*, she tried other designers, then settled on Sheila O'Brien, who had an uncanny sense of what Crawford needed for her mature years—not the flamboyant Adrian gowns that were suited for Joan's youth and the needs of Depression audiences. Sheila gave Joan dresses so plain they would have seemed drab in a department store, but the designs were enhanced by gorgeous furs and exquisite jewelry, rented or borrowed for the duration of filming. Sheila convinced Joan to eschew the big bows and other excesses she had favored in earlier years; however, Joan refused to part with the high-heeled shoes with plastic ankle straps that became her defiant trademark. She claimed she needed the straps to support her weak ankles; the plastic would be transparent when photographed.

Sheila O'Brien knew how to make the most of the Crawford figure. Although Joan was only five feet four and one-half inches tall, her erect posture made her seem taller. She appeared taller also because she was long-waisted; her legs, although perfectly formed, were out of proportion to the rest of her body. Her bust was not large, but it seemed adequate because of her wide chest and shoulders. She had slim, well-formed hips, not flat and boyish. She liked to boast: "The other girls at Metro were jealous because I wore the smallest panties."

Joan did not mourn the loss of *From Here to Eternity*. She moved to Paramount for a spy film to be directed by Nicholas Ray, *Lisbon*. When script problems developed, Joan offered the solution: "Oh, hell, Nick, give it balls! Write it for Gable, and I'll play it." But the script defied any solution, and it was sold to Republic, where it starred Ray Milland. Joan's disappointment was assuaged by her next film, a triumphant return to MGM.

Ben Thau, a longtime MGM executive, had sent her the script of *Torch Song*, about a driving, self-dedicated musical-comedy star who is transformed by the love of a blind accompanist. Joan was eager to make the film, though Thau warned her that the budget would be modest. Her only request was for Charles Walters to direct, and that was granted. Even though *Torch Song* had only a twenty-four-day schedule, Howard Strickling's publicity department treated Crawford's return like a major event. "WELCOME BACK, JOAN" read the banner over the MGM studio gate, and Dore Freeman of the publicity department arranged for a red carpet to be laid from the street to Joan's dressing room. Freeman had been the Western Union boy who coached Joan to say "Time will tell" to reporters' questions about a marriage to Franchot Tone. The most devoted of her fans and collector of a vast amount of Crawfordiana, he was befriended by Joan, who caused him to be hired by MGM in 1938.

Since Lana Turner, Ava Gardner and Kathryn Grayson were not working at the time, their rooms in the stars' building were combined for the Crawford suite. Because of the intense shooting schedule, she decided to stay on the lot overnight—it was "less disrupting for the children," she explained.

Crawford had an early conference with the director, Charles Walters; as soon as the contract had been settled, she telephoned him at his beach house and said, "I am going to bring dinner down and I'll read the script to you." She arrived with a picnic basket with champagne, caviar, pâté and other delicacies. On another night she telephoned to say she was bringing her jewels to his house so he could decide which she should use in the movie. She came in wearing an elegant housecoat and bearing a velvet box that contained her jewelry. Walters dutifully reviewed the gems and made a few comments about what might be usable. When they were finished, Joan remarked, "I think you should see what you have to work with." She opened the housecoat and displayed Joan Crawford—all of her. The director was flustered, not knowing where to look. The Crawford figure was indeed very well-formed, and he managed to say, "That's very nice, Joan." She seemed pleased.

Joan began two weeks of rehearsals for her first movie dancing in fourteen years. She was forty-eight, but she remained remarkably lithe. Never an accomplished dancer, she moved with sufficient skill to portray a musical-comedy star, and the choreographer, Eugene Loring, covered her inadequacies with a number of dramatic lifts by her male partners. Her singing voice was dubbed by India Adams, but little new recording was done for *Torch Song*; to keep the cost under a million dollars, the producers borrowed playbacks from other musicals. Chuck Walters observed Joan's growing nervousness as the start of shooting approached. A dancer himself, he became her partner in her most intricate dance number. Realizing she would worry about it through the filming, he told her, "Let's shoot it the first day and get it over with."

On the first day of shooting *Torch Song*, Fred Astaire dropped by with a basket of red roses, Ann Blyth brought a mass of orchids, and Van Johnson sent a huge telegram card. From Gable, a market basket full of chocolate delicacies from Italy. So many flowers arrived that two picnic tables had to be set up outside Joan's dressing room to accommodate the overflow. Instead of the customary bestowing of gifts at the end of a picture, Joan gave them to the entire crew on the first day. Her present to director Walters was a potted rubber tree on which hung a cashmere sweater, a dozen cellophane-wrapped loin lamb chops ("You're too thin," she told him), a stopwatch, vitamin pills and other items she felt he needed for the filming. Every man on the crew was given a carnation boutonniere.

Walters went to Joan's dressing room to summon her for the first shot. He found her in the black leotard with black-net opera-length stockings, huddled on a stool in front of the mirror. "I'm absolutely petrified," she said. "I can't face it."

"Of course you can, Joan," the director said reassuringly. "We've done this number dozens of times. You'll be terrific."

"I can't do it, unless . . . You're going to hate me, but I've got to have a drink."

"All right, Joan, I think that's warranted."

"You've got to have one with me."

"All right, Joan."

An hour later, Joan and Chuck left her dressing room and wavered to the set.

"Playback!" called Walters. "Action!"

By six o'clock the intricate number had been filmed, and the exultant Crawford left the stage with shouts of "Bless you!" to her co-workers. She went to her apartment in the stars' building and began writing dozens of notes to the crew: "It was just a wonderful opening day. . . ."

The filming proceeded swiftly, but Joan didn't mind. She enjoyed the challenge of performing her work with total efficiency. By spending twenty-four hours at the studio, she could devote herself entirely to what she enjoyed most in life: acting in films. No intrusion of children, no household responsibilities, no lovers. The dancing had exhilarated her, she adored all the attention lavished on her return to MGM.

Chuck Walters said twenty-five years later: "I've worked with actresses like Judy Garland and Shirley MacLaine, and I always figured I could get the best performance from them if I knew them better than they knew themselves. It worked with Judy Garland and Shirley MacLaine, but not with Joan Crawford. Drunk or sober, the facade never dropped."

Nicholas Ray convinced Republic's Herbert J. Yates to take two gambles with *Johnny Guitar*. The film was a western, and westerns were considered risky because of the glut of television cowboys. And the plot concerned a deadly feud between two women, not the usual male antagonists of movie westerns. The star of *Johnny Guitar* was Joan Crawford, and such a celebrated name had rarely been associated with Republic. Yates was willing to take the chance.

Philip Yordan wrote a florid script, and Ray assembled an impressive cast: Sterling Hayden, Scott Brady, Ward Bond, Ernest Borgnine, Royal Dano, Ben Cooper and, as the nemesis of Crawford, Mercedes McCambridge. The company reported to Sedona, Arizona, for location scenes, and Joan impressed her fellow workers with her professionalism. She was always on the set a half-hour before needed, she delivered her own offstage lines, and she even insisted on standing in for herself while her close-ups were being lighted. Royal Dano asked her why. "Nobody has my bone structure, so the lighting wouldn't be the same," she replied. "The camera is just like my mother. I'm nice to it. And it's nice to me. I was born in front of a camera, and I don't know anything else."

On a Sunday, Scott Brady found Joan in her motel room signing hundreds of fan letters. He asked why she didn't have a secretary sign her name. "There is only one Joan Crawford," she nobly replied.

In *Johnny Guitar*, Crawford was cast as Vienna, the aggressive operator of a gambling saloon, and McCambridge played Emma, the sexually frustrated leader of the cattle forces. Yordan's script provided fierce encounters between the two women, including a final shoot-out. Director Ray understood both Joan's jealousy of younger actresses and Mercedes' competitive ambition, and he assumed that a little off-screen antagonism could contribute credibility on the screen. His strategy succeeded too well.

The first portent of trouble came after Joan had evoked the admiration of the crew by submerging herself in icy river water for an escape scene with Hayden. The director thanked his stars for their courage, gave each a bottle of brandy and told them to return to the motel to dry out.

The next scene involved Mercedes and the posse. In the first take she spewed out the reasons for her poisonous revenge, delivering her lines expertly while keeping her horse in camera range. The entire cast and crew applauded. "Beautifully done," said Ray, who immediately felt he was being watched. He gazed over his shoulder to a nearby hill. A solitary figure was outlined against the sky, and there was Crawford shaking with fury. She turned on her heel and disappeared beyond the hill.

After shooting that day, Scott Brady was passing Crawford's room. The star was inside surrounded by her retinue. "Hey, you should have seen McCambridge work today!" he shouted. "I wouldn't be surprised if that dame won another Oscar." His announcement was greeted with pregnant silence.

At midnight Nick Ray made his nightly tour of the motel grounds like a superintendent of a summer camp, checking to see that lights were out and no all-night crap games were in progress. As he approached the highway, he saw a slender figure stumbling wobbily toward the telephone booth next to the gas station. Joan Crawford dialed the operator and shouted, "I want a Tanner car here tomorrow!" (she referred to a car-rental agency). She began screaming at the operator and pulled the receiver from the telephone. Then she staggered back toward her room. Ray shook his head in disbelief and he gazed out at the highway pavement. It was strewn with objects which he recognized upon close examination as Mercedes' costumes for the movie. The director gathered them up amid his growing concern for the future of *Johnny Guitar*.

In the morning, Ray moved out of his nearby cabin and transferred McCambridge there, reasoning it would be unwise to have the two actresses quartered in the same motel. Late that afternoon Joan summoned her director. She was sober and adamant. "I want a meeting on the script," she announced. "These are three scenes that are necessary to make this picture work."

Ray examined the proposed scenes, which were largely devoted to expanding the character of Vienna. He calculated the added cost at $600,000, an amount that would infuriate Herb Yates. Ray sent an urgent message to Hollywood.

Twenty-four hours later a small plane landed on the Sedona air strip, bringing Philip Yordan and Arthur Park, who represented not only Crawford, but such other MCA clients as Yordan, Ray and McCambridge. While Park placated Joan, Ray and Yordan fashioned the added scenes, and by combining them with footage already filmed, the new material would cost only $220,000. Yates acquiesced. His only complaint was about Ray's stylized use of black and white. "I'm paying for color, and I don't see any flowers," said the studio boss.

Crawford was content with the script additions, but her attitude toward Mercedes remained hostile. One day Joan was entertaining Borgnine, Cooper, Dano and Brady in her room, pouring her vodka—she had brought twenty cases to Sedona—and she joined the actors in telling stories. Mercedes was walking past the room as they burst into laughter. "Hi, fellas, what's so funny?" Mercedes asked.

"What the hell are you doing here?" Joan demanded, and began to scream accusations at the younger actress. The *Arizona Republic* sent a reporter from Phoenix on a scheduled interview with Crawford. After making the long trip, the reporter was told she was not available, so he interviewed others in the company and printed a story detailing the star's erratic behavior. Joan was certain that Mercedes was responsible, and the article was countered by an advertisement in the Phoenix *Gazette* by Joan's fellow workers, who proclaimed, "If there is a more cooperative, charming, talented, understanding, generous, unspoiled, thoughtful, approachable person in the motion-picture business, we have not yet met him or her. . . ."

Word of the Sedona doings reached Hollywood, of course, and reporters were ready to investigate further when the *Johnny Guitar* company returned to the Studio City lot for interior scenes. Erskine Johnson published a report that Joan had insisted Sterling Hayden's wife leave the set. Johnson received a late-night telephone call. "Is this Erskine Johnson?" the feminine voice asked.

"Yes, it is."

"This is Joan Crawford. You're a shit." She hung up.

Don Boutyette, Republic publicity man, received a telephone call in his office: "Don, this is Mercedes. Come down to the set right away or I'm going to walk off the picture." Boutyette hurried to the *Johnny Guitar* stage and found McCambridge seething. "Read this!" she commanded, hurling a copy of the Los Angeles *Herald Examiner*. Harrison Carroll's column contained Joan's comment about Mercedes: "I wouldn't trust her as far as I could throw a battleship."

Before the publicity man could prescribe remedies, a knock came at the door. Standing outside was the pudgy, bald Herbert J. Yates. Boutyette promptly retired while the studio head tried to make peace.

His efforts were unavailing. McCambridge herself was a formidable foe, a strong-willed woman with a loud voice. Most of the other actors in the film ran for neutral ground, but not Sterling Hayden. Longtime defender of the underdog, he joined with Mercedes in the attack on Crawford. So did Mrs. Hayden. "Joan Crawford hates all women, except those who can help her," declared Mrs. Hayden. "If I ever see her again, I'll probably strike her in the face."

Crawford would not change her ways. She was unsympathetic when her fellow workers complained that the frigid temperature she demanded on the *Johnny Guitar* stage was giving them colds, and she refused to let the stage be heated.

When I visited the set one day, Mercedes was still in a feisty mood. "The feud? Some days it's on, some days it's off. Joan told me once that she didn't really want me on this picture. She wanted Claire Trevor to play the part. At one point I went to her dressing room and said we should make up. She asked me to leave."

Joan tried to be offhand. "It was one of those silly personality clashes," she told me. "It was stupid. You know how some people just don't hit it off with each other? That's the way it was with us. Now it's all over. I have nothing but respect for her professional ability. She is doing a terrific job in the picture. That's the important thing." Joan related how after a long shooting day Mercedes stayed until eight o'clock in the evening to deliver off-camera lines to Joan. "Afterward I thanked her before the whole crew," Joan said.

Mercedes commented dryly, "I am paid a very handsome salary to do such things."

Torch Song had its premiere during the filming of *Johnny Guitar*, and Mercedes sent Crawford a telegram wishing her success. Joan reciprocated by inviting Mercedes to a post-premiere party at Romanoff's. For the benefit of photographers, the two actresses met in a momentary embrace. "I just hope it will stay like this until the end of our picture," Mercedes said dubiously.

There could be no peace, because Joan never forgave anyone who challenged her position. And the press would not let the feud die. The huge success of the scurrilous *Confidential* magazine had sent magazines and newspapers sifting through famous lives in search of scandal. The failing Los Angeles *Mirror* seized upon the feud as premise for five malicious articles on Crawford and her supposedly ruthless ascent to power.

All of Crawford's opponents were interviewed. Jack Palance said: "After our picture together, she complimented me on a good performance. But I also learned that she told top people in the film industry, 'I'll never work again with Jack Palance.' She accused me of copying Marlon Brando during *Sudden Fear*. In the middle of a scene—while the cameras were on us—she would stop the whole production to tell me, 'I don't want a Brando quality in this thing.' " Said Sterling Hayden: "There is not enough money in Hollywood to lure me into making another picture with Joan Crawford. And I like money. Her treatment of Mercedes was a shameful thing. . . . There is one thing about Crawford you must admire: her ability to create a myth, a legend about herself." The *Mirror* also quoted Hal LeSueur ("I haven't seen my sister in more than five years") and an unnamed former servant ("I quit after two weeks. She made me take my shoes off when I entered the house so I wouldn't get dirt on the rugs.").

Joan was devastated by the onslaught. In her long career she had never experienced such a vicious attack; indeed, few film personalities had ever been subjected to such journalistic overkill. She was especially disheartened because she had agreed to be interviewed by the reporter who wrote the series; she discovered her words twisted to fit the anti-Crawford theme. Joan brooded for days. Her instinct was to slash back at her attackers. But that, she concluded, would only give them more satisfaction. Instead, she issued a queenly response: "Let people who need publicity say those things."

She remained unrepentant and became even more vocal in her defense of the old and increasingly rejected standards of the Hollywood she revered. "Any actress who appears in public without being well-groomed is digging her own grave," she told Louella.

When Queen Elizabeth canceled introductions to stars at Command Performances, Joan said in an interview: "Too many actresses today are little more than tramps and tarts. The Queen is a lady and expects to meet ladies. . . . I was at the last Command Performance, and Arlene Dahl, Marilyn Monroe and Anita Ekberg didn't even show up for rehearsals. Monroe's hairdresser was doing her hair as the Queen came up the steps. Those girls don't even know how to curtsy."

About the new generation of stars she complained: "Half of them have to go to a psychiatrist before they can get on a movie set. What they really need is a kick in the pants. I keep hearing how it is their unhappy childhood that is at fault. Who grew up happy? How can you be two hours late on a set and blame it on your childhood? We're living in the present, not the past."

Yet it seemed that Joan herself was trying more and more desperately to recover the past, stridently opposing new and threatening values. It was a natural fear, growing out of her constant effort to maintain herself as a star. She alone had to accomplish it; there was no one who could help her. And what a toll the struggle had exacted! The vulnerability she had displayed as Flaemmchen, as Sadie McKee, even as Sadie Thompson in her redeemed stage, had vanished. From *Mildred Pierce* onward, a show of innocence was impossible. Her portrayals could no longer be complementary to men, they were competitive with men. She sought to destroy them, not to entice them.

Crawford detested her own change. She fought against the role of the castrating woman, and yet she was drawn inexorably by the image, both off the screen and on. As a woman alone in the world's most competitive business, she was forced to compete as a man, and as an aging star her only hope for survival was to find roles that stressed her invincibility. She had defied time longer than most stars, but now it was catching up with her. Male stars dominated the film world, and they wanted their masculinity enhanced by appearing with young, sexually attractive actresses. As gently as he could, Arthur Park tried to explain this to his client.

"Joan, dear," he said, "there's one thing we have no control over: getting older."

Crawford cried.

IV

The Pepsi Years:
1955–1972

20

Female on the Beach WAS JOAN'S first film for Universal Pictures. She arrived on the lot in Crawford style, commandeering the largest dressing room for her living quarters, insisting on script changes to bolster her role, requesting as her leading man the studio's number-one star, Jeff Chandler. Since she was having a romance with Milton Rackmil, president of Universal Pictures, her wishes were granted.

Joan impressed the director, Joseph Pevney, and the Universal crew with her professionalism. The only concession she asked was no close-ups after 4:30 in the afternoon. Otherwise she would do anything she was asked. A crucial scene involved a night swim by Lynn Markham, the Crawford character. It had been scheduled on the back-lot lake, and a double was prepared to substitute for Joan in the chilly water. "I'll do it myself," said Joan. To the amazement of the crew, she filmed the scene three times.

Female on the Beach continued filming through the Christmas holidays, 1954. On the day before New Year's, the company finished work at 1:30 in the afternoon. Cast and crew gathered for a holiday drink, then left the studio. Except for Joan.

She had work to do—dictating letters into her voice recorder. When darkness fell, she decided to stay all night in the bungalow rather than risk the drive to Brentwood through holiday traffic. She telephoned the children that she would be home in the morning and bade them Happy New Year.

The studio was dark and empty, except for watchmen on their rounds. After dinner Joan dictated more letters, then prepared for bed. She was startled when the telephone rang.

"Joan, darling, this is Earl Blackwell. I'm in Las Vegas and I wanted to call and wish you a Happy New Year. I'm at a party with some friends who would like to talk to you."

One of them was Alfred Steele. Joan remembered meeting him four years before at the New York apartment of Sonny Werblin, an executive of MCA. Steele was then a vice-president of Coca-Cola, married to a beauty named Lillian Nelson, and father of a one-year-old son. Joan had met Steele a few more times and knew that he had become president of Coca-Cola's competitor, Pepsi-Cola.

"What are you doing in your dressing room alone on New Year's Eve?" he asked on the telephone.

"I worked today, and I'm tired," Joan replied. "Besides, I never cared much for New Year's Eve parties."

"Listen, I expect to be out in California one of these days. I'd like to see you again."

"Fine. I'd love to see you and Lillian."

What Joan didn't know was that the Las Vegas party was a farewell celebration for Lillian and Al Steele. A few days later, Joan read that Alfred N. Steele had filed for divorce in Acapulco.

Al Steele came to California and called on Joan. She was overwhelmed by his charm and dynamism, and accepted his invitations to dinner. The gossip columnists continued reporting her romance with Milt Rackmil, unaware that she was becoming seriously involved with the soft-drink president from New York.

Joan realized she was ready for another marriage. "I was unutterably lonely," she recalled. "I was unfulfilled. Stories that I've always had scores of men waiting around to date me simply weren't true. I can't tell you how many nights after I put the children to bed I've stayed up alone, all alone. I am a woman with a woman's need, a husband."

Privately she had other reasons besides loneliness for being attracted to Al Steele. She feared she was failing in her dual role as mother and father to her children, particularly the two oldest. Christina was becoming increasingly defiant, and Christopher seemed impossible to control. Both might improve under the firm hand of a man like Al Steele. She admired Al's strength; he was unlike the three actors she had married. Each had been ineffectual in different ways, all uncertain of their own identity. Al Steele was confident and commanding. Like Joan herself, he was an achiever and had succeeded in the business world, fulfilling the American dream, which Joan Crawford completely embraced. Both Joan and Al were creatures of impulse. As leader of a huge, widespread corporation, he was accustomed to making swift decisions throughout the working day, and he relied on his instincts. Joan, too, was instinctive. Her decisions came fast, and even when they proved to be wrongheaded, she rarely repudiated them. She decided immediately to welcome Al Steele's attentions.

Joan learned more about him. He was five years older than Joan, having been born on April 24, 1901, in Nashville, Tennessee. His father, Edgar Alfred Steele, was an extroverted man who was so devoted to Sigma Nu fraternity that he named his son Alfred Nu Steele. Edgar Steele had worked as a traveling secretary for the YMCA, and he and his wife, Fanny, lived in several European countries before the First World War, taking their son with them everywhere they went. Young Al was his father's pride, a handsome, alert boy, fond of reading but also an athlete. He played football at Northwestern University, where he graduated in 1923.

Everyone agreed that Al Steele was going to be a giant in the business world. He started his career in the advertising department of the Chicago *Tribune*, then moved to Standard Oil of Indiana as advertising manager. After a stint as Detroit manager of Columbia Broadcasting System, Steele joined the D'Arcy advertising agency in New York. Among his accounts was Coca-Cola, whose executives were so impressed by his aggressive sales ideas that they hired him as vice-president for marketing.

Al Steele proved a dynamic salesman. Muscular, with a square, rugged face, he shouldered his way into the corporate world, slapping backs and calling everyone "pally"—so he would call no one the wrong name. A stylish dresser, he could charm women as well as men. He had been married twice, first to his college sweetheart, Marjorie Garvey, mother of his daughter, Sally, and then to Lillian Nelson, with whom he had a son, Alfred Nelson.

Al Steele was restive at Coca-Cola. Life in Atlanta was dull, and the company was slow to adopt his innovative proposals. There seemed to be little need to, since Coca-Cola was by far the leader in the soft-drink business.

One day in 1949 Steele listened to the chairman of the board discuss the history of the soft-drink business. He ended his dissertation with the prediction that Pepsi-Cola would collapse within twelve months.

Steele's best friend at Coca-Cola was D. Mitchell Cox, a bright, personable public-relations man, and he noticed that Al seemed bemused after the lecture from the board chairman.

"Pally, do you think we could run Pepsi?" Steele asked. Cox was astonished. He learned that Steele had been invited to join Pepsi. Both men had excellent jobs with Coca-Cola, and it seemed suicidal to leave for a losing rival. But Steele was serious and they both joined Pepsi, Steele as first vice-president and Cox as head of public relations. Within a year Steele was president, and the changes in the company were phenomenal. He reduced the sugar content of Pepsi, thereby saving money and catering to a growing diet-conscious market. The Biow advertising agency employed the svelte model Dorian Leigh, photographing her sideways to emphasize the slimming benefits of Pepsi-Cola—"reduced in calories, not heavy and sweet." The traditional design of the bottle, the cartons and the logo were modernized to give Pepsi a contemporary look, contrasting with the old-fashioned look of Coca-Cola. Steele traveled indefatigably, convincing every bottler that he had a friend at the top of the company. He captured markets that had previously been Coca-Cola monopolies, guaranteeing Pepsi dealers' loans for vending machines at $400 apiece. "The company will back you up," Steele vowed. He devoted his principal energy to "push markets"— those metropolitan areas that set the style for the satellites. He reasoned that what proved popular in Chicago would be copied in Rockford and South Bend. "You've got to spend money to make money," argued Al Steele, and some of his subordinates countered that he spent too much. But they couldn't quarrel with the results. Under his leadership Pepsi-Cola sales doubled, then tripled, providing Coca-Cola with a threatening rival for the first time in its history.

Al Steele became entranced with the idea of marrying Joan Crawford, and she was intrigued by the high-powered business leader; it was her first romance with a man who would not accede to her will. Both delighted in the secretiveness of their courtship. Even Al's close friend Mitch Cox didn't know about it until he noticed a pair of gold cufflinks in Steele's bathroom.

"What do you need those for?" Cox asked.

"Take a look at them, pally," said Steele. The inscription read: "All my love, Joan."

In the spring of 1955 Joan signed a contract with Columbia Pictures for a series of films. The first was *Queen Bee*, written by Ranald MacDougall and directed by him at Joan's insistence. She played a Georgia wife whose evil, domineering ways destroy those around her. In her scenes with Barry Sullivan and John Ireland she was surprisingly skittish. She seemed unable to remember her lines, a rare occurrence for Joan Crawford. "I'm terribly sorry," she apologized to MacDougall and her fellow actors. "I don't understand what's wrong with me."

Al Steele had become a familiar visitor at Bristol Avenue and had been accepted by the Crawford children. He and Joan agreed that they would marry on May 24 at the New Jersey home of Sonny Werblin, who had introduced them. Joan began shopping surreptitiously for a trousseau, all in white.

On the night of May 9 Joan was Al's hostess at a dinner for Pepsi-Cola executives at Romanoff's restaurant in Beverly Hills. During the meal Al and Joan began talking about flying. "I could never fly," she said. "I tried it once, twenty years ago. I flew from Catalina Island to San Pedro in the cockpit of a single-engine plane. I was green with fear. I swore I would never fly again."

"That's just silly," Steele said.

"No, I *am* afraid," she insisted.

"Not with me, you won't be," he said with a smile. "Come on, I'll show you. The Pepsi plane is at the airport. Let's fly to Vegas and get married."

"But—"

"You don't like big weddings, do you?"

"No. I'll go home and pack."

"Oh, no, you don't! We're going now. You might change your mind."

Shortly after two A.M., Joan and Al were married by a municipal judge in the penthouse of the Flamingo Hotel in Las Vegas. Later Joan told reporters, "This is the happiest moment of my life. I'm going to make him the best wife in the world."

Joan and Al sailed on the SS *United States* from New York on March 26, 1955, and they began playing Katherine and Petruchio immediately. The courting over, both could resume their normal, self-assertive identities. Al was determined to take Joan with the same sureness he applied to conquering business problems; Joan was equally insistent on exercising her own will. She had always been able to convince men to do her bidding—didn't Franchot even kneel before her? Her new husband, she discovered, was not the least bit compliant. In fact, he seemed to defy her at every turn.

Al Steele reveled in the power he had achieved at Pepsi-Cola. Usually he could achieve his ends by exercise of his considerable charm; if not, he cracked heads together. In any case, his will was law, both with business underlings and with wives—it never occurred to him that that was perhaps why his first two marriages had failed.

Aboard the *United States* sounds of verbal and physical battles emanated from the honeymoon stateroom. Yet the newlyweds were smiling as they arrived in a Cadillac at the Plaza Athénée in Paris, followed by a truck bearing Joan's luggage. Earl Blackwell hosted a party at Maxim's for the Steeles, inviting Louis B. Mayer and his wife, Lorena, and other celebrities who were in Paris, as well as Sally Steele, Al's daughter, who was touring Europe with college friends.

"It's Sally!" Joan announced to the crowd. "Look what I inherited. I only met her yesterday." She added to the embarrassed Sally, "Honey, how would you like to meet Johnnie Ray?"

While talking to one of the guests, Sally mentioned the fun of taking the Métro. She turned to her new stepmother and added, "You really ought to try it." Joan chewed gum as she eyed the girl and muttered with a half-smile, "Listen, kid, you live your life and I'll live mine."

On to Capri, Rome and more parties to honor the newlyweds, and more battles behind the doors of hotel suites. "It was sheer hell," she recalled later, shocked by his "streak of bullheaded obstinacy that frightened me." She added: "We'd arrive in Rome and he would go out to a business appointment and come back an hour later and say, 'We're having eighteen for drinks and dinner.' I'd say, 'Dammit, we are *not*! I won't give them hotel food, and I haven't got time for caterers.' He would say, 'Dammit, you *will*!' and I would do what I could."

They returned to his New York apartment at 36 Sutton Place South, where he plunged into his Pepsi-Cola business. She had to return to California to start a new film for Columbia. And Christopher had run away again.

In August Joan and Al arrived by train in Los Angeles, and she reported to Columbia studios for costume fittings on *Autumn Leaves*, produced by William Goetz and directed by Robert Aldrich. Joan was cast as a New England spinster in her early forties who marries a lonely man in his late twenties and then discovers he is psychotic. Joan wanted Marlon Brando for the role, but it was out of the question. She agreed to Cliff Robertson, a Broadway actor who had played a small role in *Picnic*.

Crawford was perplexed by her new director, Robert Aldrich. She had generally managed to get her way with directors by one means or another, but the independent Aldrich could not be persuaded. He had climbed up from the ranks as production clerk, script clerk and assistant director, and had learned movie politics from the bottom. His lack of subservience came naturally; his family were the banking Aldriches, and the Rockefellers were his first cousins.

Aldrich acquiesced to Joan's insistence on Charles Lang as cinematographer; although Lang's meticulous lighting prolonged the schedule, he was able to make Joan appear a convincing forty-two. But Aldrich would not agree to the script changes that Joan demanded. During the first days of filming, she remained aloof, addressing him as "Mr. Aldrich." Then Joan performed an emotional scene, a key moment in the plot. "Cut!" said Aldrich, and when she completed her lines she glanced toward him to discover that he was misty-eyed. Crawford rushed over and embraced him in gratitude. Thereafter she referred to Bob Aldrich as "My director."

Autumn Leaves was Al Steele's first experience with the working Joan Crawford, and he was both amazed and outraged. "Why the hell do you have to stay at the studio every night?" he demanded. "Nobody I know has to sleep where they do business."

"That's because you don't know any actors," she replied.

"Bullshit. I've asked around. No other stars sleep at their studios."

"Alfred, you knew what you were getting into. I do things *my* way. That's why I'm still in business."

"Well, it's goddamn wrong. When you're through with your day's work, your place is with your husband and your children— at home. And that's the way it's going to be."

"Like hell it is!" But later that night Joan telephoned Bob Aldrich and told him tearfully that she would be unable to report to the set in the morning. She had a blemish on her face that wouldn't allow her to be photographed. "No problem, Joan," said the director. Crawford was furious. Being struck by her husband was bad enough; to miss a day's work was totally against her code of principles.

Billy Haines had planned a party at Romanoff's to honor the newlyweds. Al Steele announced that he could not attend because he had to hurry east; the wife of a Pepsi-Cola executive was critically ill. Gossip columnists hinted that Joan and Al were having a rift, and there were reports that she planned to go to Reno for a quick divorce. "I'm not about to divorce Mr. Steele today or any other day," Joan told Hedda Hopper. "I'm the happiest woman in the world."

Joan Crawford was fifty, and film offers grew scarce. Her agents were hesitant to mention a proposal from James and John Woolf, whose Romulus Films had produced *Beat the Devil* and *Moulin Rouge*, because the project had three drawbacks: it would be filmed in England, the script contained a spectacular role for a young actress, and Joan's salary would be reduced. "I don't care. I'll go," she replied.

The movie was originally called *The Golden Virgin*, but later changed to *The Story of Esther Costello*. Joan was pleased with the casting of Rossano Brazzi as her villainous husband, and although she would be working abroad for the first time, she felt secure because David Miller, who had directed *Sudden Fear*, would function as both director and producer. Crawford was cast as a wealthy American woman who takes a deaf and blind girl out of Irish squalor and launches a fund drive for help, only to have her efforts thwarted by the Italian philanderer she married. A promising English actress, Heather Sears, was selected to play the girl.

Joan's arrival in London gave the English reporters plenty to write about. First came the white Pepsi-Cola vans bearing Crawford's thirty-seven pieces of luggage, all monogrammed "J.C." Then came the limousine with Joan and Al Steele. She carried a stuffed white poodle which replaced her own dog, left in America because of the six-month British quarantine.

The Story of Esther Costello was Joan Crawford's last film for almost three years. However, she found a new outlet for her inexhaustible energy—Pepsi-Cola.

In the beginning she referred to herself as Mrs. Alfred Steele and insisted that others do the same (she always called her husband Alfred, although all his friends knew him as Al). After three failed marriages, she sought to avoid having her husband referred to as Mr. Joan Crawford. Al Steele was unconcerned. He was too successful in the business world to fear being relegated to the consort of a movie star. Indeed, he reveled in the new attention he received with or without the presence of his famous wife, and it fed his considerable ego to be the husband of one of the most famous women in the world. "Honey, it's all right to call yourself Mrs. Alfred Steele in private life," he told Joan, "but you should be Joan Crawford in public. You ought to be proud of what you achieved— as proud of yourself as I am proud of you."

Steele admired how she had built and sustained a career in the fiercely competitive field of motion pictures, and he astutely realized what an important asset Joan could be in his endeavor. After finishing *The Story of Esther Costello,* she accompanied him on business trips to West Germany and South Africa. On previous journeys alone, he had been greeted only by Pepsi-Cola agents. When he arrived with Crawford, cheering crowds appeared at the airport and press conferences were jammed. Local dignitaries stood in line for a chance to meet her at hotel receptions, and heads of state invited the Steeles for a visit. Al Steele told a reporter: "In Denmark, where we and Coca-Cola are barred by high taxes to protect the local beer, we had a press reception in our suite. As usual, there was a small Pepsi cooler in the room. One of the reporters asked why Pepsi wasn't sold there. Joan explained that we were taxed out of the market and remarked that it hardly seemed fair, since we import so much Danish beer, ham, silver, laces and other products. The next day her reply was bannered on the front page. Crawford gave it that importance."

At 6:30 in the morning, the Steele plane arrived at Lourenço Marques, Mozambique. Sixteen thousand people crowded the airport, waving wildly and shouting "Joan Crawford!" She had come to help open a new bottling plant.

With his bulldozing persuasion, Al Steele managed to conquer or at least ameliorate Joan's fear of flying, and in a year and a half she flew 98,000 miles. Her terror of public speaking took longer to overcome. Her mentor was Mitchell Cox, Al's close friend who had accompanied him from Coca-Cola to head Pepsi's public relations. Cox had been a teacher of public speaking, and he presided at the Pepsi sales meetings and conventions. Once, however, he erred at a huge gathering in 1957 in Cincinnati, where twenty-two hundred guests were treated to a banquet in a plant garage. Cox introduced some of the dignitaries and returned to his seat. He could sense an air of tension, but didn't realize the cause until an executive took the microphone and introduced Joan Crawford, wife of Pepsi's board chairman, Alfred Steele. Cox realized that Al had been fuming over the omission, and if he hadn't been a personal friend, Cox would have been fired. He never repeated the mistake.

At first Joan merely nodded in acknowledgment of the introduction. Then Cox persuaded her to rise halfway from her chair. In the next phase Joan said to the crowd, "Thank you very much."

Much later Joan agreed to deliver speeches that Cox wrote for her. Never would she speak impromptu, although she finally agreed to answer questions, only if they were submitted beforehand. But soon she abandoned all reluctance and plunged headlong into performing for Pepsi. During one nine-city tour she gave 176 newspaper interviews, appeared on 41 television programs and 65 radio shows.

Although Pepsi's public-relations specialists accompanied her, Joan attended to many tour details herself. Before a press reception, she visited the conference room, rearranged the furniture, made sure the tables were free of dust, even dipped a finger into the flower vases to check the water level. For every interview and appearance, her hair, makeup and attire were as perfect as if she were in front of a movie camera. She never drank during the day, except during an autographing session. As the long line passed her table and she signed her name with a personal message, she sipped from a glass that looked as if it contained water—it was vodka. Often at night she boarded a train for the journey to the next city. Then she kicked off her shoes and entertained her traveling staff with champagne and caviar, which she kept cold in a Pepsi cooler. During one night journey through the Carolinas, she ran out of sour cream for the caviar. She had the train stopped so she could get some.

Crawford enjoyed talking about her life with Al Steele to interviewers: "When my husband comes home at the end of the day, we cut off the phone, mix a drink and discuss what happened. We talk about his business, because that is *my* business, too—in addition to the business of understanding him and making him happy. Not only am I interested in his work—I work with him, too. If my husband were an accountant, I'd help him total up figures. If he ran a store, I'd be behind the counter. It happens my husband must travel, so I travel with him. Before my marriage, I had been in an airplane only once—I felt if God had wanted me to fly, He would have made me a bird. Now I've been flying in more ways than one."

It became apparent early in their marriage that Al's bachelor quarters on Sutton Place would be inadequate for his life with Joan. In typical style he bought two entire apartments at 2 East Seventieth Street, just off Fifth Avenue. He had the two floors converted into a single apartment, reducing eighteen rooms to eight. Billy Haines came from California to decorate the cavernous rooms and design new furniture to fit the huge scale. Crawford had her own ideas about designing closets for her wardrobe, of course, and she enjoyed displaying them with dozens of dresses arranged by color, row upon row of plastic boxes containing hats and purses, and a single immense closet for her 304 pairs of shoes. It became legendary that all visitors had to remove their shoes before entering the apartment; her excuse was that she wanted to retain the carpet's pristine whiteness. She was also able to fulfill her need for immaculacy by scrubbing the bathrooms regularly.

Al Steele figured Pepsi should foot the bill, since he would use the apartment to promote the company's fortunes. But although Pepsi paid for construction costs, Steele learned to his shock that the money was a loan. A 1958 report to stockholders contained the note: "During 1957 Mr. Steele had extensive alterations and structural changes made in the cooperative apartment. As Mr. Steele was absent from New York on company affairs for some 165 days in 1957, the Company paid for him, and charged to his account, costs on this work. The largest aggregate amount of debt from Mr. Steele was $387,011.65. This has been repaid in full. Interest at the rate of 6% was charged."

Predictably, stockholders seized upon this at the annual meeting. John Gilbert, veteran gadfly of stockholder meetings, wanted to know if the apartment had been completed. Steele said that it had, adding that he had revealed the loan because of Securities and Exchange rules about financial transactions with officers. Gilbert said he wanted to question Mrs. Steele, who had been sitting quietly at the back of the room.

"Make it brief, boy," she advised him.

When Gilbert suggested she should be on the board of directors, she replied, "If I were, we'd have long sessions but short speeches."

"May I ask how many shares of Pepsi-Cola you own?" Gilbert said.

"It's none of your business," Crawford snapped. "Besides, I owned them before I married Mr. Steele."

Al Steele interjected: "I let my wife run her business, and she lets me run mine."

Although he acted offhand about the loan, Steele had been jolted by the company's refusal to pay for the apartment. He was earning $125,000 a year and spending much more; alimony and child support also helped to deplete his income. Now he had to borrow heavily from the banks. Fortunately there seemed to be no problem in repaying the loan. Under his stewardship Pepsi-Cola sales had soared from 87 million bottles in 1955 to 256 million in 1957, and the increase continued. Pepsi was especially aggressive in moving into foreign markets, overpowering Coca-Cola in many countries of Africa, Asia and South America. With such burgeoning prosperity, the future seemed secure for the man who had transformed a dwindling company into an international empire.

While Joan was adjusting to her new role as wife and business partner of a high-powered executive, family problems developed. Christopher continued to run away from one school after another, and Joan was disheartened and despairing. "I don't believe in heredity; I believe in environment," she told an interviewer. "And you know something? I'm wrong." I used to rush home from the studio or wherever I was to spend as much time as possible with him and his sister. I never let those two go to bed without rocking them to sleep and hearing their prayers. I was trying to make up for their having no father. I never had any family life of my own, and maybe that was why I worked so hard at creating one for them. I drove them to school every morning. When I enrolled Christopher in nursery school, I had him and Christina by the hands and the twins hanging from my shoulders.

"At first he was the most beautiful little boy—the face is angelic in the pictures taken then. And he began to change after that. How, why, I can't tell. He began to run away from school. I thought it was just excess energy, and when I would take him to school in the mornings, I would run him up the hill, to try to help him get rid of that energy. It didn't do any good. No amount of psychiatric treatment or consultation seemed to do any good. Nothing I did seemed to help. I feel as though I failed with him, but nobody can say I didn't try."

Christopher was residing with a child psychiatrist in Greenport, New York, in 1958 when he was arrested with three other youths after a shooting spree with air rifles. At fifteen Christopher was sent to a correctional institution.

"The hardest part was explaining his behavior to the twins," Joan said. "They're so sweet and innocent. What could I tell them? Yet I knew I had to tell them something. I finally said, 'Your brother didn't live up to society's expectations, and society has a way of taking care of these things. When he learns to behave the way he is expected to behave by society, he'll come back home.' "

Anna Bell LeSueur Cassin died in 1958. She had lived with Hal and rarely saw her famous daughter. After a series of strokes, her life ended in Hollywood Presbyterian Hospital at the age of seventy-four. Joan had been vacationing in Bermuda with Al, and she flew to Los Angeles for the funeral.

They had never been close. Billie Cassin could never forget how her mother always favored Hal, nor could she forget the years of working in school kitchens and the succession of "stepfathers." Even though Joan had supported her mother from her earliest years at MGM, Anna expressed no gratitude. When she took the bus to shop on Hollywood Boulevard, she complained loudly, "I'm Joan Crawford's mother; she drives around in a Rolls-Royce, and I take the bus!" Such incidents were reported to Joan, and she seethed. But at Forest Lawn cemetery in 1958, Crawford wept real tears. She was consoled by Mary Brian, who had been a Wampas Baby Star with Joan in 1926; both their mothers had been active in the

Motion Picture Mothers. "Thank heaven I have Al Steele at this time," Joan told Mary.

Hal LeSueur died of a ruptured appendix in 1963. He was fifty-nine years old. After the failure of his acting career and two marriages, Hal became a drunk, and his behavior so infuriated his sister that she forbade him to come to her house. Hal later joined Alcoholics Anonymous and managed to stay sober until his death, working at the Parkway Motel on Alvarado Street as night clerk. Nine people attended the funeral at Forest Lawn, but his sister was not among them.

It seemed strange how an actress who displayed such compassion on the screen would exhibit so little forgiveness for her own family. With untried performers, with reporters and photographers as well as devoted fans, Crawford committed acts of excessive kindness. Yet toward her two oldest children, her mother and her brother, she seemed totally vindictive, as if she had to repay them for the hurts of her childhood. *Someone* needed to suffer for the wrongs that had been inflicted on Billie Cassin. Anna had failed her, for being unable to assure the father that Billie needed so desperately. Hal's lack of compassion for his lonely sister, his self-centered nature and his alcoholism eliminated any grounds for affection. And Tina and Chris were unable to fulfill the concept their mother had created for them. All four deserved her scorn, Joan believed, and she shut them out of her mind.

21

As a salesman Alfred Nu Steele was insuperable. But his performance as executive was less impressive. He had a tendency to devise impressively ambitious programs, then play golf while his underlings were left to carry them out. For its existence Pepsi-Cola depended upon the network of independent bottlers who managed their own markets; most were hardheaded businessmen who had suffered through the lean years with Pepsi and were nervous about their newfound prosperity. Although they were grateful for the accomplishments of the board chairman and enchanted by his wife, they were concerned about his philosophy of spending money to make money. They suspected he spent too much, and his living quarters at Seventieth Street and Fifth Avenue seemed to symbolize his profligacy. Meanwhile there were reports of huge sums run up by Steele during conventions and his world travels with Joan. The bottlers loved Al Steele, but they loved their profits more.

Al Steele had been slowing his pace, but not because he was losing interest in an enterprise that no longer needed salvation. He was tired. He was fifty-seven, and he had drunk too many cocktails, eaten too many banquet meals, flown on too many jets. Joan urged him to slow down. So did the company doctor. But he was aware of the growing discontent of the bottlers, and he had to move aggressively to quell potential revolt.

Steele devised an "AD-orama" campaign, an innovative advertising drive that would further weaken Coca-Cola's monopoly on soft drinks. The chairman of the board himself would barnstorm the country for eight weeks in a campaign reminiscent of the "give-'em-hell" Truman tradition. Before starting his tour, Steele took Joan to Half Moon Bay in Jamaica for a week's rest, and she exacted a promise that after the AD-orama campaign he would establish a regime of four weeks' work followed by a week's vacation.

The AD-orama drive was a blazing success. The bottlers who most doubted Al Steele's industriousness now became his most enthusiastic supporters. "We'll beat the shit out of Coke!" they proclaimed. Al Steele was beaming. Crawford, who joined him midway in the tour, was immensely proud. But she was also concerned about his health. Each night after cocktail parties, press conferences, tours of bottling plants and banquets with speeches, he seemed exhausted.

When Al and Joan reached Atlanta, she learned that Cesar Romero was there on a tour to promote a men's clothing line. She asked her old friend to come to breakfast in the Steele suite.

It was a joyful reunion, and Crawford and "Butch" exchanged the latest gossip of the show world. Al didn't appear until midway through breakfast. He came out of the bedroom in a robe, his face gray. "I didn't sleep well last night," he admitted.

"Have you seen a doctor?" Romero asked.

"No, but I'm okay," Steele replied. "Nothing wrong with my heart. I'm just tired. This tour has taken a lot out of me."

"And it's the last one he's going to have for a while," Joan added, patting his hand. "He's been working too hard."

When they arrived in Washington, Al admitted, "I'm so tired I don't know what to talk about tomorrow."

"Go to bed, darling," Joan said soothingly. "Don't try to think now."

While he slept, she wrote out suggestions for his speech to the bottlers in the morning. She left notes on the bedside table with his milk and crackers—she always had a late snack ready for him, since he was usually sleepless during the night.

He seemed refreshed in the morning. "Thank you for the notes," he said. "They were a real help. I might well have forgotten the names of some of the men I particularly want to thank for their support."

During the long morning of group meetings, Joan could see Al's energy slide. She convinced him to share lunch with her alone in their suite, but he had an important engagement to keep that afternoon: to present a citation to Senator John F. Kennedy on behalf of the National Sclerosis Society, of which Al was chairman.

The Friday-night meeting at the Mayflower Hotel was rousing; bottlers and distributors came from the surrounding areas, and Al Steele imbued them with his messianic spirit to carry Pepsi-Cola to greater heights. He concluded his speech: "Lastly, I want to thank my beloved wife, who has helped me all along the way." The hotel ballroom erupted in applause, and everyone rose to his feet on behalf of Mrs. Alfred Steele. She wept joyfully.

That night Al and Joan celebrated the end of the tour. He felt justifiably satisfied. He had encountered no dissenters en route, and with good reason. He reminded the bottlers that when he joined Pepsi-Cola in 1949, gross sales were $40 million with a net profit of $1.2 million. Ten years later the gross was $136 million with a net of $11.5 million.

In two weeks, on May 6, 1959, the board and stockholders would demonstrate their gratitude. Al Steele would be awarded a lifetime contract and options on 75,000 shares of stock.

Al and Joan flew to New York in the company plane and went directly to 2 East Seventieth Street. Dr. Henry Nachtigall came to the apartment to examine Al briefly and discuss a Steele health plan for Pepsi executives. Al admitted that he was weary, and the company doctor was pleased that the Steeles would be leaving for a rest in Jamaica on Monday. Advertising account executives arrived at five o'clock to discuss execution of the AD-orama campaign.

"Gentlemen," Joan announced at eight o'clock, "I'm sorry, but my husband has to have dinner." She cooked a couple of steaks and tossed a salad, and they dined in front of the fireplace and watched the Perry Como television show. Joan noticed that Al seemed wearier than she had ever seen him. "Darling, you look so tired," she said. "Let's really turn in early, shall we?"

"I *am* tired," he conceded.

Joan washed the dishes and followed Al upstairs. Their suitcases lay open in their bedrooms.

"What about a hand of gin rummy before we go to bed?" he suggested.

They played one hand in her bedroom, and she was ahead twelve points when Al said, "I really am tired, baby." He took her hand and said, "Have you any idea how much I love you? Do you know how much you've given me, not only as a man but in my business? I've never been so happy. I wish there were some way I could tell you."

Her eyes brimmed. "You have, darling," she said, and she kissed him good night.

She awoke with a start at 9:15 Sunday morning. Always he called to her when he arose in the morning, and he never slept late. "Alfred, dear?"

No answer. She hurried to his bedroom and didn't find him. Pulling on a housecoat, she rushed down the stairs and found him lying on the floor in the living room. His face was ashen, his flesh cold. Crawford screamed.

She raced to the telephone and called Dr. Nachtigall, then returned to cover Alfred with blankets. "Get warm, darling, get warm," she pleaded. But his heart had stopped. Dr. Nachtigall arrived and told Joan that her husband had died instantly. Executives of Pepsi-Cola began to appear at the apartment, including Steele's handpicked president, Herbert Barnet. Messages of condolence and telephone calls soon poured in, including ones from Doug Fairbanks, Franchot Tone and Phil Terry. Joan telephoned the twins in California with the mournful news and they insisted on taking the first plane available to join her.

Crawford did not mourn. She immediately plunged into planning the funeral, telephoning friends and business associates with instructions of which limousine they were to occupy. Those around her were astonished that she could organize her husband's funeral with the same efficiency as preparing a dinner party at "21." She had immunized herself against sorrow. It was a wasteful, damaging, ultimately futile emotion. She had known enough sorrow in her early years, and it had availed her nothing. She could weep at her mother's grave, but not out of sadness for a woman she had never really loved; she wept for Billie Cassin and the childhood she had lost. No need to weep for Al Steele. He had been a realist, like Joan. That was one of the reasons she and Al understood each other so well in their last months together. Both realized their life together wouldn't last. So they buttressed themselves against the future.

Another four-year marriage had ended. Like the diamond-hard

women she had endlessly played on the screen, Joan needed to think about her own future.

Two days after Alfred Steele's death, his widow was elected to fill his vacancy on the Pepsi-Cola board of directors. "It was no sentimental or emotional gesture," said Herb Barnet, who became executive officer. He cited Mrs. Steele's travels of 125,000 miles throughout the world to promote the fortunes of Pepsi-Cola.

Crawford declared that she would be "a working member of the board, to carry on where we left off and keep the company growing." Privately she *knew* that she would have to work, for Al Steele had died broke.

It seemed incredible. Steele had been one of the most successful figures in American business, and his estate was finally valued at $607,128; but by the time the taxes and obligations were added up, nothing was left. He had even borrowed $100,000 in cash from Joan two weeks before he died, and she had no record of the loan.

Jerry Wald telephoned from Hollywood. "Joan, darling, I think at a time like this you need to work," said the producer.

"That's right, Jerry, I *need* to work," Joan replied with a bit of irony.

"I'm making a picture at Fox, *The Best of Everything*. There's a great part as Amanda Farrow, a magazine editor with great style. But I'll warn you, Joan, it's not the biggest part in the picture."

"Is the script good?"

"I think it's terrific."

"Then I'll do it. I'd rather have a small part in a good picture than star in a mediocre one."

The Best of Everything seemed like a comedown for Joan Crawford. For thirty-five years she had never known less than star billing; now she would be listed at the bottom of the cast. The lead roles would be played by newcomers Hope Lange, Suzy Parker, Martha Hyer, and Diane Baker.

Louella Parsons had heard that Joan Crawford accepted *The Best of Everything* because she needed the money. The columnist called Joan in her dressing room at Twentieth Century-Fox.

"It's true," Joan said. "I'm flat broke. I haven't a sou to my name. Only my jewels."

"But Alfred must have left you—"

"Alfred left me up to my ears in debt, Louella. He expected his company to reimburse me for the half-million dollars we spent on our New York apartment. They didn't. Everything is going to pay his debts and taxes. I'm selling my home in Brentwood because it's too big and I can't afford to keep it. I've had it for thirty years, you know."

"But what about your job with Pepsi-Cola?"

"The company has been wonderful to me, and I have agreed to go out on personal-appearance tours whenever and wherever they need me."

"Then you're really back in pictures because you need the work and the money?"

"Damn right I am! I'll take any good part, no matter how small. I'm hoping to make pictures, to work for Alfred's company, and to keep going. I'm not worried as long as I can work."

The Los Angeles *Examiner* bannered the Parsons story: "JOAN CRAWFORD FLAT BROKE."

Joan immediately had misgivings. As a movie star she could tell a reporter anything, no matter how outrageous, and the printed interview merely contributed to her glamor. But now she was spokeswoman for a giant corporation and a member of its board. She received a telephone call from an executive of Pepsi-Cola: "Joan, that story you gave Parsons makes the company look bad. It makes it seem that Al was a poor executive who couldn't provide for his own wife, much less the company. The story could have a bad effect on the Pepsi stock."

Joan was a "good soldier." She issued a statement that her financial status might be subject to some "misinterpretation." During probate of her late husband's will, she would be paid $60,000 of his annual salary, plus compensation for her services as board member and spokeswoman.

"I have two residences—an apartment in New York City and a home in Brentwood. Since my business interests will be mainly in New York, I am planning to sell my Brentwood house. As for pictures, I intend to return to Hollywood when I am offered the kind of role I feel is best suited to my talents."

Parsons, of course, was livid. Harry Brand, publicity chief of Twentieth Century-Fox, confirmed that a publicist, Don Prince, had been present when Joan admitted over the telephone that she was broke. The columnist printed the rebuttal and never forgave Crawford. Louella Parsons wrote in her memoirs: "I have known Joan Crawford for more than thirty-five years. I still don't know her at all. . . . She is the only star I know who manufactured herself. . . . She drew up a blueprint for herself and outlined a beautiful package of skin, bones and character and then set about to put life into the outline. She succeeded, and so Joan Crawford came into existence at the same time an overweight Charleston dancer, born Lucille LeSueur, disappeared from the world. It took me a long time to realize this. I believed, for some time, that Lucille existed under the skin."

Predominant among the terrors that afflicted the private Joan Crawford was the specter of poverty. She had known it as Billie Cassin in Kansas City, and it had scarred her life. Since her early years at MGM, her fear of being poor had been submerged; she had no reason to imagine that her wealth would vanish. Now her vision of comfortable mature years with Alfred Steele was shattered. After a lifetime of work, she would have to work even harder to pay off Alfred's debts and restore her own financial security.

All she had now was work. She knew she would never marry again—this time she *knew* it. She still had the twins, and they were a comfort to her. But they were twelve and would soon be less dependent on her. Christina had already proclaimed her independence and was seeking an acting career in New York, and Joan had given up hope on Christopher.

Crawford was determined to maintain a position in films, even though her age made her increasingly difficult to cast. She remained a star and expected to be treated like one. In *The Best of Everything* she insisted on a contract clause that would set her name off from the rest of the cast, making her appearance seem like an event despite the fact that she had only four scenes. She demanded that her dressing-room/trailer be parked inside the stage, so she would have less walking to the set.

The trailers for the younger actresses were parked *outside* the stage, and there was resentment about the courtesies extended to the aging star. Two or three of the actresses seemed to be playing Eve Harrington to Crawford's Margo Channing, challenging and undermining the older star's position. They discovered a formidable opponent. The director, Jean Negulesco, was staging a scene with Hope Lange and Joan, in which Joan made a speech and left.

"Would you mind letting me close the door after you exit?" Lange asked Crawford.

"No, you can't," Crawford replied. "It's my line. It's my exit. *I* close it."

"But I don't know what to do with my hands."

Crawford glared. "Why not *find* something to do with your hands?" she said acidly.

Negulesco interceded and decided against Joan. "Hope will close the door," he decreed. Joan realized she was defeated.

Negulesco had directed Joan in *Humoresque*, and she had expected another cooperative working relationship with him, but it didn't turn out that way. The Rumanian had gained more self-confidence than he had shown in his Warner Brothers years, having directed *Three Coins in the Fountain*, *How to Marry a Millionaire* and other Fox successes.

Joan argued that the character of Amanda needed more explanation, more involvement with the lives of the young career women. Negulesco was unsympathetic.

"At least give me some time alone," she asked, "so I can be better prepared for the scenes."

"Then everyone else in the cast will want the same thing," Negulesco replied. "I can't spare the time."

Joan agreed to appear in a trailer to advertise *The Best of Everything*, and Negulesco said he would direct. When he arrived for the shooting, Joan was posed before the camera with a bottle of Pepsi-Cola and a glass beside her.

"You are an actress," he exclaimed. "What do you need that stuff for?"

"I would like the bottle to appear in the shot," Joan said quietly.

"Absolutely not! This is not a TV commercial."

"Then I won't make the trailer," she said, departing in tears.

When film roles were not available, Joan appeared on television. She had made her television debut in 1953 in a segment of *Mirror Theater*, and later starred in three dramas for *GE Theater*, produced by the MCA subsidiary Revue. After Alfred Steele's death, Joan performed in two westerns for *Zane Grey Theater*, commanding the highest salary for guest appearances. Even though the programs were half-hours, with five-day schedules, she approached each of them with the same professionalism she would bring to a major movie. She also insisted on the perquisites of a cooled stage, a chauffeured limousine and tests with the cameraman before filming.

Joan also appeared with Bob Hope and on *Hollywood Palace* and other television variety shows, as well as charity telethons and beauty pageants. Such exposure was vital, she believed, to maintaining her identity as a public figure and as spokeswoman for Pepsi-Cola. She now promoted Pepsi with the same single-minded dedication that she had devoted to promoting Joan Crawford. She never missed an opportunity.

Billy Wilder was filming *One, Two, Three* with James Cagney as a promoter of Coca-Cola in Germany. Joan telephoned Wilder to protest, and the filmmaker added a final scene in which Cagney emerges from an airplane to find a Pepsi-Cola cooler at the airport, then kicks it.

Joan accepted flying and public speaking as necessities of her performance for Pepsi-Cola, but she never lost her terror of them. No matter how calm she appeared before an audience, she was totally frightened. After Steele's death, she agreed to make speeches before audiences only if Cox had prepared the text. On the rare occasions when she made impromptu remarks, she often said puzzling things out of sheer nervousness.

One of Joan's major missions was to lend glamor to the opening of bottling plants throughout the country and in foreign markets. The plants were generally located in outlying industrial areas, so Pepsi needed promotion to draw crowds. When full-page newspaper and television ads announced that Joan Crawford would appear, the results were often amazing.

At a Birmingham, Alabama, plant opening Joan signed autographs steadily for four hours and finally had to leave when her hand became too tired to hold a pen. Sixty thousand people appeared for the celebration. Five years later, bottler Jimmy Lee gave a "Thank you, Birmingham" party with Crawford as the major draw. The crowd was the largest in the city's history—73,000, more than attended the Alabama-Auburn football game. When she appeared in Miami, 103,000 toured the new Pepsi-Cola bottling plant in two days. On the following day, Spanish-speaking residents were invited, and 30,000 appeared. At a department-store appearance in Buenos Aires, Joan had to leave by the loading entrance because the crowds were so thick.

Joan developed a corporate style that was as coolly efficient as any she had employed in Hollywood. She never complained about the long hours of a bottling-plant opening with its accompanying festivities: "I'm used to working eighteen hours at a movie studio and standing on my feet. I have the self-discipline for the job."

She posed endlessly for photographs with local Pepsi officials, retaining a copy of each photograph to include in her file of people she should know. To and from airports she allowed the limousine to travel no faster than forty miles per hour, and she used the time en route to dictate letters into a tape recorder. While flying in the company plane, she received a briefing from Pepsi officials on forthcoming events and the people she would meet. When she arrived at the bottling plant she knew exactly who would be interviewing her. Each journalist received exclusive comments, and during television interviews she made sure that a bottle of Pepsi was clearly in sight. She always left time for autographs, and she developed a technique to avoid being delayed. As she signed paper napkins, dollar bills and road maps, she retreated imperceptibly, one step per autograph, thus preparing for her exit. On the flight home she fed the names and descriptions of important people she had met into her file. Then she dictated more letters.

Her trips became codified with a list of instructions issued both for her Pepsi-Cola promotional tours and her movies. The list of requirements for a movie tour fell into the hands of *Life* magazine, which published excerpts, to widespread amusement and ridicule.

The accommodations were specific: three bedrooms in the top suite of the city's best hotel. The bedrooms were to be occupied by Crawford, her personal maid, Anna ("Mamacita") Brinke, and Crawford's wardrobe. Single rooms were to be provided for publicity man Bob Kelly and two Pepsi-Cola pilots. A uniformed security officer would be stationed at the door of the hotel suite around the clock—not a city policeman or house detective.

> The following items are to be in the suite prior to Miss Crawford's arrival:
> 1. Cracked ice in buckets—several buckets.
> 2. Lunch and dinner menus.
> 3. Pen and pencils and pads of paper.
> 4. Professional-size hair dryer.
> 5. Steam iron and board.
> 6. One carton of Alpine cigarettes.
> 7. One bowl of peppermint Life-Savers.

8. Red and yellow roses.
9. Case of Pepsi-Cola, ginger ale, soda.

There is to be a maid on hand in the suite when Miss Crawford arrives at the hotel. She is to stand by until Miss Crawford dismisses her.

The following liquor is to be in the suite when Miss Crawford arrives:

1. Two fifths of 100-proof Smirnoff vodka. (Note: This is not 80-proof and it is *only* Smirnoff.)
2. One fifth Old Forester bourbon.
3. One fifth Chivas Regal Scotch.
4. One fifth Beefeater gin.
5. Two bottles Moët & Chandon champagne (Type: Dom Perignon)

Miss Crawford will be met in an air-conditioned, chauffeur-driven, newly cleaned Cadillac limousine. Instruct your chauffeurs that they are not to smoke and that they may not at any time drive in excess of 40 miles an hour with Miss Crawford in the car.

Miss Crawford will be carrying a minimum of 15 pieces of luggage. Along with the limousine you will meet Miss Crawford's plane with a closed van for the luggage. Have with you a luggage handler who can accompany the van back to the hotel. It will be his task to take an inventory of the luggage as it comes off the plane and into the van, and as it is being brought into Miss Crawford's suite. . . . Every precaution should be taken to assure that none of the luggage is misplaced. Fifteen pieces is the estimated minimum. There may be considerably more. . . .

Miss Crawford is a star in every sense of the word, and everyone knows she is a star. As a partner in this film, Miss Crawford will not appreciate your throwing away money on empty gestures. YOU DO NOT HAVE TO MAKE EMPTY GESTURES TO PROVE TO MISS CRAWFORD OR ANYONE ELSE THAT SHE IS A STAR OF THE FIRST MAGNITUDE.

22

Fasten your seat belts.
It's going to be a bumpy night.
　　　　　　　—Margo Channing, *All About Eve*

IT WAS Crawford's idea from the start. She believed a film starring Joan Crawford and Bette Davis would prove good showmanship and bring new vitality to both their careers. She further believed that Robert Aldrich was the filmmaker who could accomplish such a project, since he was daring, innovative and tough enough to control the two strong personalities. For several years after they made *Autumn Leaves* together Crawford kept urging Aldrich to find a vehicle for herself and Davis.

The two stars scarcely knew each other. During the 1930's they worked at different studios and rarely met socially, Bette preferring to live in the East between films. Joan never knew that Bette fell in love with Franchot Tone during the making of *Dangerous*, but the relationship was brief, and Franchot returned to his marriage with Joan.

Except for the luncheon with Curtis Bernhardt, Bette and Joan had little contact on the Warner Brothers lot. Both appeared in *Hollywood Canteen*, but not together. In the 1950's both Crawford and Davis had experienced an inevitable decline in their film careers. Crawford occupied herself with Pepsi-Cola and television appearances, while Davis made two films abroad and returned to the theater in *Night of the Iguana*.

Bob Aldrich was directing *Sodom and Gomorrah* in Europe when a former secretary sent him a copy of a suspense novel by Henry Farrell, *What Ever Happened to Baby Jane?* The secretary's boss had taken an option on the book against a price of $10,000. Aldrich read the book and agreed it would make a good movie. The plot concerned two reclusive sisters who were former movie stars living amid hatred and recrimination in a Hollywood mansion. Aldrich sent the book to Crawford, who recognized it as the costarring vehicle for herself and Bette Davis. Bette was equally enthusiastic about *What Ever Happened to Baby Jane?* She was familiar with the book, and a friend, William Frye, had tried to buy the property rights but had been unsuccessful. Bette urged Alfred Hitchcock to make it, but he was occupied with other projects.

Aldrich learned that the producer's option on *Baby Jane* had been dropped, and that the price was now $61,000. He and his partner in *Sodom and Gomorrah*, Joseph E. Levine, bought the rights, and Lukas Heller was assigned to write a script. When Aldrich and Levine had a falling-out, Aldrich acquired the *Baby Jane* rights and script for $85,000.

Aldrich realized that a gothic tale with two middle-aged stars would not be easy to sell to the film studios. He would have to budget the film at a price that would reduce the risk, which meant that Crawford and Davis would have to work for much less than their normal fees. They were surprisingly agreeable. Joan accepted a deal of $40,000 and ten percent of the producer's net profit. Bette wanted more immediate cash, and she agreed to $60,000 and five percent of the profit.

Aldrich calculated the leanest possible budget for the movie. By shooting in a fast thirty days in actual locations around Hollywood and at a rental studio, he figured the cost at $850,000. "Not interested at any price," said one studio head. "I don't even want to read the script," said another. "I might be interested if you'll cast two younger actresses," remarked a third executive.

All of the major studios rejected *Baby Jane*, including Warner Brothers. Aldrich's only chance was Seven Arts, a new, energetic company headed by Eliot Hyman. "I think it will make a fabulous movie," Hyman told Aldrich, "but I'm going to make very tough terms because it's a high-risk venture."

Aldrich made the contract with Seven Arts, which would release *Baby Jane* through Warner Brothers. A celebratory luncheon was held in the studio commissary, with Jack Warner welcoming back his two famous adversaries. The Hollywood press was invited to witness the confrontation.

Both actresses were surprisingly conciliatory to Warner. Bette admitted her troubles with "Papa Jack" but expressed her gratitude to him for fostering her career.

"I can't exactly call you my father, Mr. Warner," Joan said with seriousness, "because I give that credit to the late Louis B. Mayer. But you are my second father."

Both Joan and Bette sensed that *Baby Jane* could prove a much-needed bonanza to their fortunes and bring new life to their careers. They were willing to promote the film in any possible way, and they agreed to attend a command dinner-interview at the home of Hedda Hopper. Hopper noted: "The three of us were dressed in black. As we sat down to dinner, I said we looked like three black-widow spiders. But there was a difference: Joan, always the glamor star, wore a black cocktail suit, the somberness lit with diamond earrings and a diamond pin in her hair. Bette's black was unrelieved by jewelry except for a small pin." The columnist also observed that Bette drank Scotch on the rocks while Joan poured from her own flask of 100-proof vodka. "I say if you're going to have a drink, have what you want," Joan explained.

Separately and in joint interviews Joan and Bette vowed there would be no feud. The matter of billing was settled by Joan: "Of course Bette gets top billing; she plays the title role." In all other matters, treatment would be equal.

As publicist on *Baby Jane*, Linn Unkefer was apprehensive about the possibility of conflict between the the two stars, which would make his job difficult. When such feuds occurred the publicist was often the principal casualty. On the other hand, Unkefer realized the unique publicity possibilities of the Crawford-Davis combination, and he was determined to make the most of them. Unkefer alerted the local *Time*-magazine staff about the start of *Baby Jane* and the People section carried an item about the costarring of the two legendary actresses, both fifty-four.

Joan and adopted baby Christina

Joan appears on the witness stand,
April 11, 1939, to sue for divorce from
Franchot Tone

Strange Cargo (1940) with Gable again

Susan and God (1940) with Fredric March

On the set of *A Woman's Face* (1941) with director George Cukor

When Ladies Meet (1941)
with Greer Garson

A Woman's Face with Osa Massen

Reunion in France (1942) with John Wayne

Joan married Phil Terry, July 21, 1942

Mildred Pierce (1945) with Ann Blyth and Eve Arden

Joan and Oscar with *Mildred Pierce* director, Michael Curtiz

Humoresque (1946)

Humoresque (1946)   *Humoresque* (1946) with John Garfield

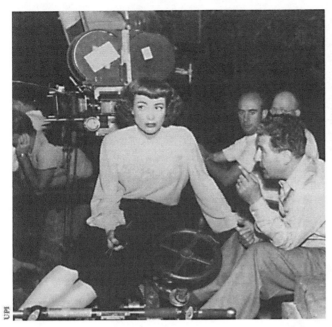

On the set of *Possessed* (1947) with director Curtis Bernhardt

Daisy Kenyon (1947) with Dana Andrews and Henry Fonda

Joan and Greg Bautzer and poodle, Cliquot, at Charlie Farrell's Racquet Club,
Palm Springs, April 22, 1949

Joan, Christina and Christopher at the Clyde Beatty Circus, May 25, 1948

The Damned Don't Cry (1950) with Steve Cochran

Flamingo Road (1949)

Harriet Craig (1950) with Wendell Corey

Joan scolding Christopher, aged 9, after he ran away from home in April of 1951

Sudden Fear (1952) with Jack Palance

Rehearsing for *Torch Song* (1953) with director Charles Walters

Johnny Guitar (1954), fording the stream with Sterling Hayden

Johnny Guitar with Mercedes McCambridge

Female on the Beach (1955) with Jeff Chandler

WW   LGC

Joan married Alfred Steele on May 10, 1955

Joan, Steele, and her four adopted children, the "twins" Cynthia and Cathy, 9, Christopher, 13, Christina, 16, sail for Europe on the *Queen Mary*, December 16, 1955   ww

Senator John F. Kennedy receives a citation from Mr. and Mrs. Steele from the National Multiple Sclerosis Society, 1959

Joan, widowed, at Pepsi's Board of Directors meeting, May 7, 1959, with Herbert Barnet (left) and Emmett O'Connell

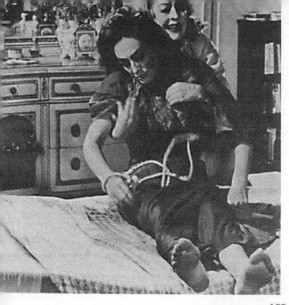

What Ever Happened to Baby Jane? (1962) with Bette Davis as Baby Jane and Joan as Blanche, her imprisoned sister

LGC

Baby Jane: "Blanche, I was cleaning the cage this morning and the parakeet got out."

LGC

Blanche beached and expiring at the end of Baby Jane

LGC

Strait-Jacket (1964)

Berserk (1968) with knife-wielding Judy Geeson

Trog (1970), Joan's final film appearance

Joan replacing daughter Christina for four episodes of the daytime television drama *The Secret Storm*, in October 1968

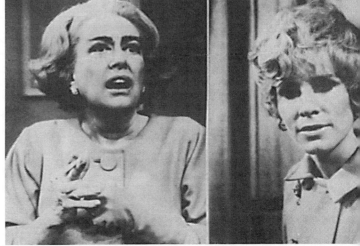

Giving a party for Rosalind Russell on September 23, 1974 —her final public appearance

Joan's last portrait

On the day after the magazine appeared, Unkefer entered the *Baby Jane* set with trepidation. He first passed the Davis dressing room and heard a stern voice: "Linn, come here!"

"Good morning, Bette," the publicist said cheerfully.

She waved the *Time* magazine at him. "Did you have anything to do with this?" she demanded.

"Yes, Bette, I did," he admitted.

She snorted. "She's five years older than me if she's a day."

Unkefer next passed the Crawford dressing room. "Could I see you a moment, Linn," she asked sweetly.

"Good morning, Joan," the publicist said, noting a copy of *Time* on the makeup table.

"Is this some of your work?" Joan asked.

"Yes, Joan."

Joan smiled. "Well, we're off to a good start, aren't we?"

Both actresses viewed their roles competitively, as was their nature. Joan realized that Bette had the more flamboyant role; thus she herself would underact and aim for sympathy. She felt it was a good change of pace for her, since she had all too often played the bitch herself. The wheelchair would be an excellent prop for her as the crippled Blanche, and she would use the prop in any way she could.

Bette realized she would be "flying on gossamer wings" as the pathological Jane Hudson. She had to perform a number of grotesque scenes, even having to imitate the child actress singing "I've Written a Letter to Daddy." How far should she go? The woman in her rebelled at making Jane appear too unappealing, and she resisted the bizarre makeup and painted mouth that Aldrich wanted. Then she said, "What the hell," for if she were to succeed as Jane, she would have to play her full-force, and in stark contrast to Joan's wan but still-glamorous appearance. Bette reasoned that "Jane never washed her face, just added another layer of makeup each day." Having been an assistant director in his early career, Bob Aldrich knew how to keep a production moving. The *Baby Jane* company moved swiftly from one location to another, and neither star complained. Davis took as much pride in her professionalism as Crawford. Both were always prompt, and neither grumbled about the primitive facilities at the Producers' Studio, a ramshackle lot used for small-budget westerns.

Crawford and Davis always maintained sets that were open to the press, and the *Baby Jane* stage attracted a stream of correspondents. One day I recorded this dialogue:

Davis: Of course you know, Joan, that everybody is trying to work up a feud between us.

Crawford: I know, dear, and isn't that ridiculous? We're much too professional for anything like that.

Davis: Exactly! Who has time for such silliness? We're much too busy making the picture.

Crawford: Of course.

Davis (guffawing): You know what the word is around New York? The situation here is so bad that your dressing room is at one end of the stage, and mine is at the other end. Now, I ask you, look at those dressing rooms! [They were twenty feet apart.]

Crawford: You know the only reason I'm over there is that I like to be near the cooling machine. It's probably too cold for you.

Davis: Oh, no! I adore it cold. I'm liable to move over there with you.

Crawford: And we'll end up the picture with our rooms side by side, fooling everyone.

Davis: I'll tell you one thing I hope this picture does: I hope it brings back women's pictures. The men have had it to themselves too long. But I must admit we women had it pretty good for fifteen years back there.

Crawford: We sure did. But now everything is war and destruction on the screen.

It was a convincing performance by two legendary actresses. The display of felicity persuaded everyone, perhaps even themselves. But it couldn't last. Inevitably, the spirit of competition entered their relationship; both were exceptionally competitive women. They competed in everything—in their interviews, in their performances before the camera, in their relationships with the cast and crew.

Joan had only one scene with Victor Buono, in which he discovers the crippled Blanche cruelly tied to her bed and near death. Joan had completed her part of the scene, had removed her makeup and was ready to leave the stage. Then she learned that Aldrich was filming a close-up of Buono's reaction. She put her costume back on, placed a veil on her head and returned to the set. She lay on the bed until Buono completed his close-up.

Bette's performance required a great deal of physical exertion. In one mad scene she had to whirl Joan around in the wheelchair, and she even lifted it off the floor. Another scene called for Jane to carry her sister from the bedroom. Playing the cripple, Joan made her body a dead weight, and Bette was strained under the exertion. As soon as Aldrich said "Cut!" Bette screamed in pain and bellowed profanities. She had hurt her back and required four days to recover. Aldrich managed to continue filming without her.

The difference in style was noticeable. As Buono observed, Joan always arrived on the set "looking as though she had just stepped out of the back of a limousine." She became the drab Blanche in her dressing room, but as soon as the day's shooting had ended, she resumed the role of Joan Crawford, and swept through the stage door like a star.

"You should see the way Bette dresses at the studio," Joan confided to a friend. "She walks around in bedroom slippers and an old ragged terry-cloth robe with makeup stains on the collar!" She resented Bette's proprietary attitude toward the *Baby Jane* project. After all, it was she who had pestered Aldrich for years to find a costarring vehicle for the two actresses. Now, Joan complained, Davis was acting as if the idea were hers.

Joan became suspicious of Bette's relationship with Bob Aldrich. After all, he had been Joan's director first, and now Bette seemed to be claiming him. Joan recognized that the Davis style probably appealed more to the burly director. Bette had a lusty laugh and became buddies with directors she liked, whereas Joan always treated them deferentially, like surrogate fathers.

As was her custom, Joan ordered a Pepsi-Cola cooler to be installed on the set, and it was stocked with bottles that were free to the company members. Aldrich had long been friendly with executives of Coca-Cola, and he asked them to send a supply to the *Baby Jane* set. Joan retaliated by ordering a giant Pepsi-Cola dispenser for the stage, accompanied by a tall stack of cartons.

The director was able to avoid a clash between Davis and Crawford until the final days of the strenuous schedule. He was filming a climactic scene in the bedroom with Jane tormenting her weakened sister. Joan had been suffering with a tenacious cold, and after several takes she asked Aldrich, "Could we have a break for a few minutes, please? I feel terrible."

Bette, who had aroused herself for the emotional scene, retorted, "You'd think after all these years we'd all be troupers."

Joan stared at Bette coldly for a moment, then walked off the set. Aldrich took Bette aside for a pacifying chat, and there was no further collision. Filming ended September 12, 1962, on schedule.

Aware that he had something extraordinary in *What Ever Happened to Baby Jane?* Aldrich assembled the film and was able to preview it thirty days later. The Seven Arts and Warner Brothers executives recognized a potential smash hit and scheduled a mass release in November. Bette agreed to tour New York City theaters on opening day to help stimulate attendance, and while Joan declined, she appeared at a press party at "21." The two stars received reporters at opposite ends of the room. At one point Bette climbed atop a table and bawled, "Everybody down here!"

What Ever Happened to Baby Jane? fulfilled everyone's hopes. Within eleven days of nationwide release, the film recovered its production cost of $825,000.

Some of the critics recognized Crawford's contribution. Paul V. Beckley wrote in the New York *Herald Tribune:* "If Miss Davis' portrait of an outrageous slattern with the mind of an infant has something of the force of a hurricane, Miss Crawford's performance could be described as the eye of that hurricane, abnormally quiet, perhaps, but ominous and desperate." But the majority of reviewers and audiences were overwhelmed by the audacious performance of Bette Davis, and she was nominated for an Oscar in 1963. Joan Crawford was not among the four other nominees. "I want this Oscar," Davis declared. "I want to be the first star to win three." She continued her appearances for *Baby Jane,* visiting Jack Paar on the *Tonight* show. She commented: "I must say we are gloating. When Aldrich tried to interest the studios in Joan Crawford and myself, the moguls said, 'We wouldn't give you a dime for those two old broads.'" Joan Crawford sent a message to Davis: "Please do not refer to me that way again."

As the April 8 date of the Oscars approached, Davis was astounded to learn that Crawford had volunteered to accept the best-actress award if the winner was absent. Such a gesture seemed traitorous to the Davis cause, and Bette was certain that Crawford was scheming against her.

Backstage at the Santa Monica Civic Auditorium, Joan took over the largest dressing room and installed two Pepsi-Cola coolers filled with liquor. She played hostess to performers on the televised show, serving drinks and hors d'oeuvres. Bette paced nervously backstage awaiting the designation of winner for best actress. She stood in the wings as the announcement was being made. Her old friend Olivia de Havilland held her hand.

"The winner is Anne Bancroft for *The Miracle Worker*."

Bette felt a hand on her arm. "Excuse me," said Crawford as she strode past Bette and crossed the stage amid heavy applause. It was a moment Bette Davis would never forget.

What Ever Happened to Baby Jane? accumulated a gross of nine million dollars and brought new vitality to the careers of Joan Crawford and Bette Davis. Quite naturally, Robert Aldrich wanted to reteam the two stars, and he found the opportunity in a four-page outline of a new story by Henry Farrell, author of *Baby Jane*. The plot concerned an aging recluse haunted by the specter of her childhood sweetheart, who had been beheaded by an unknown murderer. Originally the title was *What Ever Happened to Cousin Charlotte?* but Davis objected vigorously to the cash-in on *Baby Jane*, so it was changed to *Hush . . . Hush, Sweet Charlotte*.

This time there was no need for a tight budget. Twentieth Century-Fox financed the film for Aldrich's company, and an expert cast was assembled: Joseph Cotten, Mary Astor, Agnes Moorehead, Cecil Kellaway, Victor Buono, Bruce Dern, George Kennedy, Ellen Corby. Instead of shooting at locations around Los Angeles, Aldrich took the entire company to an antebellum mansion in Baton Rouge. Crawford and Davis would be paid $200,000 apiece.

Crawford arrived accompanied by her entourage of secretary, makeup man and maid. She seldom ventured out of her suite at the Belmont Motel, except to travel to the location. She and Bette had only one scene together in Baton Rouge, a long shot of Davis watching from above as Crawford entered the mansion. Otherwise they were never together. *Life* magazine had sent a photographer to record the return of the *Baby Jane* stars, and he had the idea of posing them in an old graveyard. The publicist, Harry Mines, was faced with the duty of asking the two women to pose on tombstones. Davis roared with laughter at the suggestion and readily agreed. Crawford disliked the idea, but she would never refuse a reasonable proposal from a publicist, especially her old friend, Harry Mines. The two actresses posed for the photographer without a word to each other. Later the *Life* man told Mines, "I'd like to do the layout again with color film. Would you ask Bette and Joan?"

"Not on your life!" the publicist replied.

Crawford remained in her dressing room on the location. When she was called for a scene, she was always slightly late, a rarity for her. Davis slouched around the set in blue jeans, chatting with members of the cast and crew. The tension between the two stars was evident in Bette's comments. She complained about how Crawford had made more money from *Baby Jane* because she had taken less cash and a bigger percentage of the profits, and about the Pepsi-Cola cooler that Joan had placed prominently on the set. She sometimes referred to Crawford as "Bless-you." "I hope 'Bless-you' doesn't insist on working in subzero temperature when we get back to the studio," she said.

Bob Aldrich had been able to avoid the confrontation at the location, but trouble began as soon as the company returned to Fox studio. The two stars spoke to each other only when in front of the camera, and set workers wondered when the clash would occur.

When Aldrich rehearsed one scene with the two actresses, Davis snapped, "My God, is that the way she's going to play it?" Joan said nothing. She was well aware of the pressure that was building, and she was afraid to make a move. It was a rare time on a movie set when she felt out of control. From *Mildred Pierce* on, she had been able to exert her power by one means or another. Now she felt powerless. She had never before encountered an adversary as steel-willed as Bette Davis. Joan suspected, with good reason, that Aldrich favored Davis as an actress and as a person, and realized that Bette had a much better role in *Sweet Charlotte*.

As often happened in times of stress, Crawford became ill. She was admitted to Cedars of Lebanon Hospital with the symptoms of high fever, lowered blood count and bad cough. The disease was reported as an "upper respiratory virus infection."

Aldrich and Fox faced a severe problem. Aldrich continued filming scenes without Crawford, but soon he would need his costar. Production was costing $50,000 a day, and although insurance would absorb part of the loss caused by Crawford's absence, if she remained unable to perform for an extended period a catastrophe could result. Joan's condition improved, and she was able to return to the studio. Aldrich worked a short day with her, but she experienced a relapse and returned to the hosptial.

"Either replace Joan Crawford or cancel the picture entirely," the insurance company instructed Aldrich and Fox. Obviously Aldrich wanted to continue. But who could replace Joan Crawford? Aldrich favored Katharine Hepburn or Vivien Leigh, but Davis would not approve. She wanted her old friend Olivia de Havilland, but Olivia was reluctant to play a murderess, and Aldrich had to fly to Switzerland to convince her.

Joan received a telephone call in the hospital from Dorothy Manners. "What do you think about Olivia de Havilland replacing you in *Hush . . . Hush, Sweet Charlotte?*" the reporter asked.

"What?" Crawford could not believe it. She had made seventy-seven movies, and she had never been replaced. And to do it without telling her!

"I cried for nine hours," she told a reporter the next day. "I still believe in this business, but there should be some gentleness. . . . I think it takes a lot of guts to make pictures, and I'm going to make a lot more of them. But I'm going to make them with decent, gentle people." She added: "I'm glad for Olivia; she needs a good picture."

Bette was livid over the Crawford statements. "The widow Steele has had her say, now I'll have mine," she told a publicist. She issued a statement welcoming Olivia to the movie and expressed regret over Miss Crawford's "reported" illness. Bette appeared at the airport to greet Olivia.

Joan retired to Palm Springs to recover her health and her morale. One night at Don the Beachcomber's she encountered a friend who had risen from the mail room of MCA, John Foreman, now a film producer. He was with Judy and Tony Franciosa, and Joan invited them for drinks at the house where she was staying. She left them in the living room and returned in a green silk pantsuit, brushing her long auburn hair. She was still hurt over the *Sweet Charlotte* replacement, which she considered a plot by Bette Davis to favor her friend Olivia.

"It was a marvelous role, and I could have done great things with it," said Joan, and she proceeded to recite her lines from the entire script.

She never forgave Bob Aldrich, and not until very late in life was she able to forgive Bette Davis.

23

CRAWFORD CONTINUED to make films and television programs through the 1960's, but she never recaptured the prestige and success of *What Ever Happened to Baby Jane?*

The Caretakers was a personal film by Hall Bartlett, dealing with mental illness. Joan had admired his work, dating from his film about an Indian boy, *Navajo*, ten years before. *The Caretakers* offered Crawford only a subsidiary role as head nurse at odds with a crusading doctor (Robert Stack), but Joan was interested in the theme and eager to work. When she arrived on the set for the first time, the film workers applauded. Joan threw up her arms and proclaimed: "It's so wonderful to be back! You're my life!"

Joan spent little time with the younger members of the cast, especially Polly Bergen, who had been a star of Pepsi-Cola television commercials and a protégée of Alfred Steele. But Joan had compassion for Herbert Marshall, who represented the Old Hollywood to her. He was desperately sick and drinking heavily, and Joan helped him through their scenes together. She had requested Bartlett to film her close-ups first—"My whole career has been built on close-ups"—but in her scenes with Marshall she asked the director to shoot his close-ups before hers.

Crawford treated her director to a unique experience: a visit to Pickfair. They were friends now, Joan and Mary, after all those years. Joan could never forget the hurt of being made to feel like an outsider, of knitting through the unbearable Sunday afternoons when the two Dougs were off playing golf and Mary was upstairs taking her nap. But the painful memories had mellowed, and Joan could admire Mary for what she had achieved. Mary had been the first great female star of films, and almost single-handedly she had managed a magnificent career. In later years Mary and Joan had met for lunch at Pickfair and had enjoyed exchanging Hollywood gossip as well as bittersweet memories of their mutual pasts.

Joan and Hall Bartlett drove in the limousine up the long, tall hill to the white mansion, Joan sipping her vodka from a glass wrapped in a napkin. When she arrived at Pickfair, she carried the glass inside, and she handed a bottle of 100-proof Smirnoff to the butler so her supply would be replenished during the evening. Joan introduced Bartlett to the other guests, most of them old and distinguished members of Hollywood society, and there was unspoken speculation about whether Mary would appear. Finally she did, standing at the top of the staircase shimmering in jewels. She came unsteadily down the stairs, a petite, still-beautiful woman, and her eyes brightened as she saw Joan.

Mary held out her arms and murmured, "Joan, darling, welcome to Pickfair."

Strait Jacket (1964) continued Joan Crawford's descent into the *grand guignol*. She played an ax murderess in the film by William Castle, who had achieved fame by dangling skeletons over audiences and wiring seats with electrical charges. Joan was paid $50,000 and a percentage of the profits, which were considerable, but the film seemed to lower her reputation. Castle used her again in *I Saw What You Did*, giving her top billing but killing her off early in the film.

Berserk (1968) provided a happy return to England, where the press had bestowed upon her the title of Her Serene Crawfordship. The British film crew adored her. She left the Grosvenor House at five in the morning and arrived at Shepperton studio in time to cook breakfast for early crew arrivals. She entertained members of the entire crew and their wives at a lavish dinner at the Grosvenor House. Pepsi-Cola was free on the movie set, of course, but the workers had to return their empty bottle to get another one. "You'd be surprised how much money we lose on unreturned empties," Joan said.

Her producer on *Berserk* was Herman Cohen, who had risen from a Detroit theater usher to make low-budget horror movies in England. He was the ideal producer for Joan Crawford—attractive, attentive, single. No romance developed between them, but Joan became possessive.

Once during the filming Cohen received a telephone call at two in the morning: "Herm, have you got your script in front of you?"

"Joan, I'm sleeping!"

"Well, get your script. I've got some things I must discuss with you." The producer realized her loneliness and spent as much time with her as he could afford from his business. He took her to dinner and to the London theater, and she was always dressed to perfection. When he tried to convince her to put on slacks and attend a weekend movie matinee, she balked. "I would never let anyone see me like that," she said.

When J. Paul Getty came to call at her hotel, Joan insisted that Cohen should be present—"it'll be good for you to know Getty." When Joan couldn't reach Cohen, she demanded, "Where were you last night? Were you out with a girl?" He told her to "cut out the goddamn nonsense."

Cohen knew Joan's drinking habits, since he carried her flask when they went out. Before entering a theater, she always determined the location of a nearby bar—she would never drink at the theater, where she could be observed by the other playgoers. Between acts she hurried to the bar and ordered glasses and ice from the bartender, then poured from the flask. She paid the bartender a couple of pounds and sipped her drink until it was time to return to the play. "I'll make a deal with you," Cohen told her before filming started. "On the picture you can never drink in the morning, and you can never drink without first getting your producer's permission." Crawford agreed, and she adhered to her promise. When Cohen asked why she didn't quit altogether, she declared that her drinking was not a problem. "I'm just a sipper," she said. "It makes me feel good." The vodka also gave her courage before a television appearance, a challenging scene, a presentation to the Queen.

Berserk was a lurid tale of murder in the circus, and while it offered little to challenge Joan's dramatic talent, she was still able to display her commendable figure in a leotard as ringmistress. "What about these?" she said, exhibiting her breasts to her producer. "And no operations on 'em, either." She wore her own clothes in the film—"Save your money, Herm; I've been hustling clothes all my life"—but she asked that Edith Head design the leotard.

Trog (1970) was the last of Crawford's eighty-one movies. She was sixty-three, but she photographed superbly. Gossip columnists claimed that she had had a face lift, but she hadn't yet; a few years later she had surgery to remove the wrinkles around her eyes. On *Berserk* and *Trog* she enjoyed the services of a gifted hairstylist named Ramon Guy, who had worked with other aging stars such as Marlene Dietrich and Edith Evans. For Crawford he devised six "lifts"—tapes connected behind the head by rubber bands—which stretched the skin and erased wrinkles.

Trog was a monster picture filmed on a budget so low that portable dressing rooms were not sent on location. Joan huddled in a car parked on an English moor and did not complain. Why would Crawford, who had invented "star treatment," submit to such conditions on a film that could not possibly add luster to her career? First, she wanted to act; it was her life. As she once said, "They were calling me 'The Last Movie Queen.' I'm no queen. I started as a hoofer in the chorus line, and by hard work and good breaks became, I hope, an actress." Also, she needed the money. Pepsi-Cola was paying her $50,000 a year with additional perquisites, but that was not enough for her to live like Joan Crawford. When no more movies were offered to her, she continued to pursue television.

The idea seemed like a good one. The writers of Lucille Ball's television show proposed a script with Joan Crawford as guest star. The plot would have Lucy and Ethel (Vivian Vance) breaking down in their car and stopping at the first house for help. They would discover Joan Crawford scrubbing floors in a house devoid of furniture. The two visitors would presume that the great actress was down on her luck, not realizing that she had a penchant for cleanliness and had disposed of her furnishings to redecorate. Lucy and Ethel would then devise a program to raise money for the destitute Joan Crawford. An ideal Lucille Ball script, but would Crawford go for it? The word came from the William Morris office—Crawford would.

Joan arrived at the Desilu studio with her usual entourage, and

Lucille Ball was indulgent and amused. But she became alarmed, then incensed as the rehearsals began. Lucille was accustomed to the precision enforced by a weekly television schedule. It required a steady progression from first reading to rough rehearsal, to camera blocking, to dress rehearsal, and finally performance before an audience with what might prove to be a minor comic masterpiece. Crawford seemed totally incapable of such discipline. Her early readings were tentative and humorless, she displayed an inability to memorize lines, and the mention of a live audience filled her with terror. And she was drinking.

Mutterings behind the camera. Urgent calls to William Morris. Lucille Ball grew more impatient. Crawford drank more.

"Get Gloria Swanson!" Lucy exclaimed.

Joan called her friend Herman Cohen in a panic. "They want to get rid of me. What shall I do?"

"Don't leave!" Cohen instructed her. "The worst thing you can do is leave. If you stay, they can't replace you." Joan stayed. She managed to stumble through the rehearsals, and prepared herself for the live performance with great trepidation. As soon as she made her first entrance, the studio audience gave her a standing ovation. Her eyes widened, and she thrust her shoulders back. She hurtled through the script, delivered every comic line with mastery, and never missed a cue or a word of dialogue. At the end she received another standing ovation. "Joan, you were terrific!" Lucille said afterward. "Can you join Gary [Morton, her husband] and me for dinner?"

Joan had invited the rest of the cast and the crew members to a celebration at Don the Beachcomber's. "Thank you," Crawford replied imperiously, "but I have an engagement."

Steven Spielberg didn't know whether to laugh or cry. He had just been told that he would direct his first television movie with Crawford in the starring role. He recalled seeing *Mildred Pierce* and *Baby Jane*, but he knew little about her except that she was a legend. Steven Spielberg was twenty-one years old.

Rod Serling had written a pilot script for a series to be called *Night Gallery*. Crawford had been hired for $50,000 to play a blind woman whose sight is restored on the night of New York City's 1965 blackout. Spielberg called her at the Hollywood apartment she maintained for film assignments. Crawford sounded exuberant about the role but concerned about the dialogue. "People just don't talk that way," she said perceptively. She suggested they discuss the problem over dinner.

Spielberg bought the book of *The Films of Joan Crawford* and studied it from cover to cover. Learning of the star's penchant for punctuality, he arrived at her apartment precisely at eight.

"Come in, Steven," said the warm, throaty voice. He opened the apartment door and peered inside. At first he didn't see her, and then he was startled to find her standing behind the couch with a mask covering her eyes. He watched in astonishment as she stumbled about the room, bumping into furniture, holding out a protective hand as she moved. "This is how a blind person walks through a room," she said. "I'm practicing for the role. How difficult it is without the benefit of sight! You feel lost in a world of blackness. I've got to do this on the set, Steven. I need to practice with the furniture two days before we shoot so I'll be able to let my eyes go blank and still find my way around like a blind person."

She removed the blindfold. Her huge eyes blinked in bewilderment as they gazed for the first time on the man who would be her director. Her smile froze as she studied the smooth, beardless face. "Hello, Steven," she said, offering a brave hand.

"Hello . . . Joan," he replied, wishing that he could escape.

"Goodness," she said, "you certainly must have done something important to get where you are so soon. What films have you directed?"

"Uh, none."

"No films at the studio?"

"No, ma'am."

"Then . . . ?"

"Well, I did make a movie that the studio liked. That's why they signed me."

"Oh? And what was that?"

"It was, uh, a twenty-minute short I made at Cal State, Long Beach."

"At school."

"Yes."

She looked at him quizzically. "Do you happen to be the son of anybody in the Black Tower?" She referred to the executive building of Universal Pictures and MCA.

"No, ma'am. I'm just working my way through Universal."

She laughed. "Steven, you and I both made it on our own. We're going to get along just fine! C'mon, let's go to dinner."

At the Luau, a Beverly Hills restaurant long favored by the movie crowd, Crawford was greeted like a duchess. "So nice to have you back, Miss Crawford." "Right this way, Miss Crawford." "Your usual drink, Miss Crawford? And for the young man?"

Spielberg muttered, "I'll have a fruit punch, please."

Crawford drank her vodka and kept the conversation going, asking about her young director's background and interests. "I guess about the only thing we have in common is that we're both members of the Pepsi generation," he remarked. Her thunderous laugh could be heard above the clamor of the busy restaurant.

Even though forty years separated them, Crawford and the young man spent the evening conversing like contemporaries. He told her of his dreams to be a filmmaker, she told him of the happiness she had known with Al Steele. When they parted she gave him assurance: "Now, I know what television schedules are, and I know the pressure that will be on you to finish the show on time. You'll want your first work as a director to be something you can be proud of, and I'll break my ass to help you. Don't let any executive bug you because the picture's not on schedule. If you have any problems with the Black Tower, let me take care of it. I'll be your guardian angel. Okay?"

"Okay," Spielberg responded with a wide smile.

While preparing for *Night Gallery*, Spielberg studied Crawford's films: *Mildred Pierce, Reunion in France, Torch Song, What Ever Happened to Baby Jane?* His assessment: "She is five feet four, but she looks six feet on the screen. In a two-shot with anyone, even Gable, your eyes fix on her. She is imperious, yet with a childlike sparkle. She is haughty, yet tender. She has no great range as an actress, yet within the range she can perform better than any of her contemporaries."

The schedule called for one day's rehearsal, seven days' shooting. Spielberg arrived early for his first day as a director, and when he opened the stage door he was blasted with a gust of cold air. The temperature was at fifty-five degrees in accordance with Crawford's contract, and crew members who had worked with her before were wearing overcoats.

At precisely 8:45 Joan Crawford walked through the stage door, wrapped in a fur coat. She was followed by her makeup man, hairdresser and wardrobe woman, then three men bearing portable coolers. Inside were dozens of bottles of Pepsi-Cola packed in ice. She began introducing herself to unfamiliar members of the crew, and by the end of the day she could repeat the first names of all fifty.

The first day's work went badly. Even such experienced actors as Barry Sullivan and Tom Bosley had difficulty with Serling's lines, and for Crawford the dialogue was an ordeal. She was rarely less than letter-perfect in remembering her lines, yet she stumbled again and again. She realized that the schedule for the television film would not permit delay, and her concern grew. So did Spielberg's. He knew that his bosses in the Black Tower were more interested in maintaining the schedule than in achieving quality, and he feared that both would elude him. If he failed on his first assignment, would he ever have another?

Barry Sullivan made a timely suggestion: write Crawford's lines on cue cards and place them off-camera. Even though she wore eye bandages, a thin layer of gauze would allow her to read the dialogue. The device improved the pace of filming, but Spielberg was falling steadily behind schedule. He himself was partly responsible. Since it was his first film, he declined the standard television formula of medium shots followed by "Ping-Pong" close-ups. He insisted on choreographing complicated camera movements which he believed would heighten the suspense, and he also spent considerable time on a scene to introduce Crawford in a regal way. "I want to present her to the audience for the first time like an *objet d'art*—or a Stutz Bearcat in a show window." The solution was to open with a shot of the back of a thronelike chair. Then a bejeweled hand pressed a button on the chair arm and the chair swiveled to face the audience, placing Crawford on view.

After two days of shooting Crawford became at ease with the dialogue and no longer required the cue cards. Spielberg also grew more relaxed, and he could enjoy directing her. He especially liked scenes of movement. He admired the cool calculation of her walk— legs straight, back stiffly erect, shoulders back. He was also fascinated by her affinity for the camera. Instead of pushing the camera toward her, he sought the effect that she was drawing the camera to her. Spielberg noticed that in the medium shots Crawford often held back. But when he called for the close-up, a generator within her seemed suddenly switched on. She glowed as the camera focused on her, and if Spielberg liked the take, she seemed ecstatic. She could always tell by the tone of his voice whether he *really* liked it or was merely saying "Cut—print!" in order to meet the demanding television schedule. If he seemed halfhearted, she said, "Oh, Steven, don't you think we can do a better one?"

Despite the difference in their ages, Joan treated Spielberg as she did every other director. She sought his counsel, deferred to his judgment. Realizing that some members of the crew would consider a twenty-one-year-old directing Joan Crawford as a bizarre joke, the pair decided early in the filming not to discuss filming problems before others. If he needed to consult with her, Spielberg told his star, "I'd like to discuss this privately." He possessed the youthful wisdom that he should never say he did not like something she did. Instead he always suggested, "Do you think it would be better if you . . . ?" They developed a rapport. Every day she found in her dressing room a single red rose in a Pepsi bottle, a gift from Steven Spielberg. She gave him an engraved bracelet, cologne. One day she startled him by finishing a Pepsi-Cola and emitting a large belch.

"Oh, that's what you should do, to show you enjoyed it," she explained. "Go ahead—you burp, too."

"But I can't," he said.

"You can't?"

"No, I never learned how to burp."

"Why, you poor boy! I'll teach you." And she did.

The pace of shooting was improving, and Spielberg was hopeful that he could make up time and meet the mandatory seven-day schedule. But one day Joan fainted. Her ailment was diagnosed as an inner-ear infection, and her doctor insisted on a one-day rest. She returned looking wan, but was eager to continue. Spielberg was asked if he would come to her dressing room for a talk about the next scene. When he arrived, he found her lying on the couch, stomach-down, the script opened before her. A doctor and a nurse were in the room.

"Steven, I wonder if we could switch a couple of lines in this next scene," Crawford commented as she turned the script pages. While she continued the discussion, her pants were lowered by the nurse, and the doctor administered an injection into the shapely Crawford behind.

Before she left the set that evening, she told Spielberg, "Tomorrow I really need your help, Steven."

"How do you mean?"

"That scene where I take off the bandages and see for the first time. It scares the hell out of me. That may be the most important shot in the picture, and I simply don't know how to do it."

"We'll work it out, Joan, don't worry," he said reassuringly. "The important thing is for you to get a good night's rest."

It was a familiar Crawford technique: to emphasize her total reliance on her director. She had received her training in silent films, when actors were indeed subject to their director's control, responding to his insistent commands as filming was in progress. Crawford never lost that need for the firm, parental voice of authority, even when the director was young enough to be her grandson.

On the following day Spielberg was badgered by the Universal production office, who demanded to know why filming was progressing so slowly. The director devoted all his time to completing a sequence so the stage could be released for another television company. He was within a half-hour of his goal when the assistant director suggested he meet with Crawford in her dressing room.

"Later," said Spielberg. "I've got to finish with this set by six."

"I think you'd better talk with Joan," the assistant said firmly, "or else you may not be able to finish with the show."

Spielberg left the set and knocked on Joan's door. He found her with tears streaming down her face.

"You have let me down," she sobbed. "I rarely ask anyone for help, but this time I needed it—badly. I asked you last night if you could spare some time today to help me with the scene where I am able to see. Now, here it is, the end of the day, and you haven't talked to me. You know how important that moment is. If the audience doesn't buy it, then the whole picture fails. And I don't know how to do it! I'll be embarrassing to watch. You won't like me, I won't like me. It will just be a godawful mess!"

The sobs shook her whole body, and Spielberg took her in his arms. "Joan, dear, I'm sorry," he said. "It was stupid of me to get so tied up with meeting that damned schedule that I forgot about what was most important. We'll take care of it right now. You stay right here, and I'll be back in a minute."

Spielberg instructed the assistant director to dismiss the company, even though the single scene remained. Spielberg returned to Joan, and they sat together for an hour, discussing the scene in great detail. He conjured every insight he could manage from his knowledge of the script and character. At the end he assured her, "Now I'll be there tomorrow, and I'll hold your hand. I don't care what the production office says. I'll give you any number of takes until we get it on film just the way you and I believe it should be."

He was painstaking the next day, calling for take after take until Joan was satisfied. The shot lasted less than five seconds in the film, but the experience proved an invaluable lesson for the young man—the director's responsibility for his actors.

Night Gallery extended two days over schedule, causing grave concern in the Black Tower. Spielberg didn't direct for a year, but later he went on to direct such successful features as *The Sugarland Express, Jaws* and *Close Encounters of the Third Kind*. They never met again, but Crawford followed Spielberg's career closely and sent periodic notes of congratulation. The last one came two weeks before her death.

Joan's daughter Christina left home to pursue an acting career. When she was advertised as "Joan Crawford's daughter" in an off-Broadway play, Joan became furious. She suggested that Christina change her name, and Christina refused: "It's the only name I've ever had."

When Christina couldn't find roles, Joan arranged a job for her as a receptionist in the New York office of MCA. Christina found she couldn't work there and seek acting jobs, so she quit. Joan cut off her daughter's allowance, and Christina struggled on her own and began to work in summer stock and on television. She secured steady employment on a daytime television serial, *The Secret Storm*. In 1966 Christina married a director, Harvey Medlinsky, and Joan attended the wedding. All the bitterness and recriminations between mother and daughter seemed to have vanished.

By 1968 Christina's marriage had crumbled and she became suddenly ill. When she had to be hospitalized for an abdominal operation, Joan telephoned Gloria Monty, director of *The Secret Storm*. "What about Tina's contract? Will she lose the role?" Joan asked.

"No, of course not," replied Gloria Monty. "It's not like the movie studios in the old days. I'll have to find another actress to fill the role until Tina can return."

"Gloria, I'll play it," Joan announced.

The director was astounded. Joan Crawford in a soap opera! "Are you sure?"

"Yes, I'll do it. If it would help Tina, I'd do anything."

Fred Silverman, chief of daytime programming at the CBS television network, was delighted with the news, and he cleared the use of a studio for rehearsals on Saturday and taping on Sunday. Gloria Monty went to Joan's apartment on the night before rehearsal and found her in a state of excitement.

"I know this character like this," said Joan, snapping her fingers. "It's Mildred Pierce!"

"Okay, let's not talk too much; let's just read the scene," said the director. She was amazed at how adroitly Joan fell into the character, and at the subtlety she lent to the soap-opera dialogue.

Crawford had asked that no publicity be issued, but of course her appearance was too tempting for the network publicists. When Joan arrived for the Saturday rehearsal, members of the press were waiting for her at the CBS studios, contributing to her growing nervousness.

"Now, Joan," said Gloria Monty, "for the rehearsal we'll have no set, just a suggestion of the scenery."

Joan shook her head. "I need walls, baby. I need furniture. I need to know where things will be."

A makeshift set was improvised, and Joan moved through the rehearsal with more confidence. Her morale was boosted when Fred Silverman arrived at the studio to thank Joan for her gracious gesture. He was certain her appearance would elevate the rating of *The Secret Storm*, and he assured her that the event would be handled with dignity: a simple announcement of the substitution would be made before the broadcast so that viewers would know why the character was being played by an actress thirty-five years older than the regular cast member.

On the day of taping, Joan grasped Gloria Monty and said desperately, "I'm in your hands." Joan's chauffeur had brought the Pepsi-Cola cooler with vodka, and Monty strove to keep Crawford on the set so she wouldn't drink too much. At one point the director replaced the vodka in Joan's glass with water, and when Joan took a sip she bawled, "Who the hell touched my glass?"

Monty watched helplessly from the control booth as Joan's performance deteriorated through the day's taping. All the precision that Joan had displayed while rehearsing the scripts in her apartment was gone. When Joan missed her cues or failed to hit her marks, the director covered by announcing, "Sorry, I made a boo-boo in here. Could we try it again?"

They worked all day and into the evening, piecing together scenes that would later be interspersed into the continuity of the serial. It was hard work for both actress and director, and when the final scene arrived, Joan took Gloria's hands and implored, "Baby, help me now."

Crawford completed her work on the show. She had suffered the ordeal for her daughter, just as Mildred Pierce had sacrificed for Veda. But meanwhile Joan had appropriated the acting role of a daughter who was struggling desperately to establish her own identity as an actress. From the hospital, Christina's reaction was restrained. "I couldn't exactly jump up and down in bed about it, but it was fantastic she would care that much."

Crawford's consumption of vodka had become prodigious. All of her acquaintances became accustomed to the ever-present flask. At "21," where she dined almost exclusively when in New York, the 100-proof Smirnoff was always at the table when she arrived. It was poured over ice, and although she was meticulous in her table manners, she stirred the drink with her finger. In other restaurants she sometimes depleted her own supply of vodka and ordered from the bar. Waiters cringed when Crawford took a sip and announced like an expert, "This is not one-hundred-proof; take it back!"

Billy Rose once invited Joan to drive from New York to Washington for a government ceremony. They traveled in the producer's Rolls-Royce, and Joan astounded Rose by consuming a quart of vodka on the trip south, and later that day, another quart on the return to New York. Banquets and formal dinners were a peculiar hazard. She bolstered her nerves with drinks before arriving, and continued pouring from the flask during the meal. At one memorable New York banquet she rose from her seat and served dessert dishes to those sitting on the dais. "This is how I worked my way through school," she explained.

An unfortunate result of Joan's drinking was her giving way to certain obsessive fears, including her fear of competition from younger women. In 1967 Crawford was invited by Lyndon Johnson to a White House dinner at which members of the Supreme Court and their wives were guests. Among them were William O. Douglas and his twenty-three-year-old bride, Cathy.

Joan had been drinking heavily, and she began to verbally snipe at the pretty young wife of the associate justice, who was sixty-eight years old. Whatever Cathy Douglas said about conservation and the environment was belittled by Joan, who also attacked the young woman's appearance and background. When Mrs. Douglas was talking to a tablemate and did not see a waiter place a finger bowl before her, Joan reached across three guests and planted the bowl firmly on a doily, where etiquette dictated it should be. "That's the way we do it!" Joan said emphatically.

Mrs. Douglas looked up in surprise. "Uh, thank you," she stammered.

Joan had reached across Joseph Califano, a presidential assistant, and he came to Mrs. Douglas' defense. So did others at the table, including Interior Secretary Stewart Udall and Sol Linowitz, ambassador to the Organization of American States. When the incident was published in Washington social columns, Mrs. Douglas was quoted as saying, "That was the first time I'd ever been insulted in Washington. Up to now everyone has been so nice."

Joan told reporters in Los Angeles: "I've never heard of anything so ridiculous. I have not even met Mrs. Douglas. I didn't attack her. Besides, who the hell am I to criticize anyone? I was a waitress from the time I was nine." Even among friends Joan could not understand why such a fuss had been raised. "When I was first at Metro, I was happy when anyone corrected me," she said.

Herman Cohen paid a visit to Joan's New York apartment. She greeted her producer affectionately and led him toward the kitchen. Cohen saw a white-haired, emaciated figure in a wheelchair. The face was hauntingly familiar, and Cohen whispered, "Who is that?"

"It's Franchot," Joan replied. "He's dying. I bring him over here, and I cook dinner for him and we talk."

They had become good friends. Crawford had offered him sympathy and support during his scandal-ridden marriage to Barbara Payton, and he had hurried to her side after the death of Alfred Steele. Joan and Franchot often dined together at Don the Beachcomber's in Hollywood and "21" in New York, and he told her,

"You are the only real, the only beautiful thing that ever happened in my life." Once while she was making *Strait Jacket* at Columbia, she was called to the telephone and heard Franchot's voice: "Will you marry me, Joan?" He realized by her silence that the answer was no.

During their marriage, Franchot had often talked about Muskoka Lake in the Canadian woods, where his family had owned a lodge since his boyhood, but Joan and Franchot had always been too busy to go there. In 1966 Franchot invited her for a vacation at the "Lake of Bays," and she was able to arrange her schedule to go. Joan lay in the sun while Franchot and his brother fished from a motorboat. At night Franchot read Shakespeare aloud and played Mozart on the phonograph.

The following year Franchot had a lung removed because of cancer. In 1968 Joan was appearing on *The Mike Douglas Show* in Philadelphia when a call came from Franchot's son. Franchot had died. Joan arranged to have his last wish fulfilled: his ashes were scattered over the woods of Muskoka Lake.

Joan Crawford returned to Stephens College in 1970 to receive the first President's Citation given to a former student. The award was "in recognition of her achievement in varied roles expected of the women of today, for her distinguished career as creative film actress, as businesswoman, as homemaker and mother, and as philanthropist."

It was the first time in forty-eight years that Joan had seen Stephens, and she was flooded by memories—of being rejected by the sorority because she waited tables, of dancing with the rich boys at the fraternities, of the scene with Daddy Wood at the station when she tried to run away. But she declined to reminisce for the student audience; instead, she played the actress, businesswoman and authority:

"I got where I am," she said, "not just by ambition, but by the desire to do my best—in roles, in my appearance, in interviews, in everything." She always seemed so assured, so self-confident.

The Balboa Bay Club on the southern coast of California honored Joan Crawford as Woman of the Year at a banquet to benefit a charitable hospital. A former governor of California bestowed the award. Claire Trevor presented a toast, Jimmy Durante played the piano and sang "Inka Dinka Doo." Documentary producer David Wolper presented a film tribute with clips ranging from *Our Dancing Daughters* to *What Ever Happened to Baby Jane?* "Butch" Romero escorted Joan, and John Wayne was in the crowd. Crawford cajoled him into joining her on the platform.

After all the speeches, Joan retired to a bedroom in the club, where she had planned to stay the night. An old friend who had once directed Joan in a film was a guest in the club. He telephoned her and she invited him to her room.

She served him champagne on the balcony overlooking the shimmering bay. She talked gaily about the evening, her travels, and they gossiped about mutual friends. Then suddenly she began to cry.

"What's the matter, Joan?" he asked. "You're lonely, aren't you?"

Her back stiffened. "I don't allow myself to feel lonely."

"But you are. Don't you have a man?"

"How can I? I'm on the road most of the time. I'm not interested in one-night stands, which is what I get offered. You don't know how people try to use me."

"I doubt if they would ever succeed."

"Oh, sure! Tough-as-nails Crawford. Well, sometimes I don't feel so tough. Sometimes I feel like Billie Cassin. Scared to death."

V

Alone: 1972–1977

24

ALFRED STEELE ONCE SAID: "The whole trick in hiring executives is to find a good man and turn him into a prick. A good man would be able to stand the course, but if a guy is a prick to begin with, he'd crumble along the way."

Steele found Donald Kendall and helped him rise from a route salesman to vice-president in charge of the international division. Like Steele, Kendall had been a football player, considered himself a self-made man and knew how to use people to his advantage. One of Kendall's close friends was Richard M. Nixon—so close that Nixon played piano at the reception for Kendall's second wedding. As Vice-President and later as President, Nixon proved helpful to his friend Don Kendall: cameras flashed when Nikita S. Khrushchev downed a Pepsi, and Leonid I. Brezhnev chatted with Kendall for hours in the Kremlin. In return, Kendall proved useful to Richard Nixon in raising campaign funds.

It was inevitable that two such dominant individuals as Joan Crawford and Donald Kendall would clash. It first happened in Nairobi, where Al Steele and Joan had flown as part of their mission to open Africa to Pepsi-Cola. Unlike other stops on the African tour, the visit to Kenya was badly organized. While Al Steele was elsewhere, Joan excoriated Kendall for the fiasco and demanded that he make amends. "Why the hell should I take orders from a goddamn actress?" Kendall responded, and he and Joan glared at each other. It was a scene that Kendall would not forget.

Nor would he forget the excruciating embarrassment of the incident at the Stork Club, when Kendall and other Pepsi executives were paying court to the wife of the board chairman. She spotted Ernest Hemingway across the room and cajoled, "Don, would you be a dear and go ask Mr. Hemingway to join our table? I'd like so very much to meet him." Kendall obediently crossed the room and conveyed the message, and Hemingway responded for the benefit of those nearby, "Tell her to bring her ass over here if she wants to meet me."

If Al Steele had lived, Crawford might have been able to convince her husband that Don Kendall was not in her opinion the best person to assume the responsibility of Pepsi-Cola. But Steele was succeeded by Herb Barnet, who felt otherwise. Kendall envisioned Pepsi-Cola as a potential conglomerate, and in 1965 Pepsi-Cola merged with Frito-Lay, manufacturer of snack foods. The corporation became PepsiCo, Incorporated, and a new board of directors was established minus Joan Crawford Steele, although she remained on the board of the subsidiary Pepsi-Cola Company. Herb Barnet, board chairman of PepsiCo, asserted that Mrs. Steele's undivided attention was needed at Pepsi-Cola "and we are a little selfish about that."

Kendall may have thought he had finally rid himself of Joan Crawford, but it was not so. Even though PepsiCo went on to acquire Wilson Sporting Goods, North American Van Lines and Monsieur Henri wines and beverages, Kendall still found he was introduced at cocktail parties as "the man with Joan Crawford's company." Meanwhile Kendall had erected the world headquarters of PepsiCo in Purchase, New York, occupying a seven-building complex designed by Edward Durell Stone on 141 acres. But every day mail arrived addressed to "Joan Crawford, President of Pepsi-Cola."

Wherever Kendall went it was the same. When he appeared at a press conference with Joan in New Orleans, he became visibly annoyed because all of the questions were directed at her. A publicist for PepsiCo asked a reporter, "For God's sake, would you please ask Mr. Kendall about the company's finances?" "Who gives a shit about him?" replied the reporter, returning his attention to Joan Crawford.

Joan delighted in such occasions, realizing Kendall's antagonism toward her. The feeling was mutual. As the enmity developed, she concocted her own name for Kendall. She called him Fang.

"Fang would like nothing better than to get rid of me," Joan remarked to a junior executive of PepsiCo.

"Joan," he replied uneasily, "I don't think it's a good idea to call Mr. Kendall 'Fang.'"

"Bullshit, I'll call him what I like. God only knows what he calls me. But I've been called plenty of things in my day; that doesn't bother me. It's true, isn't it, that he'd love to get me out of the picture?"

"Well, I guess you know that he's concerned that Pepsi-Cola is considered your company."

"I've worked hard enough for fifteen years that it should be. And if he makes a move to ease me out, he'll have the fight of his life!"

"Don't press him, Joan. That's one fight you can't win."

After the years of opening bottling plants from San Diego to Buenos Aires, of representing Pepsi at the Miss America pageant in Atlantic City and the Kaiser Cookout in Honolulu, Joan found she was being asked to do less and less.

No movie offers had come since *Trog*. She could still find work in television, and in August 1972 she returned to Universal to appear in an occult series, *The Sixth Sense*. Again she was the woman in jeopardy, and the episode was entitled "Dear Joan, We're Going to Scare You to Death."

The hour-long show paid $2,500, but Joan went in her customary style. A long black limousine took her from her bungalow to the stage to the projection room for the "dailies" (she still called them by the older Hollywood term, "rushes"). Her dressing room was a greenhouse of plants, and the visits from Lew Wasserman, Rock Hudson, and Alfred Hitchcock sent her maid, Mamacita, scurrying around to serve snacks and drinks. Joan had also brought Princess Lotus Blossom, her tiny Shih Tzu dog, along with piddle pads she had purchased at Bloomingdale's store in New York. She demonstrated them for visitors: "Tinkle, Princess." Princess tinkled precisely on the pad.

Joan had asked for a camerman she had worked with before, Enzo Martinelli. When the studio balked, she argued, "Look, I'm

253

no longer an ingenue; I need someone who knows how to light me." Martinelli was assigned to the show. She explained to him that she had recently had a tooth capped and it had been a bad job; the color differential worried her. "Don't worry, Joan," said the cameraman, "I'll take care of it."

For the benefit of the publicity man, Robert Palmer, she went through the ritual of creating Joan Crawford. At first she seemed small and fragile, a woman on the brink of old age. The transformation came before the mirror, as makeup was applied with deft strokes. The years vanished, and she seemed almost like Letty Lynton again. Except for under the chin, but she knew how to deal with that. As the lights were being focused before the camera, she called to an electrician, "Do something about that light, George; I'm a little hot under here." She patted beneath her chin, and the sag disappeared in shadow.

Palmer watched the scene. By sheer concentration and bodily tension that seemed to emerge from her diaphragm, she began to sob convulsively. She was portraying the terror of a woman who was an asthmatic and was struggling for breath.

When the scene was finished, Palmer was so moved that he started to walk away. He heard a voice call, "Bob!"

He turned and saw Crawford staring at him.

"What?" he said.

"How was I?"

"Incredible."

"Say so!"

During another scene in the seven-day schedule, Joan stood before a window watching a girl drown. Joan gazed in horror and then shrieked the girl's name in a cry that rang through the stage. "Cut!" said the director, and everyone remained silent for a moment. Then the set erupted in applause. "Thank you," said Joan with downcast eyes.

At the end-of-filming party Joan was exhilarated and slightly drunk. Yet she remembered the names of every member of the crew and their wives (all in the company would later receive personal letters of thanks). She told everyone, "I loved working with you; I hope we can do it again."

Joan was still glowing when the limousine drove her, Mamacita and Princess through the Universal gate. Joan realized anew how much she loved the studio life, even after forty-seven years. There was nowhere that she felt more alive, more loved, more fulfilled.

It was her last performance.

John Springer, a New York publicist and inveterate movie fan, scheduled a series of tributes to Legendary Ladies at Town Hall in 1972. The appearances of Bette Davis, Sylvia Sidney and Myrna Loy had proved successful, and Springer asked Joan Crawford to join the series. At first she said she couldn't bear to face an audience, but she agreed to appear as a personal favor to Springer.

The date was set—March 8, 1973—and Joan proceeded in customary style. Unlike the other three actresses, she would not entertain questions directly from the audience; she would answer anything, but the questions had to be in writing. The other women had left the selection of film clips to Springer; Joan wanted to know exactly what was to be shown.

Joan looked superb—diamond earrings, reddish hair in a woven chignon, shining black gown slit to the knee—and she was petrified.

"Johnny, I can't do it, I can't go on!" she stammered.

"Sure, you can, Joan," Springer said reassuringly. "Didn't you hear the applause every time you came on the screen? They love you, Joan. Come on."

He took her by the hand and led her to the wings. The montage of still portraits concluded and the stage lights went on. "I can't do it!" Joan said just as Springer pushed her into the spotlight. She hesitated, then threw back her shoulders, and, breasts high, walked to center stage with the familiar Crawford stride.

Fifteen hundred people rose to their feet to cheer and applaud. Joan seemed startled, like a small girl at a surprise birthday party. Members of the capacity audience rushed down the aisles and stood before the stage, wildly applauding. A shower of daffodils fell onto the stage, and the cheering rose in volume as she picked up the flowers, one by one.

When the ovation finally died down, she murmured, "I never knew there was so much love." Applause again.

Springer read questions, and Joan's responses were brief and humble. She gave credit to her designers, Adrian and Edith Head; to directors George Cukor, Clarence Brown, W. S. Van Dyke; to costars Gable, Tracy, Taylor, Stewart—"I'm the luckiest woman in the world to have had the career I've had."

To the delight of the audience, she reiterated her explanation for Gable's greatness: "He had 'em." Would she raise her children the same way she had? "Yes. I believe the reason most of the kids are on pot and other junk is because they don't have enough love or discipline at home." Her adjustment to a career as an executive? "I sold Joan Crawford for so long, all I have to do is let Joan Crawford sell Pepsi-Cola." Her reaction to being named "box-office poison" in 1938? "I was desolate, really. I thought, well, I'm through."

Joan said forthrightly, "I love competition. Competition is one of the great challenges of life. We must have competition or we don't grow." But the scars of past competitions remained. Of Norma Shearer and *The Women:* "She was married to the boss, and I was just an actress. She didn't like my dress, and she changed it nineteen times. But I ended up wearing the gold dress and turban." When she remarked, "Bette Davis in *Baby Jane* was one of the greatest challenges I ever had," the audience erupted in knowing laughter. "I meant that kindly," Joan added quickly. "Bette is of a different temperament than I. Bette has to yell every morning. I just sat and knitted. I knitted a scarf from Hollywood to Malibu."

She couldn't forget the replacement on *Hush . . . Hush, Sweet Charlotte.* In her single off-guard moment of the evening, she snapped that Robert Aldrich "has many, many insecurities," and went on to accuse him of all sorts of things. But she quickly restored the onstage image. Outside on Forty-third Street, two hundred young men surrounded her limousine and refused to let it proceed—a touching replay from the 1930's. Joan was tearfully delighted.

Later she told Springer: "That was one of the greatest evenings of my life. And I'll never go through it again."

Joan could no longer afford the luxurious apartment on Seventieth Street. She was still earning $50,000 a year from Pepsi-Cola, plus a liberal expense account, but her income from acting had evaporated, and she did not want to expend more of her savings than was necessary. Besides, the apartment was too big for her. Both of the twins were now married, and in fact, they had never even slept in the apartment. Joan and Al had rebuilt their home with no room for children; the girls lived at a nearby hotel with a governess.

Joan found an apartment at the Imperial House at 150 East Sixty-ninth Street, and made preparations to move. On her last night on Seventieth Street, Joan invited Gloria Monty to stop by for a drink. Gloria and her husband had become friends with Joan after she substituted for Christina in *The Secret Storm*.

Gloria arrived at eight and found Crawford in a morose state. She had been drinking, and she continued to sip vodka as she reminisced about how she and Al had constructed the apartment. "My bed was so big they had to bring it through the window," she recalled. "I don't know how the hell the movers are going to get it out." She seemed compelled to share her memories, and she talked about Doug and her ordeal at Pickfair. And Franchot, who had exposed her to art and literature and music. At midnight Gloria tried to leave, but Joan insisted that she stay. Crawford talked about religion and how her understanding of God comforted her amid her sense of increasing disappointment.

Finally at one A.M. Gloria made her exit. In parting, Crawford bestowed a tribute on a fellow achiever: "You're a strong, strong woman. But ten years ago I would have made mincemeat out of you."

"Fang did it! That son of a bitch Fang did it!"

Joan Crawford read the news in the New York *Times*. Her friend publicist Michael Sean O'Shea had telephoned her on Saturday afternoon and told her to buy a copy of the Sunday *Times*. On page one of the financial section was the news that Joan Crawford was being retired by Pepsi Cola in 1973 when she reached the official age of sixty-five. She was stunned. She felt that a part of her life had been shattered, for she had devoted eighteen of her best years to the company, often to the detriment of her acting career. She had performed unflaggingly with an intensity that exhausted those around her.

She had been the recipient of the sixth annual Pally award to the Pepsi-Cola employee making a significant contribution to company sales; her bronzed Pepsi bottle stood beside her *Mildred Pierce* Oscar in her trophy case. To millions of people around the world, Joan Crawford was Pepsi, and Pepsi was Joan Crawford. That, of course, had long disturbed Donald Kendall.

Crawford was devastated. Her $50,000-a-year salary would continue as a lifetime pension, but she would no longer have her $40,000 annual expense account, including limousine service in Manhattan, $1,500 monthly allowance for her apartment, $12,000 a year for her secretary, and $40 a week for her hairdresser. And Pepsi-Cola summarily dropped her access to the company telephone line, with which she could call anywhere in the country without charge.

"That goddamn Fang!" Joan raged.

When her retirement became known throughout the Pepsi-Cola organization, the bottlers wanted her to be the guest of honor at their 1974 convention in San Francisco. Mitchell Cox, the Pepsi public-relations chief, had organized a program that would salute the achievements of Joan's career and her contributions to the success of Pepsi. Several of her friends and figures from her career had been asked to be present and surprise Joan with a "This Is Your Life" program. What could the bottlers present to Joan as a token of their appreciation? They bought a rare handwritten letter from Sarah Bernhardt. Crawford never received it. She refused the invitation to appear at the convention.

Mitchell Cox tried to persuade her. "I've never known anyone who loathed surprises as much as you, Joan, so I'll tell you what we've planned," he said. Even after he described the tribute, she was adamant.

"I'm not going," she said. "I worked my ass off for the company for almost twenty years, and now they have washed me up. Well, screw 'em."

Crawford had to learn to live without Pepsi. And without Hollywood as well. She was happy to see oldtime movie friends when they passed through New York, but she was no longer concerned about her career. She didn't understand the new industry, with its parade of themes that were forbidden by the Hays Office during her heyday, and with a corporate structure now dominated by men who had once been lawyers, accountants and agents, including her own.

The press was different, too. Hedda and Louella had gone, and there was a new breed of reporter she didn't understand. She had always been free and open with interviewers, and usually they had presented her favorably. But now, though she continued to give reporters her best and brightest quotes—after thousands and thousands of interviews, Joan never allowed herself to seem bored—they were ridiculing her.

Joan began to withdraw. She wasn't selling Pepsi or promoting movies or television shows, so why set herself up for young reporters who wanted to make names for themselves by pulling down monuments? The interviews became less and less frequent.

She found plenty to do. Her correspondence alone was enough to occupy her full-time.

The Crawford letters had become as much of a trademark for her as the Adrian padded shoulders and the scrubbing of floors. Each month she mailed between five thousand and ten thousand of the light-blue notes with the simple heading JOAN CRAWFORD. They were addressed to Pepsi dealers, television stars whose performances she had admired, fans who had remained loyal for forty-five years. She wrote to old friends, new friends and, occasionally, enemies. Christmas was an extraordinary binge. She sent six thousand greetings, the majority of them with a personal message, typed or handwritten. Joan replied with a thank-you note for every Christmas card she received. And if the recipient happened to write thanks for the thank-you, another note came from Joan. She employed two full-time secretaries, one in New York and one in California, to handle the volume. Every letter was signed by Joan personally, and many contained handwritten postscripts. Her closest friends received notes written entirely in longhand.

Joan's relations with her two youngest children remained close. Cindy now lived in Iowa, Cathy in Pennsylvania, and Joan talked to them often on the telephone. When her daughters had babies, Joan refused to be referred to as a grandmother; the children were her "nephews and nieces."

Christina had once again fallen out of favor with her mother. Both women were strong-willed, and Joan expected the same obedience she had exacted when Christina was a child. But Christina was no longer a child; she was in her thirties and striving to establish a life of her own.

Joan would not discuss Christopher. She felt she had done everything possible for him, and now he was on his own. She knew that her son had served in Vietnam, and she hoped that experience would help "straighten him out." There were reports that he had settled down as a carpenter on Long Island, that he had established a family.

One day Christopher appeared with his wife and child at the Imperial House. He told the doorman that he had an appointment to see his mother, Joan Crawford. The doorman telephoned the apartment. Christopher was instructed to wait. After an hour he asked the doorman to telephone Miss Crawford again.

"I'm sorry," the doorman said, hanging up the telephone. "Miss Crawford says she doesn't want to see you."

Although she complained about the polluted air and would not go on her apartment terrace because of it, her existence became more and more centered within the nine rooms of her New York apartment, a world she could keep immaculate and orderly. The place was decorated in shades of green and bright yellow, giving an impression of a California garden. The living area was devoid of remembrances of Joan's acting career—"I hate Hollywood people who live surrounded by memories." Her only concession was a bronze bust of herself sculptured by Salamunich in the 1930's.

After forty years, "21" remained her favorite restaurant. She always arrived by limousine, and she always let the management know she was coming. One night William Dozier had made a reservation and called for Joan at her apartment. As they drove away, Joan dialed the limousine telephone for information. "Would you give me the number of the restaurant "21," please?" she asked.

"But, Joan, we're only a few blocks away," Dozier remarked.

"That's all right. I want them to know we're on our way."

The "21" employees and owners were always ready for the Crawford entrance. She swept through the door and up the stairs, calling everyone by name. Her table was always in the upper room facing the stairs, where she could see and be seen by everyone. Her usual order was a medium-cooked steak covered with butter.

She was always stunningly attired. Leonard Spigelgas escorted her to "21" and marveled at how a large red picture hat gave her face such an attractive radiance. "Why the fuck do you *think* I wear it?" she replied.

Joan always had dinner early, conscious that she looked her best before the evening wore on. She insisted that she had to be home by ten to see her favorite television show, but her friends accused her of a Cinderella complex. She smiled, but she was always home by ten. Any change in her routine perturbed her. She was scheduled to dine at "21" with Leo Jaffe, president of Columbia Pictures, and his wife, Irving Mansfield and Jacqueline Susann, and Jaffe agreed to bring the limousine. At the last minute a driver was not available, and Jaffe did the driving. Joan pouted all the way to the restaurant. "What does she want me to do—wear a chauffeur's cap?" Jaffe grumbled.

Like other New Yorkers, Joan had become apprehensive about the city's crime. She rarely answered the telephone herself. After the secretary had left for the day, she put the telephone on an answering service. Or, if she answered herself, she often responded like a Southern maid: "Miz Crawfode isn't heah raht now; who is callin'?" Her friends recognized the disguise, others did not.

She became increasingly concerned about the chances of burglary or kidnapping. In 1974 she received a telephone message threatening her life. Police theorized that the threat was related to reports that PepsiCo was negotiating to buy a brewery, and Joan was petrified with fear. FBI agents guarded her apartment house for weeks, and nothing suspicious occurred. But Joan never overcame the fear. She spent $3,500 on sophisticated locks and a security system that would prevent any stranger from reaching her apartment.

Crawford began to withdraw more and more. She telephoned Stan Kamen at the William Morris Agency and told him, "There isn't much for me to do in pictures or television anymore, so why don't we just cool it? I love all you guys; you've been wonderful to me. But I'm just not terribly interested in working unless it's something I couldn't possibly resist."

She began paring down her correspondence. Her Christmas letter of 1974 went to many of her friends with the surprising message: "With the economy and the world situation as they are, next Christmas and thereafter, the time and energy I spend greeting each of you will be devoted instead to the charities which are so important to the less fortunate people, especially children, of the world. This, I believe, is the true meaning of Christmas."

Joan enjoyed seeing old friends, especially women. She had always liked the company of men and savored competing with them on their own level, but she couldn't really trust them. She had been disappointed by men too many times, including her four husbands. In interviews she continued to romanticize about her marriage to Al Steele ("He was the greatest lover I ever knew"), but privately and after a few drinks she complained, "The son of a bitch left me nothing but debts." When a friend playfully accused her of being a millionairess, she snapped, "I would be—except for four husbands."

Dorothy Manners visited Joan from California. Joan's old friend from the Cocoanut Grove days had succeeded Louella Parsons as the syndicated Hearst Hollywood columnist. Joan served Bloody Marys and cooked a brunch of Mexican food, which the two women adored. As Joan spread a hot sauce and powdered chili over the *huevos rancheros*, she said, "Only a couple of dames like us who were born in Texas could eat this food for breakfast and not die."

Joan didn't need to dress up for Dorothy Manners. She wore a yellow smock, her long hair tied back, with no makeup to hide the Crawford freckles. The two women sat before the huge window and talked nostalgically until daylight swept the panorama of Manhattan. Joan remarked that she was grateful for the past but couldn't live in it. "You don't see any photographs around here of me as a glamor girl, do you?"

Of the new breed of star she declared, "I feel so sorry for them. They seem to derive no joy, no real pleasure from what they're doing. They ignore their fans, they don't want to give interviews, they seem to feel guilty about being stars. They consider it dross. Well, believe me, Dorothy, it's not dross, it's gold. Pure gold."

In September 1974 John Springer planned another of his Evenings with Legendary Ladies, with Rosalind Russell as the lady. Springer asked Joan Crawford if she would act as hostess at a party at the Rainbow Room to honor Miss Russell, her costar of *The Women*.

"I'm really not going out much anymore," Joan said.

"It would mean so much to Roz," said Springer. "She hasn't been well, you know."

"All right, I'll do it."

Joan was the first to arrive at the Rainbow Room, and she made certain all the arrangements were satisfactory. Resplendent in red chiffon and diamonds, she posed for every shot requested by photographers, signed autographs on napkins and envelopes, greeted each of the guests.

Shortly before midnight, Joan said to Springer, "Have I lived up to everything expected of me?"

"And more so, Joan," said the grateful publicist.

"Then may I leave now?"

"Certainly, Joan." Having performed her duty, she left.

Roz Russell had been suffering from arthritis, and the drugs she used for treatment had distorted her lovely face. Under the glare of the flashbulbs Joan knew she herself did not look her best. The newspapers and magazines chose to print photographs that made the faces of both stars resemble grotesque masks. Crawford was wounded. "If that's the way I look," she remarked, "I won't be seen anymore."

No more public appearances. She would go out to dinner with friends, but as the months wore on, it became more difficult to make an engagement with her. Irving Mansfield, whose wife, Jacqueline Susann, had died, suggested dinner.

"Sounds fine," said Joan. "Why don't you get a limousine and we'll go to '21.' "

"That's such a big production, Joan. Why don't we just walk around the corner to that Chinese place?"

"You mean just walk right in off the street?"

"Sure, why not? Do you want to have dinner or don't you?"

"I think not."

Leo Jaffe and his wife made several dinner dates with Joan, and each time she canceled. "I'm working from five in the morning until eleven at night on my correspondence," she said.

The financial pinch continued, and Joan moved from the nine-room apartment on the twenty-second floor of Imperial House to a five-room apartment down the hall. She disposed of much of the furniture, giving her fourteen-foot dining table to her friend Cardinal Cooke for St. Patrick's Cathedral.

Joan admittedly was becoming more reclusive. She told her friend Peter Rogers, "Look, I've spent my whole life being told what to do. Now I have time to learn who I am."

Any residual loyalty Joan may have felt for Pepsi-Cola was destroyed with the appearance of an *Esquire* article by Robert Scheer about Donald Kendall. Scheer placed Joan Crawford among the things that Kendall didn't want to talk about, along with his first wife, the resigned President Nixon and Coca-Cola sales. A Kendall associate was quoted: "He took an awful lot of crap from Joan Crawford."

"Fang strikes again!" said Joan. She was devastated that her contributions to Pepsi would be so rudely dismissed.

Joan's circle of friends grew smaller. She talked on the telephone twice a day to Michael Sean O'Shea, who had been a Crawford admirer from the early 1930's. Joan became good friends with her neighbors at Imperial House, Curtis and Anne Anderson, and Selma and Martin Mertz.

Joan often called Anne Anderson to come to her apartment for advice on cooking, but often she seemed to call out of loneliness. One day after Joan had moved to the smaller apartment, her belongings were in a heap and she picked up a photograph album of her children. She described each photograph to Anne, and she dwelled on Christina as a child. "Yes, I was strict," Joan said. "But I didn't want to coddle my children. I wanted them to be independent, as I had been."

She talked about child actors she had known at MGM, especially Judy Garland. Had Judy's death come from suicide or an accidental overdose of pills? If it was suicide, Joan had no sympathy. "That's the coward's way out," she argued. "I believe that human beings can conquer almost anything. Everyone should make the most of his life."

Selma and Marty Mertz occupied the apartment across the hall from Joan's, and they became good friends. Joan was so comfortable with the Mertzes that she would come to dinner without makeup, wearing only a caftan and glasses. When the Mertzes went to Joan's apartment, they learned to live by her rules. You accepted a napkin with every drink. You deposited your glass in the kitchen but did not wash it; Joan alone did the washing. Above all, you never tried to tune the television set: "Everyone has his own fine tuning."

Joan was content with her new life. She felt at ease with her neighbors, and she liked to toss out an occasional expletive or outrageous statement for shock value. Most of all, she enjoyed being alone. She had done it all. Her career had lasted longer than any other star's. She had been among the most photographed and most interviewed people in history. She had won the Oscar and succeeded in the business world. For fifty years she had sold Joan Crawford with spectacular success, often at great sacrifice to her life as a woman. What more was left for her? She knew she was finished in films; an actress of her age could expect nothing but roles as mothers or harridans. Perhaps she could eke out a few more roles in television, but cameramen could no longer photograph her the way she envisioned herself. Besides, she was weary of rising before dawn to arrive on the set as the Joan Crawford people expected. For fifty years she had striven to please producers, directors, interviewers, fans. Now she wanted only to please herself.

Joan returned to the faith she had discovered in the 1930's, Christian Science. She had never really abandoned the doctrines of Mary Baker Eddy, but in the struggle to succeed in the worlds of motion pictures and business, she had often lost sight of those teachings. Now they appealed to her more than ever. With her working career over, she needed to sort out her life, to justify the sacrifices and the mistakes she had made. The absolutism of Christian Science was ideal for her. She could believe that disease and evil could be eradicated by God's love. All error was erased in the realization that God is omniscient, omnipotent and omnipresent. Joan was comforted by the belief that her entire being was in the benevolent control of a loving deity.

She went to a Christian Science church in New York—once. "The other people were more interested in what I was wearing than in the service," she complained. Instead of worshiping in public, she sought counsel from a Christian Science practitioner, Mrs. Markham. She was well suited as the spiritual adviser of Joan Crawford, for she was warm, compassionate, knowledgeable of human foibles and of the pressures of being a celebrity, and firm in her belief in the wisdom of *Science and Health with Key to the Scriptures.*

Mrs. Markham invited Joan to meetings of her youth group, and Joan came and sat on the floor and joined in the discussion about God. One of the girls told her father about attending a discussion with Joan Crawford, and he told her, "She was the most beautiful woman I ever saw." When the girl reported it at the next meeting, Joan remarked, "Well, I hope he didn't say that in front of your mother."

Joan often brought food she made to Mrs. Markham. One day Mrs. Markham gave a cup of Joan's potato salad to a girl named Emily. Later the girl said, "I sat in the park eating it and I thought to myself, 'If people going by only knew that I was eating a potato salad made by Joan Crawford!' " When Joan heard about her remark, she invited Emily to visit her. Joan was dressed in a housecoat, but before Emily arrived she decided she couldn't let the girl see her like that. She put on a Halston gown and full makeup.

Tom was sixteen and rebellious. Joan learned at the discussion group that Tom needed work, and gave him a job cleaning and polishing her apartment. "No, dammit, that's not the way to clean a window!" she bawled at him, and showed him how to do it. When he complained about being worked so hard, she told him, "Listen, kid, when I was nine years old, I was working a helluva lot harder than you are." After he finished, she poured him a glass of milk and said, "Now, tell me what's bugging you." He blurted out his antagonisms and she advised him to stop feeling sorry for himself. His friends at Sunday school began to remark on Tom's change.

Joan had changed, too. She stopped smoking and drinking. No more the hundred-proof vodka, no more Dom Perignon. She quit in 1975, and her children and her friends were amazed she could give up longtime addictions. "I realize that drinking and smoking are against Christian Science teachings, so I quit."

"Could you please come up to my apartment?"

Anne and Curt Anderson were surprised by the request from Joan. She had been invited to a dinner party that evening at their apartment. When they arrived at 22H, they were shocked to see Joan with an eye swollen shut as though from a beating.

"What happened?" they asked.

"I don't know," she said. "I was sitting at the table writing notes, and I must have blacked out. The next thing I knew, I was on the floor, and I must have hit my eye on the edge of the table in falling. So you can see, I can't possibly make your dinner party. I'm terribly sorry." The Andersons saw little of Joan after that accident in the fall of 1976. Joan remained inside her apartment all the time. She spent much of her time alone.

On October 28, 1976, Joan signed her will. She bequeathed her personal property to the nearest and most attentive of her daughters, Cathy. To both Cathy and Cindy she left $77,500, to be given in increasing amounts at five-year intervals until they were forty-five years old. To her secretaries, her makeup man, her wardrobe woman, and Michael Sean O'Shea she left amounts varying from $5,000 to $35,000. Whatever remained after the bequests would be divided among the Heart Association, the Muscular Dystrophy Association, the Cancer Society, the Motion Picture Country

House and Hospital, the USO and the Wiltwyck School for Boys, New York City.

And then the unforgiving mother: "It is my intention to make no provision herein for my son Christopher or my daughter Christina for reasons which are well known to them."

The Christmas notes were fewer in 1976, and many bore the message that it would be the last such greeting, that she would devote her energies to charity. To her closest friends she sent a photograph of herself and Princess, which John Engstead had taken in September. Joan had suggested a sitting whenever the photographer visited New York, and he spent an hour in her apartment. Engstead had first photographed Joan in 1944 and many times over the years. This time he found her striving to repeat the tricks she had learned so well, but they didn't work with a woman whose hair was turning white. Engstead sought more natural expressions and tried to get shading in the eyes. These last photographs, which required surprisingly little retouching, show Joan's beauty intact. But there is also something disturbing in the tight-lipped smile, the eyes still large and clear but now familiar with pain.

All her life Joan had refused to burden others with her sorrow, and now she kept her pain private. It had become her constant companion, and hence she never went out and had no visitors. When she talked with friends on the telephone, she always sounded cheerful and busy. "I'm happy to stay home with Princess and answer the mail and watch the soap operas and all my favorite TV shows," she said.

She loved the daytime serials and often spotted promising young performers; she copied their names from the credits and sent them letters of admiration. She liked Walter Cronkite and *Bonanza*; *The Waltons* was her favorite show, partly because it featured her long-time friend, Ellen Corby. Joan even watched the Saturday-morning children's shows.

She also watched Joan Crawford movies, not out of narcissism but as a means of testing her memory about past events. "Watch what Tracy does in this next scene," she would tell Michael Sean O'Shea on the telephone and then she would call him back to explain how it had been filmed. Joan was amused when Carol Burnett presented a parody of *Mildred Pierce*, and she telephoned the comedienne to tell her so.

267

"I'm glad you liked it," said Burnett. "Now we're going to do a takeoff on *Torch Song*."

"Great!" said Crawford. "That was one of my best bad movies." But when she saw the *Torch Song* travesty she found it cruel and grotesque. Nor was Joan pleased when CBS presented the American Film Institute's tribute to Bette Davis.

Joan was cheered by the outpouring of flowers and greetings on her birthday, March 23, 1977, but her health was rapidly deteriorating. A hospital bed allowed her to sit up and watch television with less pain, but her back hurt constantly. Her weight declined as her illness progressed. What was afflicting her? Neither she nor anyone else knew. She would not see a doctor. She would not take any medicine; none was in her apartment, except aspirin. Most likely Joan Crawford had cancer of the liver or pancreas.

"Am I dying?" she asked her practitioner.

"Knowing God is life," Mrs. Markham replied. "The human spirit is like a sunbeam, and God is the sun. Your spirit has to go on—a sunbeam doesn't die. Your spirit is eternal. It doesn't exist in this fleshly body."

Joan thought for a long time, and then she smiled. "That's the first time I could see that," she said.

Her only companions were her housekeeper and a longtime fan from Brooklyn who had attached herself to Joan and ran errands for her. Cathy came for a visit with her husband, Jerome LaLonde, and their two children. Friends like Nancy Kelly and Anita Loos tried to call Joan by telephone but reached only her secretary or answering service. She continued corresponding with close friends in Hollywood, and after the holidays she sent a handwritten letter to Sally Blane, whose husband, Norman Foster, had died in 1976: Joan recalled her loss of Alfred eighteen years before and added that she had been saved from despair by remembering their "glorious experiences and joys together." Her advice to Sally: "Dwell only on the joys."

Joan wrote to Virginia Grey of her life in a smaller apartment. She said she had spent a year finding places for "only the essentials." Joan declared she was "content beyond belief" and had found wisdom in the advice of her lawyer's wife, who had also moved to smaller quarters: "Never love anything that can't love you back."

In April Mitch Cox called from a vacation he and his wife were sharing with a few Pepsi-Cola bottlers in the South. Joan seemed delighted to hear from her companions in the Pepsi crusade, and she talked to ten of them. "Joan, it's been too long since I've seen you," said Cox. "You've been putting me off, but it's time to get together for old times' sake."

"Mitchell, I promise you we will get together," Joan said. "Just give me a call when you get back."

April was the cruelest month, as Joan's strength waned and her weight declined to eighty-five pounds. When a close friend pleaded with her to see a doctor, Joan replied, "I'll be damned if I'll let myself end up in a cold hospital room with a tube up my nose and another up my ass."

By the end of the month, Mrs. Markham was coming to Joan's apartment every day. Joan would not let her tell anyone, especially the children, how ill she was. Mrs. Markham pleaded with Joan to enter a Christian Science nursing home.

"You're not going there to die, you're going there to be healed," the practitioner argued. "You have an obligation to go to a nursing home. You are an important person. You have an obligation to Christian Science."

"No, I will do anything but that," Joan said. "I prefer to be at home."

She sat at her desk, attending to the correspondence until her pain became too great. Then she continued signing the notes on a bed table across her lap. She declined the use of a bedpan, preferring to go to the bathroom.

Joan seemed to have acquired a new kind of gentleness. She was no longer the competitor in a hard world. She could find joy in small pleasures: "What a wonderful day! I got one letter from Barbara Stanwyck and another from Katharine Hepburn, all in the same day!" Joan could even forgive: "I'm so at peace with the world that I'm even thinking good thoughts about Bette Davis and Donald Kendall."

Her neighbors across the hall, Selma and Marty Mertz, were greatly concerned about Joan. They knocked on her door and were surprised when Joan herself appeared. She was pale and she seemed like a tiny replica of Joan Crawford.

"Joan, is there anything we can do?" Mertz asked.

"No, darling, everything is fine," she said with a smile.

Afterward Selma Mertz told her husband, "She's dying; this

269

woman is dying, Marty. We must do something." He replied, "There's nothing we can do. You know Joan. She does everything *her* way. Even dying."

Joan worried about Princess. She could no longer pick up the dog, and she was concerned about what would happen to Princess, who had never known life outdoors. Joan decided to give Princess to a woman who cared for stray dogs and cats and would be certain to provide affectionate care.

On the morning of May 10, 1977, Joan insisted on getting out of bed to make breakfast for the housekeeper and the longtime fan, who had both stayed overnight. Joan returned to the bedroom to begin watching her soap operas, and she called to the two women to make sure they were eating the breakfast she had prepared. Then she died.

A medical examiner attributed the death to acute coronary occlusion. The remains were cremated, as stipulated in Joan Crawford's will, and the urn was placed next to that of Alfred Steele at a cemetery in Ferncliff, New York.

Christina, now Mrs. David Koontz, flew from California for the funeral, and she convinced Christopher to attend, although he hadn't talked with his mother in twenty years. Cathy came from Pennsylvania, and Cindy, Mrs. Joel Jordan, arrived from Newton, Iowa. The funeral was supposed to be private, but two hundred people arrived at Frank E. Campbell's funeral parlor. Among them was Tom, the boy from Sunday school whom Joan had befriended; he had asked Mrs. Markham if he could attend.

Mrs. Markham addressed the gathering:

"As some of you know, our beloved Joan Crawford found great comfort and inspiration in the teachings of Christian Science and embraced the religion for a significant part of her life, as indeed the religion embraced her. It was at the request of her children that a Christian Science service be read for her, and it is a service that emphasizes the continuity and eternality of life, rather than a beginning and an end. You will note from the Scriptures read and the correlative passages from the Christian Science textbook that we strive for a tribute to a courageous and loving life that so expresses the Divine."

A memorial service was held at All Souls Unitarian Church, and fifteen hundred attended. They heard tributes from Cliff Robertson, Geraldine Brooks and Anita Loos. Pearl Bailey sang "He'll Understand" and a minister read "Desiderata."

> . . . Therefore be at peace with God, whatever you conceive him to be. And whatever your labors and aspirations, in the noisy confusion of life, keep peace in your soul. With all its sham, drudgery and broken dreams, it is still a beautiful world. Be cheerful. Strive to be happy.

They stood in line around the block to see Joan Crawford on a warm, uncommonly humid June evening in Beverly Hills, 1977. The line of people swept around the faceless glass tower that houses the Academy of Motion Picture Arts and Sciences. They were Joan's contemporaries, many of them co-workers during her long years in the studios. They filed into the foyer of the Academy, where glasses of California champagne were served, then upstairs to the Samuel Goldwyn Theater.

Kathleen Nolan, president of the Screen Actors Guild, told the gathering that the memorial service "will not have the slightest hint of sadness, for Joan Crawford would not have approved of that at all. She never looked back. Regret was not in her vocabulary."

Then George Cukor, who had organized the evening, read his eloquent tribute:

> . . . She was the perfect image of the movie star, and, as such, largely the creation of her own indomitable will. She had, of course, very remarkable material to work with: a quick native intelligence, tremendous animal vitality, a lovely figure and, above all, her face, that extraordinary sculptural construction of line and planes, finely chiseled like the mask of some classical divinity from fifth-century Greece. It caught the light superbly, so that you could photograph her from any angle, and the face moved beautifully. . . . The nearer the camera, the more tender and yielding she became—her eyes glistening, her lips avid in ecstatic acceptance. The camera saw, I suspect, a side of her that no flesh-and-blood lover ever saw. . . .

271

The theater darkened, and that superb legendary face appeared in an epic montage on the screen, first as an overweight chorus girl in *Pretty Ladies*, wearing an absurd Madame Pompadour wig . . . as a flapper in *Our Dancing Daughters*. Crawford stands above the crowd on the dance floor. The band starts to beat out frenzied syncopation, and Crawford remains motionless as rhythm seems to invade her lithe body. Suddenly she begins to quiver, then vibrate, finally breaking into a whirl of motion, elbows flailing, feet flying. . . . As Crystal Allen in *The Women*. She plays the entire scene in a bubble bath, sparring verbally with Rosalind Russell, each too clever to be wounded. . . . As the rich, bored Helen Wright in *Humoresque*, watching John Garfield hungrily as he plays a violin concerto at a society party. She says to a gigolo, "I'm constitutionally given to enthusiasm about nothing. . . . Be a good boy and wipe my glasses for me." . . . As the tough, self-centered Jenny Stewart in *Torch Song*, dancing a duet with Chuck Walters.

Crawford and Robert Young appeared on the Academy screen in *Goodbye, My Fancy*, he trying to rekindle an old romance. She answers with warm understanding, "You might have had a very good chance, Jim, except that—you see, we only met today." . . . Crawford in a suave, intricate, energetic dance with Tony De-Marco in *The Shining Hour*. . . . The confession scene in *Mildred Pierce*. Joan tells her story in the police station, her broad shoulders swathed in mink, her cheeks outlined by the overhead light: "We lived in a section where the houses were all alike. I was always in the kitchen. . . ."

A clip from *Reunion in France* with John Wayne and Crawford in a taxi on the deserted Champs-Elysées, the Arc de Triomphe painted on an MGM backdrop. . . . Clark Gable reading Song of Solomon to Crawford on a desert island . . . Wally Beery dictating a letter to Flaemmchen while trying to seduce her . . . Crawford as Peggy O'Neal beguiling Robert Taylor on a hayride . . . playboy Franchot Tone telling the *Dancing Lady* chorine: "You think you're a dancer, huh? You'll never be an artist until you find out what life is about."

Then a series of Crawford portraits flashed on the Academy screen. If she had appeared in no movies, the photographs would have made her famous. The broad patrician brow that belied her beginnings, the pencil-line eyebrows, lifted with an air of hauteur, the bones almost visible beneath the sculptured cheeks, the firm, determined chin and the sensuous painted mouth. Most of all, the eyes. Those huge, luminous, omniscient eyes that had known so much agony, not all of it self-inflicted, and the endless, unrealized pursuit of love.

Acknowledgments

The kindness of strangers and of friends is an utter necessity in research-ing a biography of a contemporary figure such as Joan Crawford, and the author has been blessed in that regard. For help in investigating Joan Crawford's early life, I am grateful to fellow journalists Ben King Jr. of the San Antonio *Express-News*; Bill Crawford of the Lawton *Constitution*; and Scott Kraft of the Kansas City bureau of Associated Press; also to Gretchen Merwin of Stephens College; researcher Nancy Thomas; Dore Freeman of MGM; the New York Library of the Performing Arts; the Academy of Motion Picture Arts and Sciences Library; Robert Knudsen and the film library of the University of Southern California; the Los Angeles Public Library, main branch; and to:

Jack Albin	Polly Bergen	Scott Brady
Robert Aldrich	Milton Berle	Mary Brian
William Aldrich	Earl Blackwell	Clarence Brown
Anne Anderson	Dorothy Blair	Helen Gurley Brown
Curtis Anderson	Robert Bloch	David Butler
Dana Andrews	Ann Blyth	Richard Chamberlain
Eve Arden	Eleanor Boardman	Don Christie
Irving Asher	Beulah Bondi	Herman Cohen
Fred Astaire	Margaret Booth	Carl Combs
William Bakewell	Ernest Borgnine	Renée Conley
Hall Bartlett	Orin Borsten	Joseph Cotten
Gregson Bautzer	Don Boutyette	D. Mitchell Cox

George Cukor
Jerry Dale
Royal Dano
Delmer Daves
Olivia de Havilland
Brad Dillman
John Engstead
Dale Eunson
Mia Farrow
George Folsey
Henry Fonda
John Foreman
Sally Blane Foster
Dore Freeman
Harry Friedman
Betty Furness
John Gilroy
Edith Goetz
Ivan Goff
Virginia Grey
Sidney Guilaroff
Ramon Guy
Ben Halpern
William Harbach
Radie Harris
Howard Hawks
Sterling Hayden
Edith Head
Andy Hervey
Dona Holloway
Rock Hudson
Ross Hunter
George Hurrell
Rick Ingersoll
Glenda Jackson
Leo Jaffe
Candy Jones
Stan Kamen
Nancy Kelly

George Kennedy
Florence Kriendler
Peter Kriendler
Madison Lacey
Charles Lang
Sol Leon
Irving Lipman
Jack Lord
Myrna Loy
James MacArthur
Dorothy Mackaill
Joseph L. Mankiewicz
Dorothy Manners
Irving Mansfield
Jacques Mapes
May McAvoy
Tim McCoy
Harold Mendelsohn
Martin Mertz
Selma Mertz
Lewis Milestone
David Miller
Harry Mines
John Mitchell
Gloria Monty
Charles A. Moses
Kay Mulvey
Ken Murray
Jack Oakie
Sheila O'Brien
Robert O'Neill
Michael Sean O'Shea
Robert Palmer
Arthur Park
Eleanor Parker
Harriet Parsons
Buddy Pepper
Joseph Pevney
Otto Preminger

Robert Preston
Leroy Prinz
Anthony Quinn
Bob Rains
Nicholas Ray
Allen Rivkin
Henry Rogers
Peter Rogers
Rosalind Rogers
Cesar Romero
Adela Rogers St. John
Dore Schary
Walter Seltzer
Eddie Sherman
Pete Smith
Steven Spielberg
Leonard Spigelgas
John Springer
Michael Stevens
James Stewart
Howard Strickling
Barry Sullivan
Sheldon Tannen
Ben Thau
Maxine Thomas
Lyn Tornabene
William Tuttle
Linn Unkefer
Nancy Walker
Charles Walters
John Wayne
J. Watson Webb
Milton Weiss
Meredith Willson
Liza Wilson
Betty Young
Robert Young
Albert Zugsmith

APPENDIX A
The Films of Joan Crawford

Note: Writing credits include authors of original material as well as scenarists. Early MGM films usually lacked producer credits.

1925

Pretty Ladies (MGM)

DIRECTOR: Monta Bell
WRITERS: Adela Rogers St. John, Alice D. G. Miller
CAST: Zasu Pitts, Tom Moore, Ann Pennington, Lilyan Tashman, Bernard Randall, Helen D'Algy, Conrad Nagel, Norma Shearer, George K. Arthur, Lucille LeSueur

Old Clothes (MGM)

PRODUCER: Jack Coogan Sr.
DIRECTOR: Eddie Cline
WRITER: Willard Mack
CAST: Jackie Coogan, Lucille LeSueur, Max Davidson, Lillian Elliot, Alan Forrest, James Mason, Stanton Heck

The Only Thing (MGM)

DIRECTOR: Jack Conway
WRITER: Elinor Glyn
CAST: Eleanor Boardman, Conrad Nagel, Edward Connelly, Arthur Edmond Carew, Louis Payne, Vera Lewis, Lucille LeSueur

Sally, Irene and Mary (MGM)

DIRECTOR: Edmund Goulding
WRITERS: Eddie Dowling, Cyrus Woods, Edmund Goulding
CAST: Constance Bennett, Joan Crawford, Sally O'Neil, William Haines, Douglas Gilmore, Ray Howard

1926

The Boob (MGM)

DIRECTOR: William A. Wellman
WRITERS: Kenneth Clarke, George Scarborough, Annette Westbay
CAST: Gertrude Olmstead, George K. Arthur, Joan Crawford, Charles Murray, Antonio D'Algy, Hank Mann, Babe London

Tramp, Tramp, Tramp (First National)

PRODUCER: Harry Langdon Corp.
DIRECTOR: Harry Edwards
WRITERS: Frank Capra, Tim Whelan, Hal Conklin, J. Frank Holliday, Gerald Duffy, Murray Roth
CAST: Harry Langdon, Joan Crawford, Edwards Davis, Carlton Griffith, Alec B. Francis, Brooks Benedict, Tom Murray

Paris (MGM)

DIRECTOR: Edmund Goulding
WRITER: Edmund Goulding
CAST: Charles Ray, Joan Crawford, Douglas Gilmore, Michael Visroff, Rose Dione, Jean Galeron

1927

The Taxi Dancer (MGM)

DIRECTOR: Harry Millarde
WRITERS: Robert Terry Shannon, A. P. Younger
CAST: Joan Crawford, Owen Moore, Douglas Gilmore, Marc McDermott, William Orlamond, Gertrude Astor

Winners of the Wilderness (MGM)

DIRECTOR: W. S. Van Dyke
WRITER: John Thomas Neville
CAST: Tim McCoy, Joan Crawford, Edward Connelly, Frank Currier, Roy D'Arcy

The Understanding Heart (MGM)

DIRECTOR: Jack Conway
WRITERS: Peter B. Kyne, Edward T. Lowe Jr.
CAST: Joan Crawford, Francis X. Bushman Jr., Rockcliffe Fellowes, Carmel Myers, Richard Carle, Harry Clark

The Unknown (MGM)

DIRECTOR: Tod Browning
WRITERS: Tod Browning, Waldemar Young
CAST: Lon Chaney, Joan Crawford, Norman Kerry, Nick de Ruiz, John George, Frank Lanning

Twelve Miles Out (MGM)

DIRECTORS: Jack Conway
WRITERS: William Anthony McGuire, Sada Cowan
CAST: John Gilbert, Joan Crawford, Ernest Torrence, Betty Compson, Bert Roach, Eileen Percy

Spring Fever (MGM)

DIRECTOR: Edward Sedgwick
WRITERS: Vincent Lawrence, Albert Lewin, Frank Davies
CAST: William Haines, Joan Crawford, George K. Arthur, George Fawcett, Eileen Percy

1928

West Point (MGM)

DIRECTOR: Edward Sedgwick
WRITER: Raymond L. Schrock
CAST: William Haines, Joan Crawford, William Bakewell, Neil Neely, Ralph Emerson, Edward Richardson

Rose-Marie (MGM)

DIRECTOR: Lucien Hubbard
WRITERS: Otto Harbach, Oscar Hammerstein II, Lucien Hubbard
CAST: Joan Crawford, James Murray, House Peters, Creighton Hale, Gibson Gowland, Polly Moran, Lionel Belmore

Across to Singapore (MGM)

DIRECTOR: William Nigh
WRITERS: Ben Ames Williams, E. Richard Schayer
CAST: Ramon Novarro, Joan Crawford, Ernest Torrence, Frank Currier, Dan Wolheim, Duke Martin

The Law of the Range (MGM)

DIRECTOR: William Nigh
WRITERS: Norman Houston, E. Richard Schayer
CAST: Tim McCoy, Joan Crawford, Rex Lease, Bodil Rosing, Tenen Holtz

Four Walls (MGM)

DIRECTOR: William Nigh
WRITERS: Dana Burnet, George Abbott, Alice D. G. Miller
CAST: John Gilbert, Joan Crawford, Vera Gordon, Carmel Myers, Robert Emmett O'Connor

Our Dancing Daughters (MGM)

DIRECTOR: Harry Beaumont
WRITER: Josephine Lovett
CAST: Joan Crawford, Johnny Mack Brown, Dorothy Sebastian, Anita Page, Nils Asther, Dorothy Cummings

Dream of Love (MGM)

DIRECTOR: Fred Niblo
WRITERS: Eugene Scribe, Ernest Legouve, Dorothy Farnum
CAST: Joan Crawford, Nils Asther, Aileen Pringle, Warner Oland, Carmel Myers, Harry Reinhardt

1929

The Duke Steps Out (MGM)

DIRECTOR: James Cruze
WRITERS: Lucien Cary, Raymond Schrock, Dale Van Every
CAST: William Haines, Joan Crawford, Karl Dane, Tenen Holtz, Eddie Nugent, Jack Roper, Delmer Daves

Hollywood Revue of 1929 (MGM)

PRODUCER: Harry Rapf
DIRECTOR: Charles F. Reisner
WRITERS: Al Boasberg, Robert Hopkins
CAST: Conrad Nagel, Bessie Love, Joan Crawford, William Haines, Buster Keaton, Anita Page, Karl Dane, George K. Arthur, Gwen Lee, Ernest Belcher's Dancing Tots, Marie Dressler, Marion Davies, Cliff Edwards, Charles King, Polly Moran, Gus Edwards, Lionel Barrymore, Jack Benny, the Brox Sisters, the Albertina Rasch Ballet, Natacha Natova and Company, the Rounders, Norma Shearer, John Gilbert, Laurel and Hardy

Our Modern Maidens (MGM)

PRODUCER: Hunt Stromberg
DIRECTOR: Jack Conway
WRITER: Josephine Lovett
CAST: Joan Crawford, Rod LaRocque, Douglas Fairbanks Jr., Anita Page, Edward Nugent

Untamed (MGM)

DIRECTOR: Jack Conway
WRITERS: Charles E. Scoggins, Sylvia Thalberg, Frank Butler
CAST: Joan Crawford, Robert Montgomery, Ernest Torrence, Holmes Herbert, John Miljan

Joan Crawford

1930

Montana Moon (MGM)

DIRECTOR: Malcolm St. Clair
WRITERS: Sylvia Thalberg, Frank Butler, Joe Farnham
CAST: Joan Crawford, Johnny Mack Brown, Dorothy Sebastian, Ricardo
Cortez, Benny Rubin, Cliff Edwards, Karl Dane

Our Blushing Brides (MGM)

DIRECTOR: Harry Beaumont
WRITERS: Bess Meredyth, John Howard Lawson
CAST: Joan Crawford, Robert Montgomery, Anita Page, Dorothy Sebas-
tian, Raymond Hackett, John Miljan, Albert Conti, Edward Brophy,
Hedda Hopper

Paid (MGM)

DIRECTOR: Sam Wood
WRITERS: Bayard Veiller, Lucien Hubbard, Charles MacArthur
CAST: Joan Crawford, Robert Armstrong, Marie Prevost, Kent Douglass,
Hale Hamilton, John Miljan, Purnell B. Pratt, Polly Moran, Robert
Emmett O'Connor

1931

Dance, Fools, Dance (MGM)

DIRECTOR: Harry Beaumont
WRITERS: Aurania Rouverol, Richard Schayer
CAST: Joan Crawford, Lester Vail, Cliff Edwards, William Bakewell, Wil-
liam Holden, Clark Gable

Laughing Sinners (MGM)

DIRECTOR: Harry Beaumont
WRITERS: Kenyon Nicholson, Bess Meredyth, Martin Flavin
CAST: Joan Crawford, Neil Hamilton, Clark Gable, Marjorie Rambeau,
Guy Kibbee, Cliff Edwards, Roscoe Karns

This Modern Age (MGM)

DIRECTOR: Nicholas Grinde
WRITERS: Mildred Cram, Sylvia Thalberg, Frank Butler
CAST: Joan Crawford, Pauline Frederick, Neil Hamilton, Monroe Owsley, Hobart Bosworth, Emma Dunn, Albert Conti, Adrienne D'Ambricourt, Marcelle Corday

Possessed (MGM)

DIRECTOR: Clarence Brown
WRITERS: Edgar Selwyn, Lenore Coffee
CAST: Joan Crawford, Clark Gable, Wallace Ford, Skeets Gallagher, Frank Conroy, Marjorie White, John Miljan

1932

Grand Hotel (MGM)

DIRECTOR: Edmund Goulding
WRITERS: Vicki Baum, William A. Drake
CAST: Greta Garbo, Joan Crawford, Wallace Beery, John Barrymore, Lionel Barrymore, Lewis Stone, Jean Hersholt

Letty Lynton (MGM)

DIRECTOR: Clarence Brown
WRITERS: Marie Belloc Lowndes, John Meehan, Wanda Tuchock
CAST: Joan Crawford, Robert Montgomery, Nils Asther, Lewis Stone, May Robson, Louise Closser Hale, Emma Dunn

Rain (United Artists)

DIRECTOR: Lewis Milestone
WRITERS: John Colton, Clemence Randolph, W. Somerset Maugham
CAST: Joan Crawford, Walter Huston, William Gargan, Beulah Bondi, Matt Moore, Kendall Lee, Guy Kibbee, Walter Catlett

1933

Today We Live (MGM)

DIRECTOR: Howard Hawks
WRITERS: William Faulkner, Edith Fitzgerald, Dwight Taylor
CAST: Joan Crawford, Gary Cooper, Robert Young, Franchot Tone, Roscoe Karns, Louise Closser Hale

Dancing Lady (MGM)

PRODUCER: David O. Selznick
DIRECTOR: Robert Z. Leonard
WRITERS: James Warner Bellah, Allen Rivkin, P. J. Wolfson
CAST: Joan Crawford, Clark Gable, Franchot Tone, May Robson, Winnie Lightner, Fred Astaire, Robert Benchley, Ted Healy, Gloria Foy, Art Jarrett, Grant Mitchell, Maynard Holmes, Nelson Eddy, Moe Howard, Jerry Howard, Larry Fine, Sterling Holloway

1934

Sadie McKee (MGM)

PRODUCER: Lawrence Weingarten
DIRECTOR: Clarence Brown
WRITERS: Viña Delmar, John Meehan
CAST: Joan Crawford, Gene Raymond, Franchot Tone, Edward Arnold, Esther Ralston, Earl Oxford, Jean Dixon, Leo Carrillo, Akim Tamiroff

Chained (MGM)

PRODUCER: Hunt Stromberg
DIRECTOR: Clarence Brown
WRITERS: John Lee Mahin, Edgar Selwyn
CAST: Joan Crawford, Clark Gable, Otto Kruger, Stuart Erwin, Una O'Connor, Marjorie Gateson, Akim Tamiroff

Forsaking All Others (MGM)

PRODUCER: Bernard H. Hyman
DIRECTOR: W. S. Van Dyke

WRITERS: Edward Barry Roberts, Frank Morgan Cavett, Joseph L. Mankiewicz

CAST: Joan Crawford, Clark Gable, Robert Montgomery, Charles Butterworth, Billie Burke, Frances Drake, Rosalind Russell

1935

No More Ladies (MGM)

DIRECTORS: Edward H. Griffith, George Cukor
WRITERS: A. E. Thomas, Donald Ogden Stewart, Horace Jackson
CAST: Joan Crawford, Robert Montgomery, Charlie Ruggles, Franchot Tone, Edna May Oliver, Gail Patrick, Reginald Denny

I Live My Life (MGM)

PRODUCER: Bernard H. Hyman
DIRECTOR: W. S. Van Dyke
WRITERS: A. Carter Goodloe, Gottfried Reinhart, Ethel Borden, Joseph L. Mankiewicz
CAST: Joan Crawford, Brian Aherne, Frank Morgan, Aline MacMahon, Eric Blore, Fred Keating, Jessie Ralph, Arthur Treacher, Hedda Hopper, Frank Conroy

1936

The Gorgeous Hussy (MGM)

PRODUCER: Joseph L. Mankiewicz
DIRECTOR: Clarence Brown
WRITERS: Samuel Hopkins Adams, Ainsworth Morgan, Stephen Morehouse Avery
CAST: Joan Crawford, Robert Taylor, Lionel Barrymore, Franchot Tone, Melvyn Douglas, James Stewart, Alison Skipworth, Louis Calhern, Beulah Bondi, Melville Cooper, Sidney Toler, Gene Lockhart

Love on the Run (MGM)

PRODUCER: Joseph L. Mankiewicz
DIRECTOR: W. S. Van Dyke

WRITERS: Alan Green, Julian Brodie, John Lee Mahin, Manuel Seff, Gladys Hurlbut
CAST: Joan Crawford, Clark Gable, Franchot Tone, Reginald Owen, Mona Barrie, Ivan Lebedeff, Charles Judels, William Demarest

1937

The Last of Mrs. Cheyney (MGM)

PRODUCER: Lawrence Weingarten
DIRECTOR: Richard Boleslawski
WRITERS: Frederic Lonsdale, Leon Gordon, Samson Raphaelson, Monckton Hoffe
CAST: Joan Crawford, William Powell, Robert Montgomery, Frank Morgan, Jessie Ralph, Nigel Bruce, Colleen Clare, Benita Hume, Ralph Forbes

The Bride Wore Red (MGM)

PRODUCER: Joseph L. Mankiewicz
DIRECTOR: Dorothy Arzner
WRITERS: Ferenc Molnar, Tess Slesinger, Bradbury Foote
CAST: Joan Crawford, Franchot Tone, Robert Young, Billie Burke, Reginald Owen, Lynne Carver, George Zucco

Mannequin (MGM)

PRODUCER: Joseph L. Mankiewicz
DIRECTOR: Frank Borzage
WRITERS: Katharine Brush, Lawrence Hazard
CAST: Joan Crawford, Spencer Tracy, Alan Curtis, Ralph Morgan, Mary Phillips

1938

The Shining Hour (MGM)

PRODUCER: Joseph L. Mankiewicz
DIRECTOR: Frank Borzage
WRITERS: Keith Winter, Jane Murfin, Ogden Nash
CAST: Joan Crawford, Margaret Sullavan, Robert Young, Melvyn Douglas, Fay Bainter, Allyn Joslyn, Hattie McDaniel

1939

The Ice Follies of 1939 (MGM)

PRODUCER: Harry Rapf
DIRECTOR: Reinhold Schunzel
WRITERS: Leonard Praskins, Florence Ryerson, Edgar Allan Woolf
CAST: Joan Crawford, James Stewart, Lew Ayres, Lewis Stone, Bess Ehrhardt, Lionel Stander

The Women (MGM)

PRODUCER: Hunt Stromberg
DIRECTOR: George Cukor
WRITERS: Clare Boothe, Anita Loos, Jane Murfin
CAST: Norma Shearer, Joan Crawford, Rosalind Russell, Mary Boland, Paulette Goddard, Phyllis Povah, Joan Fontaine, Virginia Weidler, Lucille Watson

1940

Strange Cargo (MGM)

PRODUCER: Joseph L. Mankiewicz
DIRECTOR: Frank Borzage
WRITERS: Richard Sale, Lawrence Hazard
CAST: Joan Crawford, Clark Gable, Ian Hunter, Peter Lorre, Paul Lukas, Albert Dekker, J. Edward Bromberg, Eduardo Ciannelli

Susan and God (MGM)

PRODUCER: Hunt Stromberg
DIRECTOR: George Cukor
WRITERS: Rachel Crothers, Anita Loos
CAST: Joan Crawford, Fredric March, Ruth Hussey, John Carroll, Rita Hayworth, Nigel Bruce, Bruce Cabot, Rita Quigley, Rose Hobart, Constance Collier, Gloria DeHaven

1941

A Woman's Face (MGM)

PRODUCER: Victor Saville
DIRECTOR: George Cukor
WRITERS: Francis de Croisset, Donald Ogden Stewart
CAST: Joan Crawford, Melvyn Douglas, Conrad Veidt, Osa Massen, Reginald Owen, Albert Basserman, Marjorie Main, Donald Meek

When Ladies Meet (MGM)

PRODUCERS: Robert Z. Leonard, Orville O. Dull
DIRECTOR: Robert Z. Leonard
WRITERS: Rachel Crothers, S. K. Lauren, Anita Loos
CAST: Joan Crawford, Robert Taylor, Greer Garson, Herbert Marshall, Spring Byington

1942

They All Kissed the Bride (Columbia)

PRODUCER: Edward Kaufman
DIRECTOR: Alexander Hall
WRITERS: Gina Kaus, Andrew Solt, P. J. Wolfson
CAST: Joan Crawford, Melvyn Douglas, Roland Young, Billie Burke, Andrew Tombes, Allen Jenkins, Helen Parrish

Reunion in France (MGM)

PRODUCER: Joseph L. Mankiewicz
DIRECTOR: Jules Dassin
WRITERS: Ladislas Bus-Fekete, Jan Lustig, Marvin Borowsky, Marc Connelly
CAST: Joan Crawford, John Wayne, Philip Dorn, Reginald Owen, Albert Basserman, John Carradine

1943

Above Suspicion (MGM)

PRODUCER: Victor Saville
DIRECTOR: Richard Thorpe
WRITERS: Helen MacInnes, Keith Winter, Melville Baker, Patricia Coleman
CAST: Joan Crawford, Fred MacMurray, Conrad Veidt, Basil Rathbone, Reginald Owen, Cecil Cunningham

1944

Hollywood Canteen (Warner Bros.)

PRODUCER: Alex Gottlieb
DIRECTOR: Delmer Daves
WRITER: Delmer Daves
CAST: Joan Leslie, Robert Hutton, Dane Clark, Janis Paige. Guest stars: the Andrews Sisters, Jack Benny, Joe E. Brown, Eddie Cantor, Kitty Carlisle, Jack Carson, Joan Crawford, Bette Davis, John Garfield, Sydney Greenstreet, Paul Henreid, Peter Lorre, Ida Lupino, Irene Manning, Joan McCracken, Dennis Morgan, Eleanor Parker, Roy Rogers and Trigger, Barbara Stanwyck, Jane Wyman

1945

Mildred Pierce (Warner Bros.)

PRODUCER: Jerry Wald
DIRECTOR: Michael Curtiz
WRITERS: James M. Cain, Ranald MacDougall
CAST: Joan Crawford, Jack Carson, Zachary Scott, Eve Arden, Ann Blyth, Bruce Bennett, George Tobias, Lee Patrick, Moroni Olsen, Jo Ann Marlow, Barbara Brown

1946

Humoresque (Warner Bros.)

PRODUCER: Jerry Wald
DIRECTOR: Jean Negulesco
WRITERS: Fannie Hurst, Clifford Odets, Zachary Gold
CAST: Joan Crawford, John Garfield, Oscar Levant, J. Carroll Naish, Joan Chandler, Tom D'Andrea, Peggy Knudsen, Ruth Nelson, Craig Stevens

1947

Possessed (Warner Bros.)

PRODUCER: Jerry Wald
DIRECTOR: Curtis Bernhardt
WRITERS: Rita Weiman, Silvia Richards, Ranald MacDougall
CAST: Joan Crawford, Van Heflin, Raymond Massey, Geraldine Brooks, Stanley Ridges, John Ridgely, Moroni Olsen

Daisy Kenyon (20th Century-Fox)

PRODUCER: Otto Preminger
DIRECTOR: Otto Preminger
WRITERS: Elizabeth Janeway, David Hertz
CAST: Joan Crawford, Dana Andrews, Henry Fonda, Ruth Warrick, Martha Stewart, Peggy Ann Garner

1949

Flamingo Road (Warner Bros.)

PRODUCER: Jerry Wald
DIRECTOR: Michael Curtiz
WRITERS: Robert Wilder, Sally Wilder
CAST: Joan Crawford, Zachary Scott, David Brian, Sydney Greenstreet, Gladys George, Virginia Huston, Fred Clark

It's a Great Feeling (Warner Bros.)

PRODUCER: Alex Gottlieb
DIRECTOR: David Butler
WRITERS: I. A. L. Diamond, Jack Rose, Mel Shavelson
CAST: Dennis Morgan, Doris Day, Jack Carson, Bill Goodwin. Guest appearances: Gary Cooper, Edward G. Robinson, Joan Crawford, Danny Kaye, Errol Flynn, Ronald Reagan, Jane Wyman, Eleanor Parker, Patricia Neal

1950

The Damned Don't Cry (Warner Bros.)

PRODUCER: Jerry Wald
DIRECTOR: Vincent Sherman
WRITERS: Gertrude Walker, Harold Medford, Jerome Weidman
CAST: Joan Crawford, David Brian, Steve Cochran, Kent Smith, Hugh Sanders, Selena Royle

Harriet Craig (Columbia)

PRODUCER: William Dozier
DIRECTOR: Vincent Sherman
WRITERS: George Kelly, Anne Froelick, James Gunn
CAST: Joan Crawford, Wendell Corey, Lucille Watson, Allyn Joslyn, William Bishop, K. T. Stevens

1951

Goodbye, My Fancy (Warner Bros.)

PRODUCER: Henry Blanke
DIRECTOR: Vincent Sherman
WRITERS: Fay Kanin, Ivan Goff, Ben Roberts
CAST: Joan Crawford, Robert Young, Frank Lovejoy, Eve Arden, Janice Rule, Lurene Tuttle, Howard St. John

Joan Crawford

1952

This Woman Is Dangerous (Warner Bros.)

PRODUCER: Robert Sisk
DIRECTOR: Felix Feist
WRITERS: Bernard Firard, Geoffrey Homes, George Worthing Yates
CAST: Joan Crawford, Dennis Morgan, David Brian, Richard Webb, Mari
Aldon, Philip Carey

Sudden Fear (Produced by Joseph Kaufman for RKO Pictures)

PRODUCER: Joseph Kaufman
DIRECTOR: David Miller
WRITERS: Edna Sherry, Lenore Coffee, Robert Smith
CAST: Joan Crawford, Jack Palance, Gloria Grahame, Bruce Bennett, Virginia Huston, Touch Connors

1953

Torch Song (MGM)

PRODUCERS: Henry Berman, Sidney Franklin Jr.
DIRECTOR: Charles Walters
WRITERS: I. A. R. Wylie, John Michael Hayes, Jan Lustig
CAST: Joan Crawford, Michael Wilding, Gig Young, Marjorie Rambeau,
Henry Morgan, Dorothy Patrick

1954

Johnny Guitar (Republic)

PRODUCER: Herbert J. Yates
DIRECTOR: Nicholas Ray
WRITERS: Roy Chanslor, Philip Yordan
CAST: Joan Crawford, Sterling Hayden, Mercedes McCambridge, Scott
Brady, Ward Bond, Ben Cooper, Ernest Borgnine, John Carradine,
Royal Dano

1955

Female on the Beach (Universal-International)

PRODUCER: Albert Zugsmith
DIRECTOR: Joseph Pevney
WRITERS: Robert Hill, Richard Alan Simmons
CAST: Joan Crawford, Jeff Chandler, Jan Sterling, Cecil Kellaway, Natalie Schafer, Charles Drake

Queen Bee (Columbia)

PRODUCER: Jerry Wald
DIRECTOR: Ranald MacDougall
WRITERS: Edna Lee, Ranald MacDougall
CAST: Joan Crawford, Barry Sullivan, Betsy Palmer, John Ireland, Lucy Marlow, William Leslie, Fay Wray

1956

Autumn Leaves (Wm. Goetz Prod. for Columbia Pictures)

PRODUCER: William Goetz
DIRECTOR: Robert Aldrich
WRITERS: Jack Jevne, Lewis Meltzer, Robert Blees
CAST: Joan Crawford, Cliff Robertson, Vera Miles, Lorne Greene, Ruth Donnelly, Shepperd Strudwick

1957

The Story of Esther Costello (A Romulus Production for Valiant Films, Released by Columbia Pictures)

PRODUCER: David Miller
DIRECTOR: David Miller
WRITERS: Nicholas Monsarrat, Charles Kaufman
CAST: Joan Crawford, Rossano Brazzi, Heather Sears, Lee Patterson, Ron Randell, Fay Compton, John Loder

1959

The Best of Everything (20th Century-Fox)

PRODUCER: Jerry Wald
DIRECTOR: Jean Negulesco
WRITERS: Rona Jaffe, Edith Sommer, Mann Rubin
CAST: Hope Lange, Stephen Boyd, Suzy Parker, Martha Hyer, Diane Baker, Brian Aherne, Robert Evans, Brett Halsey, Louis Jourdan as David Savage, Joan Crawford as Amanda Farrow

1962

What Ever Happened to Baby Jane? (Seven Arts and Aldrich Prod., Released by Warner Bros.)

PRODUCERS: Kenneth Hyman, Robert Aldrich
DIRECTOR: Robert Aldrich
WRITERS: Henry Farrell, Lukas Heller
CAST: Bette Davis, Joan Crawford, Victor Buono, Marjorie Bennett, Maidie Norman, Anna Lee

1963

The Caretakers (Hall Bartlett Production, Released by United Artists)

PRODUCER: Hall Bartlett
DIRECTOR: Hall Bartlett
WRITERS: Henry F. Greenberg, Hall Bartlett, Jerry Paris, Daniel Telfer
CAST: Robert Stack, Polly Bergen, Joan Crawford, Janis Paige, Diane McBain, Van Williams, Constance Ford, Sharon Hugueny, Herbert Marshall, Robert Vaughn

1964

Strait Jacket (William Castle Production, Released by Columbia)

PRODUCER: William Castle
DIRECTOR: William Castle
WRITERS: Robert Bloch, William Castle

CAST: Joan Crawford, Diane Baker, Leif Erickson, Howard St. John, John Anthony Hayes, Rochelle Hudson, George Kennedy

1965

I Saw What You Did (Universal)

PRODUCER: William Castle
DIRECTOR: William Castle
WRITERS: Ursula Curtiss, William McGivern
CAST: Joan Crawford, John Ireland, Leif Erickson, Sara Lane, Andi Garrett, Sharyl Locke

1968

Berserk (Columbia)

PRODUCER: Herman Cohen
DIRECTOR: Jim O'Connolly
WRITERS: Aben Kandel, Herman Cohen
CAST: Joan Crawford, Ty Hardin, Diana Dors, Michael Gough, Judy Geeson

1970

Trog (Warner Bros.)

PRODUCER: Herman Cohen
DIRECTOR: Freddie Francis
WRITERS: Peter Bryan, John Gilling, Aben Kandel
CAST: Joan Crawford, Michael Gough, Joe Cornelius, Kim Braden, Bernard Kay

Appendix B
Television Performances by Joan Crawford

Note: This list does not include variety and interview programs.

Mirror Theater, "Because I Love Him," September 19, 1953, CBS
GE Theater, "The Road to Edinburgh," October 31, 1954, CBS
GE Theater, "Strange Witness," March 23, 1958, CBS
GE Theater, "And One Was Loyal," January 4, 1959, CBS
Zane Grey Theater, "Rebel Ranger," December 3, 1959, CBS
Zane Grey Theater, "One Must Die," January 12, 1961, CBS
Route 66, "Same Picture, Different Frame," October 4, 1963, CBS
The Man from UNCLE, "The Five Women Affair," March 31, 1967, NBC
The Lucy Show, "Lucy and Joan Crawford," February 26, 1968, CBS
The Secret Storm, October, 1969, CBS
Night Gallery, November 6, 1969, NBC
The Virginian, "Nightmare," January 21, 1970, NBC
The Sixth Sense, "Dear Joan, We're Going to Scare You to Death," September 30, 1972, ABC

APPENDIX C
Printed Sources

The newspaper and magazine articles that proved helpful in writing this book are far too numerous to be listed here. These books proved informative:

Astaire, Fred, *Steps in Time*, Harper and Brothers, New York, 1959.

Blotner, Joseph, *Faulkner, A Biography*, Random House, New York, 1974.

Capra, Frank, *The Name Above the Title*, Macmillan, New York, 1971.

Carey, Gary, *Cukor & Co.*, The Museum of Modern Art, New York, 1971.

Castle, William, *Step Right Up! . . . I'm Gonna Scare the Pants Off America*, Putnam, New York, 1976.

Clurman, Harold, *All People Are Famous*, Harcourt Brace Jovanovich, New York, 1974.

Crawford, Joan, with Jane Kesner Ardmore, *A Portrait of Joan*, Doubleday, Garden City, New York, 1962.

————, *My Way of Life*, Simon and Schuster, New York, 1971.

Crowther, Bosley, *The Lion's Share*, Dutton, New York, 1957.

Gargan, William, *Why Me?* Doubleday, New York, 1969.

Graham, Sheilah, and Gerold Frank, *Beloved Infidel*, Henry Holt, New York, 1958.

Hancock, Ralph, and Letitia Fairbanks, *Douglas Fairbanks, The Fourth Musketeer*, Henry Holt, New York, 1963.

Harris, Warren G., *Gable and Lombard*, Simon and Schuster, New York, 1974.

Lambert, Gavin, *On Cukor*, Putnam, New York, 1972.

Latham, Aaron, *Crazy Sundays*, Viking, New York, 1971.

Lesley, Cole, *Remembered Laughter*, Knopf, New York, 1976.

Logan, Josh, *Josh*, Delacorte Press, New York, 1976.

Parsons, Louella O., *The Gay Illiterate*, Garden City Publishing, Garden City, New York, 1945.

———, *Tell It to Louella*, Putnam, New York, 1961.

Quirk, Laurence J., *The Films of Joan Crawford*, Citadel, New York, 1968.

Swindell, Larry, *Body and Soul, The Story of John Garfield*, Morrow, New York, 1975.

Thomas, Bob, *Selznick*, Doubleday, New York, 1970.

———, *Thalberg*, Doubleday, New York, 1969.

Tornabene, Lyn, *Long Live the King*, Putnam, New York, 1976.

Turnbull, Andrew, ed., *The Letters of F. Scott Fitzgerald*, Scribner, New York, 1963.

Index

C

L

M

N

Made in United States
Orlando, FL
29 April 2023

32616149R00212